The Man Who Found Thoreau

REVISITING NEW ENGLAND: The New Regionalism

SERIES EDITORS

Lisa MacFarlane • University of New Hampshire
Dona Brown • University of Vermont
Stephen Nissenbaum • University of Massachusetts at Amherst
David H. Watters • University of New Hampshire

This series presents fresh discussions of the distinctiveness of New England culture. The editors seek manuscripts examining the history of New England regionalism; the way its culture came to represent American national culture as a whole; the interaction between that "official" New England culture and the people who lived in the region; and local, subregional, or even biographical subjects as microcosms that explicitly open up and consider larger issues. The series welcomes new theoretical and historical perspectives and is designed to cross disciplinary boundaries and appeal to a wide audience.

Richard Archer, *Fissures in the Rock: New England in the Seventeenth Century*

Nancy L. Gallagher, *Breeding Better Vermonters: The Eugenics Project in Vermont*

Sidney V. James, *The Colonial Metamorphoses in Rhode Island: A Study of Institutions in Change*

Diana Muir, *Reflections in Bullough's Pond: Economy and Ecosystem in New England*

James C. O'Connell, *Becoming Cape Cod: Creating a Seaside Resort*

Christopher J. Lenney, *Sightseeking: Clues to the Landscape History of New England*

Priscilla Paton, *Abandoned New England: Landscape in the Works of Homer, Frost, Hopper, Wyeth, and Bishop*

Adam Sweeting, *Beneath the Second Sun: A Cultural History of Indian Summer*

Mark J. Sammons and Valerie Cunningham, *Black Portsmouth: Three Centuries of African-American Heritage*

Pauleena MacDougall, *The Penobscot Dance of Resistance: Tradition in the History of a People*

Donna M. Cassidy, *"On the Subject of Nativeness": From Regionalism to Race in Marsden Hartley's Late Art*

Jennifer C. Post, *Music in Rural New England Family and Community Life, 1870–1940*

Donald W. Linebaugh, *The Man Who Found Thoreau: Roland W. Robbins and the Rise of Historical Archaeology in America*

The Man Who Found
THOREAU

Roland W. Robbins

and the Rise of

Historical Archaeology

in America

Donald W. Linebaugh

University of New Hampshire Press

Durham, New Hampshire

Published by University Press of New England

Hanover and London

University of New Hampshire Press

Published by University Press of New England,
One Court Street, Lebanon, NH 03766
www.upne.com
© 2005 by Donald W. Linebaugh
Printed in the United States of America

5 4 3 2 1

Library of Congress Cataloging-in-Publication Data

Linebaugh, Donald W.
The man who found Thoreau : Roland W. Robbins and the rise of historical archaeology in America / Donald W. Linebaugh.
    p.   cm.
Includes bibliographical references and index.
ISBN 1–58465–425–2 (alk. paper)
1. Robbins, Roland Wells, 1908–   2. Archaeologists—United States—Biography.
3. Archaeology and history—United States.   4. Historic preservation—United States.
5. United States—Antiquities.   6. Excavations (Archaeology)—United States.   I. Title.
CC115.R63L56 2004
974'.01'092—dc22   2004016272

The publication of this book was made possible in part by a grant from the Massachusetts Foundation for the Humanities, state-based affiliate of the National Endowment for the Humanities.
Additional funding was provided by: Eastern National. Eastern National provides quality educational products and services to the visitors to America's national parks and other public trusts;
the Walden Woods Project and Roland Wells Robbins Memorial Fund. The Walden Woods Project preserves the land, literature and legacy of Henry David Thoreau. Through its Thoreau Institute, the Project maintains the Roland Wells Robbins Collection and administers the Roland Robbins Memorial Fund;
the School of Architecture, Planning and Preservation, University of Maryland; and the College of Arts and Sciences, University of Kentucky.

To Suzanne and Claire, with love

Contents

Acknowledgments

I wish to express my sincere thanks and appreciation to the family of Roland W. Robbins, particularly his wife Geraldine and daughter Bonita. Mrs. Robbins has been especially generous, giving me total access to her husband's papers and talking with me about his career and their life together. Bonita Robbins and sister Jean provided interpretative ideas about many aspects of their father's life, particularly his sketchy early years and his intense interest in Thoreau. The Robbins family has been very open and hands-off in terms of my approach to their husband and father's career and life story, and have encouraged me to be open and forthright in my interpretation of his work.

This book has been made much richer through interviews with several of Robbins's archaeological and Thoreauvian colleagues and friends. Thoreau scholar Thomas Blanding introduced me to the Robbins family and helped with the project from its very inception, providing keen insights regarding Robbins and Thoreau. Family friend and local artist Kristina Joyce spoke with me about her friendship and work with Robbins. A gifted artist and calligrapher, Kristina lettered the text for the 1986 reprint of Robbins's book of poetry *Thru the Covered Bridge*. I had the pleasure of interviewing the late Dr. Walter Harding Jr. of the State University of New York College at Geneseo, a nationally known Thoreau scholar and Thoreau biographer. Dr. Harding provided useful insights into Robbins's career, particularly his work on the Thoreau House site and many years of participation in the Thoreau Society. He also generously offered his correspondence files relating to Robbins and the Thoreau House project for my use. Dr. Paul Heberling of Juniata College discussed his memories and stories about Robbins, whom he met in 1976 during

Robbins's stay at Juniata College as lecturer-in-residence. Dr. Heberling, a university-trained archaeologist, provided a very fascinating and enlightening perspective on Robbins. Architect Floyd Johnson, the project director of the Shadwell project during Robbins's work, met with me to discuss Robbins and the project, and read my draft manuscript dealing with Shadwell. The late Thomas Hopkins, a local stonemason who worked with Robbins on many restoration projects in New England, took great pleasure in describing their work together. Finally, the late Evan Jones, Robbins's coauthor of *Hidden America*, took the time to meet with me and to travel back to the last few years of the 1950s and discuss the process of creating and marketing this important early work on historical archaeology.

Scholars at several of the sites excavated by Robbins have been helpful in providing additional archival information and opportunities to examine the artifacts and sites themselves. Numerous staff members at the Saugus Iron Works National Historic Site have contributed to this project; in particular Lead Park Ranger Curtis McKay White and Cultural Resources Program manager Carl Salmons-Perez have provided help with sources and in thinking about Robbins's archaeology and the restoration at this site, and superintendent Steven Kesselman has provided support and encouragement along the way. The librarian and archivist at Strawbery Banke in Portsmouth, New Hampshire, Susan Grigg, provided assistance during my visit to the site and answered my long-distance inquiries. Archaeologist Susan Kerns, formerly of the Thomas Jefferson Memorial Foundation, provided a great deal of help with the Shadwell project. She directed the most recent excavations at the site and was able to offer important insights into the site's structure and the previous excavations by Kimball, Schumacher, and Robbins. At Historic Hudson Valley's Philipsburg Manor Upper Mills, curator Kate Johnson and archivist Claudia Dovman were extremely helpful and enthusiastic. They shared the archival material relating to the site and ferried me to the artifact repository at the Rockefeller Archives. Matthew Kierstead of PAL provided assistance with the Oliver Mill Park project, and generously shared his ideas and recent report on work at the site.

My dissertation committee, particularly Dr. Robert A. Gross, was very supportive and helped me focus my thoughts and develop my ideas. Dr. Gross pushed me to undertake this study, read and reread the manuscript, and offered excellent advice on both substance and the craft of writing. He has continued to be a mentor and colleague to me since graduation. Dr. Marley R. Brown III has shared his memories of Robbins with me during the project and has always been willing to talk about the project and read my drafts; we have had many spirited conversations. Dr. Dennis O'Toole, formerly of Colonial Williamsburg, and Dr. Virginia Kerns and Dr. James P. Whittenburg of the College of William and Mary also provided helpful comments and support during the dissertation work.

The staff at the Thoreau Society and Thoreau Institute at Walden Woods have been tremendously supportive during my work. They provided lodging during my repeated visits to use the archives and have encouraged the project in every way. In particular, Thoreau Institute executive director Kathi Anderson, former staff member and Thoreau scholar Bradley Dean, and staff member Dan Schmid were enthusiastic backers of the project and helped with numerous questions related to Robbins's Walden excavation. Curator of collections Jeffrey S. Cramer deserves special mention as he has been an extraordinary help during my many research trips to the institute. Jeff has been a sounding board on many issues and is a marvel as a reference librarian and curator.

Numerous colleagues have discussed Robbins and his work with me over the years, and this interchange has been very helpful in my analysis and interpretation. In particular, I would like to thank W. Barksdale Maynard, Steven Pendry, Marley R. Brown III, Mary Beaudry, David Starbuck, and David Poirier. While the late James Deetz declined to be interviewed because he felt he had said all there was to say about Robbins in the past, he encouraged the project. My colleagues at the William and Mary Center for Archaeological Research and the Department of Anthropology were very supportive during the many years of dissertation research and writing, and subsequent investigations. In particular, I would like to thank codirector and colleague Dennis B. Blanton for his enthusiastic support of this project.

The staff of the Massachusetts Historical Commission has also been supportive of the project. I would like to thank executive director Cara Metz, state archaeologist Brona Simons, and senior archaeologist Edward Bell. Ed has been an excellent sounding board for my ideas, and he has helped with research questions along the way.

The Commonwealth Center for the Study of American Culture at the College of William and Mary funded portions of the research for this project through its summer fellowship and travel grants programs. In addition, the College of William and Mary provided two Minor Research

Grants to cover my travel for various interviews. The Office of the Vice President for Research at the University of Kentucky and the College of Arts and Science generously provided travel support at critical times during the research.

Funding to support the publication of this book has been generously provided by the Thoreau Institute at Walden Woods, the University of Kentucky College of Arts and Sciences, Eastern National, the Massachusetts Foundation for the Humanities, and the School of Architecture, Planning, and Preservation at the University of Maryland. Without this critical support, the project would not have been possible.

Series editor Stephen Nissenbaum read and commented on several versions of the manuscript, and he pushed me early on to do some necessary reworking that has greatly improved the final book. Series editor Dona Brown and an anonymous reviewer also provided important feedback to me during the preparation of the manuscript. These thoughtful reviewers have had a real impact on the shape of the final book. Ellen Wicklum, my editor at the University Press of New England, has been wonderful to work with and supportive throughout each phase of the project. Her calm and steady advice has been greatly appreciated during the final weeks of the project.

Finally, my wife Suzanne has been a best friend and confidante throughout the project. She has read and reread drafts, critiqued portions of the book, and listened critically to many versions of my lectures on Robbins. It is a joy to be able to share the ups and downs of a research project of this magnitude with someone who understands the pleasure of working through an idea and choosing just the right word.

The Man Who Found Thoreau

Introduction

To his admirers, Roland W. Robbins was known as the "Man Who Found Thoreau" and the "Pick and Shovel Historian," respected for his commonsense approach to historical and archaeological research, and liked for his charismatic personality.[1] To his critics he was a destroyer of archaeological sites, a "difficult and tempestuous" man, and a charlatan of the first order.[2] The truth, of course, lies somewhere between these extremes and depends heavily on perspective and context. Robbins's discovery of Thoreau's house at Walden Pond in 1945 marked the beginning of a controversial career in archaeology that encompassed excavations at important sites across New England and the northeastern United States. Robbins was in many ways a pioneer in historical archaeology and restoration, can be counted among the first industrial archaeologists in America, and created one of the earliest public archaeology programs in the United States. He excavated numerous early domestic and industrial sites in the Northeast using an approach that suited his restoration-oriented goals, captured the public's imagination with the excitement of historical archaeology, and, in retrospect, embodied many characteristics of modern historical and industrial archaeology practice. As archaeologist Marley R. Brown III commented in 1978, Robbins was "one of the leading authorities on seventeenth- and eighteenth-century industrial sites in New England."[3]

Nevertheless, Robbins ultimately failed to achieve much stature among professional archaeologists. His career reflects historical archaeology's early ties to historic preservation and the almost complete lack of appreciation for or interest in industrial sites, and reveals the developing boundaries and growing tensions that existed between academic practi-

tioners, amateurs, and the public. Robbins's forte and focus was archaeology in the service of building restoration and reconstruction, particularly within the context of industrial sites; his strict adherence to the goal
of reconstruction and restoration and his intense distrust of the academy eventually sealed his fate as the organized disciplines of historical
and industrial archaeology emerged in the late 1960s and early 1970s.
His career is emblematic of the ways in which emerging academic disciplines and practitioners attempt to legitimize themselves and, in the
process, exclude both early pioneers like Robbins and the public. His use
of mechanical equipment for excavation, stubborn adherence to his own
unique approach to archaeology, and inclusion of the public in his
archaeological projects did little to enhance his reputation and in many
instances damaged the sites he studied. Yet, the story of his career is
also one of innovation and experimentation, astute visual skill, and a
commonsense approach to research problems, focused on identifying
and reconstructing or memorializing New England's historic sites and
Yankee heritage. He embraced a practical and philosophical commitment to make "history come alive . . . making something live again in
people's imaginations."[4]

In many ways, Robbins was the quintessential Yankee, "handy, resourceful, inventive, practical, ready to turn his hand to anything, and
possessed of a keen, inquiring mind that made the most of whatever
events and ideas came his way."[5] His innovative and commonsense approach cast him as an influential and fascinating figure in the construction of a regional identity for New England, one that was increasingly
grounded in physical sites and objects. This regional identity, which ex-
tolled a simple, pastoral New England countryside inhabited with hardworking, self-taught, irascible Yankee characters like Robbins, had its
beginnings in the nineteenth century and was refined in the early twentieth century by popular works such as the poetry of Robert Frost and
the enormous success of regional publications such as *Yankee* magazine.[6] With the advent of the Cold War, regionalism gave way to the construction of a more cohesive national identity, and Robbins's work at the
Saugus Iron Works and other industrial sites documents this trend toward the celebration of American exceptionalism and military strength.
In the case of Saugus, the core values of hardworking Yankee ingenuity
were writ large to celebrate the American steel industry. The exploration
of Robbins's part in crafting historic sites in New England against the
backdrop of historical archaeology and historic preservation extends

our understanding of the ways in which tangible and physical memorials to the past have structured the New England regional identity. In his carefully crafted persona as an untutored, irascible Yankee character, Robbins served as a sort of cultural *bricoleur* or handyman, fashioning and sculpting an impression of the New England past from whatever came to hand at the various sites that he explored.

Taking his intellectual lead from Thoreau, the self-educated Robbins discovered that he could realize his ambitions in the field of letters within the expanding discipline of historical archaeology. He explains that

it was a curiosity about my own community that led me to dig in Massachusetts when I had no more equipment than a shovel and a questioning mind. At the time I had a thriving business as a house painter and handy man—and no archaeological training whatsoever. But I found that simple tools and the rudiments of a scientific approach, cautiously exercised, could ferret out history that had evaded others; and, as time passed, the opportunities to do so became so demanding that I ceased to be an expert at washing other people's windows and renovating other people's houses, and was established as a working archaeologist.[7]

Although he was entirely self-taught, Robbins's early work earned the respect of scholars in history and archaeology. For instance, in 1948, Smithsonian curator C. Malcolm Watkins wrote of his visit to the Saugus Iron Works dig, "I cannot begin to tell you how impressed . . . I [was] with your project and the wonderful results that are everywhere apparent."[8] Several years later, J. C. Harrington, a founding father of historical archaeology in America, wrote of the Saugus work that "I was amazed at the results of your work and very much impressed with the fine job of reconstructing you were doing."[9] Clearly impressed with Robbins's work, Harrington and Jamestown curator J. Paul Hudson along with Harvard's J. O. Brew enthusiastically recommended Robbins for the Shadwell excavation in Virginia and other new projects.

By the mid-1960s, however, Robbins was increasingly snubbed by professional archaeologists (including John Cotter, a central figure in the discipline's early history), who were engaged in formally establishing historical archaeology as an academic discipline.[10] From this period to the present, many academic archaeologists have characterized Robbins as the worst kind of pothunter and destroyer of sites, and accused him of a variety of archaeological atrocities. Although his techniques initially were little different from those of the developing academic practice, he did not embrace changing professional standards, choosing to maintain his own philosophy and approach to archaeology and site restoration in the face of rejection by the new professionals. He was, he understood, a self-taught Yankee possessing common sense but no academic credentials, neither a college education nor a permanent, stable position. Robbins's untutored approach to archaeology and his adoption of an unyielding Yankee persona did not sit well with academics eager to develop and professionalize their discipline. He came to represent everything that they rejected in the amateur and antiquarian approach to archaeology, and they saw him as a danger to archaeological sites. In this sense, Robbins is a transitional figure in the professionalization of historical and industrial archaeology, poised between the gentleman scholar of the later nineteenth and early twentieth centuries and the academic professional of the late twentieth century. Had Robbins practiced his craft a mere twenty to thirty years earlier, he would have been viewed as a very enlightened amateur and been accorded more respect and acclaim as a pioneer figure in the discipline.

The polarity between Robbins and the profession grew in the 1960s, as an anthropological approach began to supersede a restoration focus in historical archaeology. While Robbins continued to seek ruins as a means of rekindling the past and adding a tangible, physical aspect to historical memory, a process that he saw as more akin to art than science, academic archaeologists dug with scientific precision to carefully expose and dissect the past, looking for evidence of cultural and social processes. Two fundamental differences separated Robbins from his academic brethren throughout his thirty-five-year career: his devotion to identifying and restoring physical ruins over the scientific collection of artifactual data and, related to this, his conviction that archaeology-and-restoration was as much art as science. As the methodological and ideological gulf widened, Robbins became bitter and resentful of what he perceived to be academic control of the past. In the process, he moved away from archaeology to what he labeled more broadly as heritage studies. Robbins also responded to his vocational crisis by increasingly identifying with Henry David Thoreau. A model of the practical intellectual, who had scorned the authority and gentility of cultural elites for the hard-won experience of working people, Thoreau appealed to the high-school dropout Robbins. Paradoxically, it was through Thoreau that the self-educated Robbins first discovered that he could realize his desire for a meaningful intellectual career within the infant discipline of historical archaeology. The search for Thoreau's house at Walden Pond, Robbins's first and most famous excavation, provided the opportunity that he sought, and he seized it with determination.

Robbins's entry into historical and industrial archaeology was tempered by his personal experiences as a child and young adult, as well as the larger social and cultural trends of the early twentieth century. His lack of stability and rootedness in early life, and struggles to survive during the Great Depression, motivated him to seek security and control over his life through hard work and a curiosity about the American past. He probed historical incidents for representations of economic, social, and physical stability, literally seeking foundations—both personal and actual. His tenacity and personal history, his identification with Thoreau, his adoption of a self-educated Yankee demeanor in the midst of a rebirth of regional studies and redefinition of New England, the larger cultural needs that he served in the historic preservation movement, as well as the emergence of historical archaeology in the academy and the early lack of interest in industrial sites by academic archaeologists—all of this launched Robbins on a controversial career devoted to the preservation and restoration of ruins across New England and the northeastern United States. His career was a manifestation of both his personal craving for stability and equilibrium in a changing world and of what historian Michael Kammen sees as the growing national concern for heritage and memory in the face of "worries about security, freedom, swift social change, and a sense of radical discontinuity with the world as it had hitherto been known."[11]

Robbins was, as noted earlier, a pioneer in historical archaeology and can be counted among the first industrial archaeologists in America, excavating more early ironworks sites than any other archaeologist of the period. He became thoroughly familiar with the process of iron making and studied sites ranging from the birth of the iron industry in America at Falling Creek, Virginia, and Saugus, Massachusetts, to its specialization in the early nineteenth century at Dover Union Iron Company in Dover, Massachusetts. Robbins also excavated many important domestic sites, including the 1627 John Alden House and Shadwell, the birthplace of Thomas Jefferson. His data have subsequently been utilized for new analysis and interpretation at a number of important sites including Shadwell, Saugus, Philipsburg Manor, and Walden. The results of Robbins's lifetime of research at over sixty sites promise to enhance our understanding of early New England life and industry by providing current scholars with important evidence for ongoing research and for interpretation to the public.

Robbins's archaeological legacy, however, has proven as controversial as his life. The ultimate worth of his meticulous records—field notes, maps, photographs, and accompanying collections—has been questioned, and in some cases entirely written off, by professionals who regard his methods as deplorable and Robbins himself as a poseur and showman. While this reputation is not entirely undeserved, particularly in terms of his later work, a review of Robbins's motives, training, and approach to excavation helps to clarify both the important contributions that he made to early historical and industrial archaeology and the often problematic nature of his work. Armed with a more thorough understanding of his reasons for embracing archaeology and his methods of research and excavation, researchers can profitably revisit Robbins's investigations at important sites. By placing Robbins's work in context and carefully considering the records of his work, this study extends our knowledge the uses of restoration archaeology for building physical monuments to New England's past, and opens our eyes to the hidden value of Robbins's work.

On a more personal note, his extended career in archaeological and historical research allowed Robbins to support himself and his family and cultivate a vocation that temporarily offered him both the stability and equilibrium he craved and the satisfaction, success, and recognition he sought. While his work was rejected by many academically trained archaeologists, it was eagerly welcomed by the general public. Reviews and comments on his publications and presentations indicate that he was skilled at bringing the excitement and importance of historical archaeology to his audiences, truly making "history come alive."[12]

In some cases, however, by continuing to "find things out in his own way," Robbins, like other early pioneers, destroyed important and irretrievable archaeological data. The work of early practitioners is always fraught with problems from a modern methodological and theoretical perspective and presents a host of dilemmas for those interested in the history of the discipline. By its very nature, archaeology is a destructive research tool; we have only one chance to excavate a site and cannot redo it if we make errors along the way. Still, the available data with all its flaws is always better than no data at all. For instance, the Saugus Iron Works reconstruction could have been based almost entirely on historical documents with little or no attention to the archaeological record at the site itself, thus destroying or heavily damaging the site and resulting in a much more problematic loss of data. As Robbins and others, for example the late historical archaeologist James Deetz, have pointed out, it is likely that very little would have been documented at a huge and complicated site such as the Saugus Iron Works utilizing standard hand excavation methods drawn from the practice of prehistoric archaeology.[13] As it was, Robbins's work at Saugus was pushed along by the sponsors, and he was always under pressure to work faster. Although irreplaceable evidence was clearly lost as a result of his excavation approaches, Robbins's meticulous documentation at Saugus and sites like it provides a tremendous archive of information for new research and interpretation. Even with its methodological faults, the quality of his documentation—notes, maps, and photographs—is such that his excavations have the potential to provide as much or perhaps more usable data than that available from the many "professionally" excavated sites of the period.

To the dismay of the professional archaeological community, Robbins also actively encouraged the general public to become "pick and shovel historians," declaring that the past was not the exclusive property of university-trained archaeologists. He was clearly ahead of his time in taking archaeology to the streets and schools, but he ultimately paid a heavy price for his public-oriented approach. His populist bent as a self-taught Yankee earned him the title of the "People's Archaeologist" and created a tension between himself and university professionals that would run through and ultimately shatter his career. As the academy drew the discipline of historical archaeology within its gates, it began the slow professionalization process that sought to control and standardize archaeological knowledge—the field's "secrets" were restricted to those with symbols of professional proficiency (e.g., college degrees), and membership in this new "community of the competent" was guarded.[14] Robbins, a high-school dropout and laborer, believed that the ownership of the past should be in the hands of the common man, thus, to use Carl Becker's phrase, making "everyman his own historian."[15] Robbins's unrestricted approach, sharing archaeology with the masses and suggesting that with a bit of Yankee know how and determination they could themselves be archaeologists of sorts, ran counter to all that was held sacred in the professional culture.[16]

Because of his public orientation, his restoration and antiquarian interests, his outdated and often destructive excavation techniques, his reliance on mechanical excavation, and his unabashed self-promotion and combative style, Robbins's work has largely been forgotten or ignored by "scientific" researchers who consider it useless for science if not totally worthless. While his later projects did fail to keep up with the rapidly changing standards of the discipline, there is much to learn about the creation of physical shrines to the early New England and American past from Robbins's numerous projects and his accumulated archaeological and historical data. Robbins was an actor, often in a supporting role, in a much larger drama that sought to represent and present New England in a very specific light. His story is one that can help us to better understand the uses and values of historical sites in developing a foundation to underpin a carefully crafted New England identity.

Robbins's life and early work reveal that he had a variety of reasons for embracing historical archaeology as a career. Clearly, he operated within a system that desired to create monuments and shrines as symbols of the New England and American past. He worked with and was often directed by the many small historical societies, museums, and family associations that desired to identify and interpret the physical remains associated with their sites, organizations engaged in crafting a twentieth-century vision of New England's heritage. Like any pioneer, Robbins also desired to build a shrine to his personal success and flaunt his connection to the man who represented the independence and self-determination that he sought. "Do I think [Thoreau] wanted me to find [the cabin]? You're damned right I do! I think he wanted me to stay right there until I found the damned thing!"[17]

In Robbins's view, business success, historical knowledge, and popular appreciation of the past went hand in hand. His rivals eschewed both business and popularity in pursuit of professionalism. This contest over professionalism concealed many similarities of practice between Robbins and his critics. Ironically, the professionals in the field have ultimately embraced many of Robbins's positions and practices in terms of consulting, the meaning and use of ruins, and the importance of public participation in and support for archaeology.

The results of his work, still visible in many state parks and historical sites and shrines, now provide a new generation with symbols of the American past. In constructing and accepting these symbols, Robbins made himself an emblem of Thoreauvian self-determination, an unlettered, self-educated man of action with common sense and a thoroughly Yankee background who could be called the "People's Archaeologist."

CHAPTER 1

The Road to Ruins and Restoration

Historic Preservation and Historical Archaeology
on the Road to Walden Pond

Roland Robbins's career in historical archaeology had its origins in an amalgam of personal experiences and larger social and cultural trends. His family situation, vicissitudes of early life, and ordeals during the Great Depression set the stage for him to seek stability and control over his life through hard work and mastery of physical symbols of the American past. Within this idiosyncratic framework, Robbins fashioned his career as the "Pick and Shovel Historian," probing the historical record for representations of economic and social equilibrium, seeking foundations—both past and personal. Significantly, Robbins's individual quest for security coincided with several larger and interconnected ideological movements: Progressive reforms, the new regionalist movement, and the Colonial Revival. Moreover, the preservation activities spawned by these movements would provide an early raison d'être for historical archaeology, and thus a raison d'être for Robbins himself. Progressive reformers, fueled by concerns with rapid growth, industrialization, and middle-class anxieties over eastern and southern European immigration, pursued symbols of the United States's heritage. The convergent Colonial Revival, with its "heady blend of nativism, antimodernism, and elitism . . . [likewise] represented a longing for stability and roots."[1] The resulting historic preservation movement, engaged in a search for emblems and ruins of the past, increasingly embraced historical archaeology and championed the protection and preservation of buildings and sites that venerated colonial America. These emblems were also carefully crafted to serve as symbols for a growing regionalist movement that by the 1930s had repositioned New England's identity in terms of the simple, rural life of Vermont, Maine, and New Hampshire.[2]

In New England, writes historian James M. Lindgren, "tradition-minded Yankees wanted a past that was usable," and early buildings and sites provided icons for their interpretation and reinvention of the past.[3] Harvard professor Charles Eliot Norton championed the need for tangible connections to the past in 1889, writing that "more is needed than a mere intellectual recognition" of the importance of the past in defining individual lives. "Our sentiments draw nourishment from material things, from visible memorials, from familiar objects to which affection may cling," he explained.[4]

The historic preservation movement began slowly in the mid-nineteenth century and gained momentum during the first half of the twentieth century, as adherents worked to protect and preserve historic structures and sites that represented their vision of the early American past.[5] As one New England commentator explained, these shrines were "a reminder to new citizens of the service due from them and their children to the Commonwealth."[6] Turn-of-the-century immigration from eastern and southern Europe impinged on both the recently established middle class and the elite, which "calmed its own anxieties by a veneration of the past."[7] As immigrants flooded cities like Salem, Portsmouth, and Boston, "native Yankees moved west. . . . By 1910, 70 percent of Boston's population was either foreign born or first generation."[8] In contrast, the historic preservation societies that emerged around the turn of the century were "almost entirely WASP and middle to upper class."[9] These new organizations sought to protect important sites and "build a coalition of forces to include not only the affluent and educated, but also institutions such as schools, churches, and governments."[10] Within an increasingly heterogeneous and complicated modern world, "preservationists sought to maintain a tradition they interpreted as homogeneous and simple."[11] Historian T. J. Jackson Lears argues that "antimodern impulses helped WASP elites to become a unified and self-conscious ruling class."[12] These progressives "prized their memory, sweetened by myth and wishful thinking, of an earlier unvarying harmony in New England."[13]

The first half of the nineteenth century saw little interest in preservation, partly because of the country's relatively brief existence. Recently minted Americans wished to shed their outmoded customs of the past, "break free of the burdens of history," and establish their own traditions in literature and art.[14] Nathaniel Hawthorne wrote that old houses were "'heaps of bricks and stones' that a man builds 'for himself to die in, and for his posterity to be miserable in.'"[15] By midcentury, however, a concern for the past was slowly growing as the founding fathers died and the Revolution began to fade in the memories of Americans. The national campaign to save George Washington's Mount Vernon in the early 1850s established the pattern for preservation during the remainder of the nineteenth century.[16] "In the period following the Civil War," writes preservation historian Charles B. Hosmer Jr., "the scope of the Mount Vernon movement, together with the influence of the centennials of various phases of the Revolution, combined to create a deeper appreciation of historic sites."[17] The Civil War's aftermath, furthermore, presented complex circumstances in which Americans not only used

historic shrines to assert our legitimacy in an international community of venerable nations, but also, as individuals and groups, we looked to associative history for reassurance. In the face of post–Civil War affluence, established families pursued genealogy and the preservation of their ancestral homesteads as a challenge to "new money's" claims of legitimacy.[18]

A complex set of events fueled the preservation movement's growth in the late nineteenth century. By 1880, the rapid growth of the country's population and the advance of industrial capitalism were speeding the destruction of early buildings and sites across the country. These changes also placed enormous stress on the existing social structure and gravely alarmed the country's elite. The Brahmins of New England, the descendants of the Southern planter class, and the handful of multimillionaire industrialists alike became increasingly determined to gain custodianship of the past as a way to restore and underpin their political and cultural authority, to resurrect "the golden days when their ancestors had been undisputed masters of the region."[19] As a result, preservation and protection advanced rapidly; in 1895 there were twenty house museums in the country, and by 1910 there were over one hundred.[20]

The last decades of the nineteenth century marked a period of intense interest in patriotic societies throughout the eastern United States.[21] Groups such as the Colonial Dames, Sons of the American Revolution (SAR), and Daughters of the American Revolution (DAR) became involved in a multitude of preservation-related activities, including restoration of Independence Hall and the Betsy Ross House.[22] In turn-of-the-century New England, the local historical society was the most influential and active agency engaged in the work of preserving and caring for old buildings.[23] While the range of sites included those associated with great men, noteworthy ancestors, and patriots, most "appealed to local pride or commemorated the service of early inhabitants."[24] Local preservation efforts across New England grew out of the inspiration provided by the campaign to save Boston's Old South Meeting House in 1877, and resulted in the early preservation and protection of many of the structures and sites that Roland Robbins would later investigate and excavate. For instance, the Lexington (Mass.) Historical Society purchased and relocated the Hancock-Clarke House in 1897, when the owner decided to stop maintaining the structure. Several years later, the society became the first in New England to own a historic house other than its headquarters with the purchase of the Munroe Tavern, facing the famous Lexington Battle Green.[25] It is not simply a coincidence that Robbins came to excavate both the Hancock-Clarke site and Munroe Tavern. Small historical societies realized the potential importance of archaeological excavations for restoration, reconstruction, and interpretation, a trend that would have considerable influence on Robbins's career.

Other groups active in saving New England's historic buildings during the late nineteenth and early twentieth centuries included family and literary associations organized at local, regional, and national levels. A host of family associations, including the Fairbanks Family in America, the Mayflower Society, the Pilgrim John Howland Society, and the Alden Kindred of America, Inc., entered the preservation arena in New England at this time. These groups conducted intense genealogical research to secure an elevated position in American family history, and supported local preservation efforts related to family properties.[26] Because such organizations usually lacked a professional staff, they regularly sought preservation experts such as Robbins in a host of specialized areas.

By the beginning of the twentieth century, preservation groups fell into three categories with respect to their reasons for selecting buildings for preservation: historic and inspirational values, tourism, and architectural qualities. Probably the single most important factor for preserving a building during this period was its potential as a historic-house museum that would contribute to a reinvented past. Preservationists frequently referred to their sites as shrines or meccas, and a host of books, such as Edwin Bacon's *Historic Pilgrimages in New England,* served as guides for anxious and excited pilgrims.[27] The buildings that early preservation organizations preserved and protected "reified old-time New England values, including a respect for law, civic pride, and honest labor," and were "appropriate vehicles for informing foreigners and less enlightened natives as to American traditions and values."[28]

Another increasingly important reason for preservation and a criterion for saving specific buildings was the appeal of the growing tourist trade. Lindgren argues that tourism benefited directly from traditionalism, the "hymn of the civil religion."[29] In 1924, for instance, thirty thousand visitors toured Hawthorne's House of the Seven Gables.[30] Massachusetts lieutenant governor Curtis Guild Jr. saw the Paul Revere House as a mecca for "thousands of pilgrims from all over the Country seeking the shrines of American history."[31] A proper restoration of the Abraham Browne House, preservationist William Sumner Appleton wrote in 1916, "would be of greatest educational value—a Mecca for tourists and a joy to all."[32]

The least common criterion for preserving a building was as an architectural monument. As the chairman of the American Institute of Architects (AIA) Preservation Committee lamented, "the public is not readily persuaded where matters of beauty are a concern. People appreciate old buildings for sentimental reasons. . . . They do not understand, nor treasure, them for their construction or outstanding architectural value."[33]

One of the most influential organizations in the New England preservation scene was the Society for the Preservation of New England Antiquities (SPNEA), the brainchild of William Sumner Appleton. "Laboring side-by-side with patriotic and ancestral societies," Lindgren observes, "SPNEA often articulated the era's civil religion."[34] Appleton's birth into a leading Brahmin family in Boston and his Harvard education "influenced his later career by strengthening his loyalties to Yankee traditions."[35] Caught in the struggle between antimodern sentiments and industrial power, Appleton initially failed to "find his niche in life." Lindgren observes that, "like Wallace Nutting and other soon-to-be antiquarians, he [Appleton] suffered a nervous collapse," an affliction that Robbins would also confront in his early career.[36] Appleton's and Nutting's "neurasthenia" resulted from their failure to succeed in business, while Robbins's resulted from his search for a meaningful calling and subsequent struggle with the demands of his new career. All three relied on essentially the same remedy, immersing themselves in historical study, "work that consumed their energy, fascinated their interest, and offered personal meaning."[37]

With a lifetime trust fund from his father, Appleton founded SPNEA in 1910, putting all his resources into the project.[38] He strongly criticized the "one-house" approach of many small societies, which neglected other important structures, and stressed the important "opportunities unveiled by archaeologically accurate, scientifically informed preservation work."[39] For Appleton, Lindgren asserts, preserved buildings "could become actual documents which . . . could tell a visual story about early New England life."[40] Appleton's reorientation of "preservation to the professional disciplines of archaeology, architecture, and history" encouraged scholars in these fields to study our country's past, launching "a wave of interdisciplinary research."[41] While he still valued sentimental attachments, Appleton generated a professional movement that "increasingly stressed science," including historical archaeology.[42] As Roland W. Robbins would experience throughout his career, however, this movement toward professionalism "helped to marginalize those who had been the pioneers of the [preservation] movement."[43]

In the years prior to Rockefeller's influential Williamsburg restoration and Robbins's venture to Walden Pond, historical archaeology was largely a pawn of eager preservation and historical societies. Although examples of historical archaeology extend back into the nineteenth century (for example, James Hall's 1853 excavation of the Miles Standish House in Duxbury, Massachusetts), it was not until well into the twentieth century that "historic-sites archaeology" took hold to any significant degree. An address by historian Carl Russell Fish to the Wisconsin Archaeological Society in 1910 provided an early call to historians and archaeologists for the excavation of historic sites, but Fish's words went largely unheeded at the time by archaeologists primarily interested in prehistory:

it is not only in the periods void of written sources, that archaeology can perform its services. . . . I wish to call the attention of American archaeologists to some possibilities that it offers . . . even in America we have monuments which are worthy of preservation, and which can add to our knowledge of our American ancestors, as well as of our Indian predecessors.[44]

During the late nineteenth and early twentieth centuries, the usefulness of historical archaeology was also embraced by two remarkable amateur archaeologists, William L. Calver and Reginald Pelham Bolton. "In a period when individual activity had not yet been submerged within an institutional structure," archaeologist Jacob Gruber writes, "amateurs like Calver and Bolton . . . so pushed their own enthusiasms that they can be said to have invented an historical archaeology."[45] Working on important military and domestic sites around New York City, these gentleman scholars demonstrated the value of archaeological research at historic sites, and their work went beyond simple antiquarian collection and classification of artifacts for museum display to emphasize the study of chronology and interpretation.[46] In a period when public exploration of farmland to collect ancient artifacts had reached faddist proportions, Calver, Bolton, and their Field Exploration Committee joined "the products of their controlled excavations with the documents of history in order to expand both the knowledge and the understanding of the human activity."[47] Bolton explained their goals in a 1923 address:

The method of discovery is by use of old maps and historical books locating some old site approximately, then by searching the surface for indications of human occupation, and by prodding the soil with a light steel rod, known as a "sounder," we attain a considerable degree of expertness in deciding the character of objects below the sod, then the shovel is brought into play exposing the buried layer or deposit, and in the sifter even such small objects are caught [as] buttons, nails, and pins. . . .

One interesting line of work consists in measuring old sites, forts, and buildings and making maps or drawings of them. This requires a little knowledge of surveying or engineering, but its results are important. And of course, some of the workers must keep note of every incident and discovery, and write up the subject for publication by the Society or newspapers.[48]

The principles of Bolton and Calver's work would be rekindled and expanded on by Roland Robbins at Walden Pond beginning in the mid-1940s. Bolton's description of the work of the Field Exploration Committee largely articulates the approach that Robbins would employ some twenty years later at Walden Pond.[49]

Another major influence on both historic preservation and the development of historical archaeology was the enactment of several important pieces of federal legislation during the early twentieth century including the Antiquities Act of 1906 and the later Historic Sites Act of 1935. The historic-sites movement was bolstered in 1906 with the enactment of the federal Antiquities Act, which for the first time offered protection of archaeological sites on federal land. Along with the increased stimulus from the federal government, preservation and restoration activities were gaining momentum through the work of organizations such as the American Scenic and Historic Preservation Society, SPNEA, and the Association for the Preservation of Virginia Antiquities (APVA). These organizations slowly began to seek the aid of archaeologists for restoration and reconstruction projects. Historic-sites archaeology grew during the first three decades of the century due to the increased political and financial support provided through federal legislation, and via new concerns for and interests of Americans in their heritage.[50] These archaeology projects included early work at Jamestown by the APVA in the 1890s, Samuel Yonge's 1903–1906 work at Jamestown, the 1920s excavation of the seventeenth-century Aptucxet Trading Post in Massachusetts by Percival Lombard, and several projects in Canada including work at the Saint Marie I site.[51]

The Jamestown excavations of Samuel Yonge are an excellent example of the state of historical archaeology as the new century began. Yonge, an engineer employed to supervise the construction of a seawall along the James River at Jamestown, exposed the brick foundations of the large Philip Ludwell House while working along the shoreline. He notes that this led to his "making personal researches among all available sources of information, which occupied the leisure moments of a period of two years."[52] He continued his excavations over the next several years, identifying other important seventeenth-century structures. Archaeologist J. C. Harrington, who later excavated at Jamestown, wrote that

the apparent goals of the early digs at Jamestown were very little different from later projects; namely, to uncover foundations and secure architectural information about the original buildings. Recovery of artifacts was not ignored, but it was incidental to the major objective.[53]

In this passage, Harrington lays out a theme that would be repeated throughout historical archaeology's early years, namely, the focus on delineating building foundations for reconstruction, while paying less attention to the recovery and the use of artifacts and their contexts (relationships to features such as foundations, wells, etc., and to each other) for the interpretation of human society and culture.

John D. Rockefeller Jr.'s Williamsburg restoration project was just gearing up as the pioneering work of Bolton and Calver came to a close in the late 1920s and early 1930s. Williamsburg proved to be influential in both the scope of its task and its increasingly professional approach to preservation and the use of archaeology. In 1928, finding the necessary "contractors, historians, archaeologists, furniture experts, draftsmen, landscape architects, and engineers" to carry out the Williamsburg project was a difficult task indeed.[54] Historians did not yet view buildings and material objects as documents, most archaeologists still focused on the prehistoric inhabitants of this country, and decorative arts professionals had just begun to seriously consider early American objects. Of these, architecture proved the field most prepared for the challenges of the Williamsburg restoration, and it was architect Fiske Kimball, one of Robbins's predecessors in excavating Shadwell, who first recommended that the project hire an archaeologist to keep a thorough record of the restoration. "Historic-sites archaeology did not yet exist as a profession," writes preservation historian Charles B. Hosmer Jr., "so [archaeologist Prentice Duell] had to retrain himself in order to interpret brickwork as he found it in the Wren Building."[55] Singleton P. Moorehead, director of Colonial Williamsburg's Department of Architecture and son of the well-known archaeologist Warren K. Moorehead, said of Duell that

[he] has the sharpest eyesight I have ever seen. . . . He is at ease in studying strata, soil differences and all the minutiae of "digging" that even the average well-trained investigator would probably miss . . . ! The type of soil encountered was, fortunately, extremely favorable for making sound judgements on the difference between disturbed and undisturbed earth thus enabling the archaeologists in tracing out foundation walls from which the brick had later been salvaged.[56]

At Williamsburg, archaeology was integrated into detailed architectural monographs on each building project.[57] The objective of this work remained focused on the identification of architectural data, not archaeological deposits and features, such as trash pits or living surfaces or the artifacts they contained.[58] In prehistoric archaeology, this set of data— features, artifacts, and their contextual relationships—constituted the principal evidence for the study of human culture and was the focus of the discipline. The individuals who participated in the early investigations at Colonial Williamsburg ranged "from a trained archaeologist to unsupervised laborers to landscape architects to a CCC crew."[59] Retired Colonial Williamsburg archaeologist Ivor Noël Hume has noted that

archaeology as a tool of the architectural restorer was developed in Williamsburg in the 1930s. . . . The method, known as cross-trenching, involved the digging of parallel trenches a shovel blade in width and a shovel length apart, and throwing the dirt up onto the unexcavated space between them. . . . The trenching was done by laborers who paid little attention to the salvage of artifacts and none to the layers whence they came.[60]

Archaeologists Marley Brown and Linda Derry have documented that these early investigators did have some recognition of stratigraphic layering of soils but were generally focused on the locations and interpretations of former structures; artifacts were not typically associated with the stratigraphic sequences and, in fact, were typically provenienced to the house lot, destroying or limiting their usefulness in the dating and interpretation of activities in and around the buildings that they sought to reconstruct.[61]

During the 1930s and 1940s, restoration- and preservation-oriented archaeology focused on architectural reconstruction dominated the nascent field of historical archaeology.[62] The rapidly growing preservation movement and the social crises of the Great Depression fostered a need to reinforce and give physical shape to America's sense of tradition and history, and archaeology provided a means to recover the tangible remains of the past. The economic and social stresses of the Depression precipitated the development of many public work relief programs, including the Civilian Conservation Corps and the Works Progress Administration, which embraced archaeology as a way to put people to work. In the process, these projects created physical reminders of the past and object lessons in American traditions.[63] This approach to historic-sites archaeology was also supported by the passage of the Historic Sites Act in 1935, which made the preservation of significant historic sites a national policy.[64] The Historic Sites Act strengthened the protection and investigation of archaeological sites and historic structures begun by the Antiquities Act of 1906 and, for the first time, brought together the diverse preservation activities of the federal government under the management of one agency, the National Park Service.[65]

As can be seen at Colonial Williamsburg, expertise in historic-sites archaeology had not yet developed, and few professional archaeologists were prepared to lead the thousands of unskilled laborers soon to be hired for this new endeavor. During the 1930s, the federal government began to employ trained investigators for some excavations, which meant relying largely on archaeologists who specialized in prehistory.[66] At this time, American archaeology was struggling to define itself within the broader discipline of anthropology and was the exclusive territory of scholars focused on the prehistoric peoples of the world. Prehistorians sought to integrate themselves within the social science of anthropology, and thus increasingly focused on establishing a rigorous theoretical and methodological approach.[67] These scholars carefully dug in thin arbitrary levels and recorded artifacts by these levels, employing grid-based excavation units for horizontal positioning of artifacts, and attempting to use the artifacts to develop sequences of human cultural development based on basic chronological and stylistic traits. All of this was done within an increasingly scientific paradigm that sought to document, explore, and understand human culture and society. This focus on theory and method was largely overshadowed in historical archaeology by the goal of restoration, although the social-science approach later became more prevalent as historical archaeology was embraced by the anthropological community. If historical archaeology had a central research goal at this time, it was the interpretation and restoration of buildings.

The situation at Jamestown in 1935 exemplifies the need for trained archaeologists who could excavate a historic site, as well as what would become a long-term divide between architects and archaeologists regarding the use of archaeology in preservation and restoration projects.[68] National Park Service (NPS) officials began to worry about the quality of the ongoing archaeological work at Jamestown after receiving disturbing reports from the field, and in response sent anthropologist W. J. Winter and "technical foremen" Alonozo Pond and H. Summerfield Day to direct the archaeological fieldwork.[69] Project architects, under the direction of Henry Chandlee Forman and John Zaharov, had established their territory early on and fought bitterly with Winter and his anthropological cohorts to control the excavation work. After much wrangling, the NPS officially divided the excavating responsibilities: the architects would excavate everything within a three-foot perimeter of each foundation, and the anthropologists would attend to everything else.[70] Although Winter felt that the arrangement made no theoretical or practical sense at all, he tried for a time to work within the system.

The archaeologists had vastly different goals from those of their ar-

chitectural colleagues, focusing their search on evidence that "would define tracts of land" and identify cultural features, including ditches,
fencerows, wells, and trash pits, that contained artifacts that would allow
a more thorough study of the lives and activities of these early settlers.[71]
Although the two groups worked side by side for several months, their
goals and methods were irreconcilable. During the summer of 1936,
when the fray had literally reached the point of physical violence, the
NPS temporarily closed the project. Colonial Williamsburg archaeologist Ivor Noël Hume later recounted that although both sides came out
looking bad, the anthropologists "were remarkably enlightened" in their
approach.[72] Winter produced an interesting summary of the situation at
Jamestown, writing that

. . . the most important things . . . are not the brick foundations. We are attempting to make a study of culture, to gain all of the information that the
ground has to yield. The only way to do this is to make use of the skill of trained
archeologists. The evidence of Indian occupation should not be ignored. The
very first English habitations had no brick foundations, yet a trained archaeologist can read in the ground any evidence of wooden structures and secure
data that would escape the best architects. . . . We have need of architects and
consultants, it is true, [but] . . . their work, however, comes after that of the
archeologist.[73]

The battle for Jamestown left NPS officials in a quandary about who
should supervise the archaeological work. The Smithsonian Institution
suggested J. C. Harrington, a University of Chicago graduate student in
anthropology and also a registered architect. Harrington, an early colleague of Roland Robbins, arrived at Jamestown in late 1935 and worked
there until 1941. As he later noted, "when it came to digging a colonial
site and carrying out related research, we were all babes in the woods."[74]
Using his background in history, architecture, and anthropology, Harrington went on to excavate about 10 percent of the site, outlining the
general layout and evolution of the early-seventeenth-century town.[75]
Harrington recalled that

[my] greatest deficiency was in my dismal ignorance of nonarchitectural artifacts. I came to Jamestown with the ability to recognize the difference between
a corrugated and a simple stamped Indian potsherd, but such terms as "delft-
ware" and "stoneware" were completely foreign to me; they were all just "china."[76]

The practice of historical archaeology in the northeastern United States was little different from its practice elsewhere in the United States at this time, although large-scale federal projects, such as Jamestown, were missing from the Northeast. Several local projects were completed in New England during the late 1930s and early 1940s by archaeologists who would soon become friends, colleagues, and promoters of Robbins. In the early 1940s, Henry Hornblower II, the founder of Plimoth Plantation, initiated excavations at several sites in Plymouth, Massachusetts. Hornblower became interested in archaeology in 1934 and, with the help of his father, became acquainted with Warren K. Moorehead of Phillip's Academy in Andover and Frederick Johnson of Harvard, who taught the young Hornblower excavation methods and preservation techniques. Hornblower went on to study at Phillip's Academy and later Harvard, where he worked with American historian Samuel Eliot Morison. While at university, Hornblower formed the Harvard Excavators' Club, a group of archaeologists who investigated several important historic sites including the John Howland House site (ca. 1637–1687) and the John Clark site (ca. 1627–1650) in 1940, and the "RM" site from 1941 to 1942.[77] Similarly, J. O. Brew of the Peabody Museum excavated the Edward Winslow House (ca. 1637–1700) in 1941, work done in conjunction with an archaeological field course. These early projects resulted in detailed field notes on the excavations and extensive artifact assemblages but, with the exception of several of the projects by Hornblower, few site reports.[78]

Great amounts of manpower and funding were invested in historic sites through both federal agencies and local historical and preservation groups primarily interested in immediate tangible results, for example, restoration and reconstruction, and with little interest in intensive research and publication.[79] While this pattern was repeated across the country, it was especially evident in New England, where archaeology focused on building restoration and reconstruction was the standard. According to Schuyler, "even excavations that involved careful technique and recognition of the significance of associated artifacts were . . . mainly for filling park museum cases or exhibiting the restored site to the public."[80] Thus, artifacts were used as interesting illustrations or footnotes and not for the interpretative data they could provide when considered in context. This was just as true for the smaller historic-house museums and sites of New England as it was for Jamestown. The Jamestown project clearly demonstrates a number of attitudes that were encountered by researchers working before World War II: a bias among anthropological archaeologists that historical archaeology was not real archaeology and against historians and architects practicing archaeology, a view that archaeology in support of restoration or park development for the public was tainted, an identity crisis over whether historical archaeology was history or anthropology, a complete lack of knowledge about historic artifacts, and a continuing emphasis on artifact collecting and description rather than interpretation.[81]

Both the Jamestown and Williamsburg projects were at the forefront of a trend that epitomizes the changing face of historic preservation. By the 1920s, businessmen were increasingly involved in the delivery of the past to the general populace.[82] Following World War I, corporate capital became king, and "business leaders began to exude a smug assurance that they were the sole and legitimate heirs of the American tradition."[83] As a way to increase tourism, preservation was seen as good for business, and it began to register as making economic sense as well. Sounding for all the world like a late-twentieth-century tourism director, SPNEA's Appleton remarked to a group of merchants in Cambridge, Massachusetts:

The preservation of such a house [Cooper-Austin] must surely increase the number of visitors going to Cambridge, lengthen the time they stay there, and increase somewhat the amount of money they spend there. All of this is good business, and accordingly we appeal to you as a business man to help this enterprise as a business proposition for Cambridge.[84]

The Williamsburg restoration quickly became a model for preservation programs across the country, serving as a sort of clearinghouse for restoration and preservation information.[85] With little doubt, the biggest achievement of the Williamsburg restoration was the successful blending of many disciplines in a manner that resulted in a thorough approach to restoration and preservation on an enormous scale. From 1935 to 1950, Colonial Williamsburg's president Kenneth Chorley "visited, advised, and inspired any number of preservation groups from St. Augustine, Florida, to Deerfield, Massachusetts," including several New England sites that would later be excavated by Robbins.[86]

The privately funded preservation projects of the twentieth century had numerous federally sponsored counterparts that grew out of Depression-era social programs. The work of the NPS in the 1930s, the preservation activities of the Works Progress Administration, Civilian

Conservation Corps, and Historic American Buildings Survey during the 1930s, the passage of the Historic Sites Act in 1935, and establishment of the National Trust for Historic Preservation in the late 1940s all served to create a major federal role in historic preservation. These efforts resulted in the first sizable and national group of trained professionals in preservation and some of the very first historical archaeologists.[87]

On one hand, the early historic preservation movement in America was dedicated to protecting, preserving, and studying structures and sites of importance to the country's early history and laid the groundwork of much preservation activity today, yet, on the other hand, it sought to create national shrines and monuments, more specifically, to create a set of symbols that supported and legitimized specific social ideas and values. Historic preservation in New England was more than just protecting buildings, argues historian James Lindgren. "It embodied a contest, sometimes of crisis proportions, over the definition of past, present, and future."[88] Historian Michael Kammen writes that people at the turn of the twentieth century

seemed to thrive upon the backward glance, not so much for purposes of escapism . . . but because the creative consequences of nostalgia helped them to legitimize new political orders, rationalize the adjustment and perpetuation of old social hierarchies, and construct acceptable new systems of thought and values. It is precisely because so much that genuinely mattered was new that people needed notions of the past that would help to define their national identities in positive ways, and required secure traditions to serve as strong psychological anchors. Otherwise, as one momentous century ended and the prospect of a new and uncertain one loomed, they faced the future as culturally displaced persons.[89]

One of the principal, and most visible, results of this social contest was the creation of "great public monuments of various sorts: statues, memorials, obelisks, fountains, cemeteries, and other structures."[90] Interestingly, Roland Robbins's research on the Minute Man sculpture in Concord, Massachusetts, one of the early nostalgic monuments to gain national recognition during World War II, actually grew from similar circumstances. He was searching for "strong psychological anchors" to ground himself following the social and economic displacement that he had faced during the Depression years.

By the 1930s, Kammen argues, "public sculpture [like the Minute Man statue] . . . became less allegorical and more functional. Its purpose was not so much to perpetuate myths as it was to inspire or assist the process of remembrance."[91] In this sense, the memorial and historical markers along the country's new highway systems became "a kind of surrogate for conventional public sculpture," and linked tradition with travel.[92] Historian David Lowenthal explains that "designation locates the antiquity on our mental map and lends it status. . . . The marked antiquity becomes an exhibit contrived for our attention."[93] During the Massachusetts Bay Colony tercentenary year of 1930, for instance, the Tercentenary Commission "erected permanent iron signs and markers in 96 cities and towns to indicate over 200 places or events significant in the history of Massachusetts."[94] "Markers celebrating this relic or forbidding access to that one profoundly influence what we make of them," writes Lowenthal. "Mere recognition thus transforms the visible past."[95] Coupling tradition and nostalgia to travel using highway markers brought historical sites to the attention of the American public on a previously unimagined scale.

During the first several decades of the twentieth century a small group of private collectors and museums had "fundamentally transformed the presentation of Americana to the people of the United States," setting new precedents and standards for the explication of history.[96] Historic preservationists engaged in "the deliberate use of preserved symbols, . . . display[ed] in appealing settings," and attempted to make them relevant.[97] Regional and local sites, from Sturbridge Village to Williamsburg, opened across the country, and the public response was overwhelming. As American business increasingly supported preservation, the "commercialization of the past became a by-product of this general attraction to the candle of the quaint."[98] In the worst cases, the new historical sites represented the trivialization of tradition, and in the best the democratization of tradition.[99]

Completely immersed in a restoration and preservation outlook, the nascent field of historic-sites archaeology was put on hold in the early 1940s with the American entry into World War II. The war marks a significant disjunction in the history of the development of historical archaeology. As discussed above, the practice of historical archaeology before 1935 was largely the province of interested antiquarians, collectors, and amateur archaeologists, with only the beginnings of "professional interest" in digging (e.g., Colonial Williamsburg and Jamestown). The prewar era was in many ways a fluid, transitional period from the days of gentleman scholars and dilettantes, such as Calver and Bolton, Appleton, and later Harry Hornblower, to one of academically trained professionals such as J. C. Harrington. Yet, even the "professionals" of the period, prehistorians by and large, were lacking in the specific training and knowledge necessary to excavate a historical site.

The range of techniques used during this period include the probing, careful digging, and historical research of Calver and Bolton in New York, the excavation and careful measured engineering drawings of Samuel Yonge at Jamestown, the simple and destructive cross trenching of Colonial Williamsburg archaeologists searching for foundations, the studied and accurate mapping and excavations of Harry Hornblower in Plymouth, and the fairly refined and accurate investigations of J. C. Harrington at Jamestown. These digs represent a cross section of basic research approaches in use at the time, and their outcomes map a range of successes. Few of the projects resulted in published manuscripts that described the work and offered interpretations. As J. C. Harrington lamented, "the apparent goals of the early digs at Jamestown were very little different from later projects; namely to uncover foundations and secure architectural information about original buildings."[100]

Historic-site projects completed prior to World War II were undertaken by a range of individuals including unpaid, volunteer researchers; trained prehistorical archaeologists/anthropologists using unskilled labor, as in the case of Harrington; and trained architects working on their own or with archaeologists. Harrington commented later in his career that "when it came to digging a colonial site and carrying out related research, we were all babes in the woods."[101] Yet, Harrington's work at Jamestown laid the groundwork for much of the historical archaeology to follow. He employed more refined excavation techniques based on artifact recovery and contextual relationships between artifacts and features that he had learned from digging at prehistoric sites, and, impressed with Samuel Yonge's careful documentary research, combined these excavation techniques with what he called a "historical orientation report," developed from his staff's careful historical documentary research.

In many ways, Harrington notes, the advent of World War II gave historical archaeologists a much-needed "chance to step back and size up what we (Jamestown) had been doing for the past eight years."[102] The "pellmell digging of the Thirties," he continued, brought with it a whole host of questions regarding the future of historical archaeology:

Was the excavation of historic sites really worth the cost and effort? What was the impact of this new field of archaeology on other disciplines, particularly history and traditional archaeology? How might the results of historical archaeology be used, other than for restoring buildings and providing interesting relics for museums?[103]

Harrington summed up the prewar period as having made a start "toward developing methods and techniques applicable to this new kind of archaeology."[104]

By 1942, when Roland Robbins began a historical research project on the Minute Man sculpture in Concord, "most field crews and indeed most professional archaeologists were serving the war effort in some capacity. Archaeology at both historic and prehistoric sites was almost at a dead standstill in America."[105] As excavations resumed at the end of the war, Robbins's taste of the research process involving the Minute Man statue and the overall state of preservation placed him in a perfect position to apply archaeology in the service of historic-sites restoration.

Robbins ventured to the shores of Walden Pond in 1945, a time when historical archaeology was still largely unknown, particularly in New England. Although projects such as the major Works Project Administration excavations at Jamestown were begun during the Great Depression, historical archaeology's development into a recognizable discipline would take decades. Historical archaeology slowly grew out of and for many years developed in parallel with the historic preservation movement. As archaeologist Marley R. Brown III has stated, until the 1970s most historical archaeologists, including Robbins, "allowed their sites to be selected for them by organizations committed to the preservation and restoration of historic buildings and sites."[106] Thus, historical archaeology found itself stimulated by many of the same concerns and motivations that were pressing preservationists into action.[107]

CHAPTER 2

House Hunting for Henry David Thoreau

Heightened interest in Thoreau and his works in the late nineteenth and early twentieth centuries ushered in a period of national prominence that culminated in 1945 in the one-hundredth anniversary celebration of his sojourn at Walden Pond. This renewed interest in Thoreau created a sizable audience for Roland Robbins's eventual discovery of Thoreau's house site. Wanting to embark on a career as a writer and still suffering from the loss of his brother John, Henry D. Thoreau had ventured to the woods at Walden Pond in 1845. Taking up his mentor Emerson's offer to use his new woodlot on the shores of Walden Pond, Thoreau began to construct his small house in March of 1845. On July 4, 1845, Thoreau moved into his new house and began his two-year stay at the Pond. While living at Walden, Thoreau gardened, studied natural history, wrote in his journal, and drafted his first book, *A Week on the Concord and Merrimack Rivers*. Thoreau frequently visited friends and family in Concord, welcomed visitors to his home in the woods, and continued to work as a surveyor. He moved out of the house in September 1847 and gave it to Emerson who still owned the land. Emerson later sold the house and it was moved from the Pond circa 1849. It was not until 1854, that *Walden*, Thoreau's story of his stay at the Pond, was first published.

By the beginning of the twentieth century, Walden Pond had developed into a shrine, a mecca for Thoreauvian disciples.[1] Thoreau had attained sainthood in the eyes of his followers, and the house site had become a major stop for literary pilgrims. In the early 1870s, a stone cairn was begun to mark the house location. Stone cairns, often just simple piles of fieldstones and rock, had a long history of use as memorials or shrines beginning in prehistoric times.[2] As Bronson Alcott, Thoreau's transcendentalist friend and colleague, explained in his journal for July 12–13, 1872,

Mrs. Adams suggests that visitors to Walden shall bring a stone for Thoreau's monument and begins the pile by laying down stones on the site of his hermitage, which I point out to her. The tribute thus rendered to our friend may, as the years pass, become a pile to his memory. The rude stones were a monument more fitting than the costliest carving of the artist. Henry's fame is sure to brighten with years, and this spot be visited by admiring readers of his works.[3]

Alcott later recorded that "after bathing we contribute severally our stone to Thoreau's cairn. The pyramid is insignificant as yet but could Thoreau's readers add theirs the pile would rise above the treetops to mark the site of his hermitage."[4] By the 1880s and 1890s, the Walden house site had become a popular destination and was listed in numerous literary guidebooks. Theodore F. Wolfe's popular *Literary Shrines* notes that "another generation of visitors comes now to this spot,—pilgrims from far, like ourselves, to the shrine."[5]

As Walden Pond emerged as a physical shrine for thousands of Thoreau admirers, the author's writings became the focus of the American literary community. For many years, the academy had dismissed Thoreau as a minor disciple and imitator of Emerson. The publication of the fourteen-volume transcription of Thoreau's *Journals* in 1900 and later of multiple editions of *Walden* brought renewed attention to his writing.[6] Vernon Parrington's influential *Main Currents in American Thought* (1927) was the first major twentieth-century publication to acknowledge the importance of Thoreau's literary contribution. Thoreau's message of Yankee individualism, resourcefulness, and self-reliance also thrust him into the public's eye during the Depression years of the 1930s.[7]

Escalated interest in Thoreau culminated in the publication of F. O. Matthiessen's *American Renaissance* in 1941, the same year in which a small group of individuals interested in fostering research and scholarship on Thoreau and his writings established the Thoreau Society. According to historian Eric Cheyfitz, Matthiessen's work effectively canonized, legitimized, and normalized the works of Thoreau, and likewise New England authors such as Poe, Hawthorne, Emerson, and Whitman, in the academic literary community.[8] Although literary scholars were mostly interested in Thoreau and *Walden* as intellectual fodder, the idea

of the physical site of Thoreau's experiment still tantalized. In his introduction to Robbins's *Discovery at Walden,* Thoreau scholar Walter Harding wrote that as a person "more stimulated by ideas than things," he was
skeptical of the value of the excavations at the house site. Yet, he notes,
"when Roland Wells Robbins took me out to Walden Pond last summer
and before my very eyes excavated nails, plaster, bricks and glass from
the site of Thoreau's cabin, I felt that little shiver of excitement which
one reserves for the most special occasions run up and down my spine
like an ecstatic butterfly."[9]

Pilgrimages to Walden, begun in the late nineteenth century, continued throughout the early twentieth century, becoming more frequent in
the decades before World War II. This growth was a direct result of the
expansion of travel and tourism and an indirect outgrowth of artists and
scholars who sought to experience American traditions themselves and
incorporate and interpret them in their writing and painting.[10] With interest in American literature and literary figures flourishing, and historical archaeology at a virtual standstill, thirty-seven-year-old Roland Robbins began the search for the remains of Thoreau's house in 1945.

Robbins was born into a working-class New England family in 1908.[11]
Although his parents were, Robbins notes, from families "with an old
and strong New England Yankee heritage," they did not have the Brahim
or elite background typical of those who forged the early preservation
movement.[12] Robbins's parents, Fred Flint Robbins (b. 1866) and Lucy
May (Davis) Robbins (b. 1873) (figure 2.1), met while working at the Concord Junction Depot, his mother as telegraph operator and his father as
baggage master.[13] His father's later career as a railroad machinist required the family to move repeatedly, and thus the family never owned
a home or established a sense of rootedness. Nevertheless, Robbins
fondly recalled his early home life with brothers Lawrence, Harland,
Kenneth, and Reginald Leonard:

I have nothing but pleasant memories of my younger years growing up. There
was no family fighting nor heavy squabbling, nor did I have frightening night-
mare fantasies haunting me in my youth. My parents seemed to be well suited
to each other and happy with their family life.[14]

Robbins did not have much in common with his older brothers, because of their age differences, but he and his younger brother Leonard

FIG. 2.1. Lucy May Davis and Fred Flint Robbins (couple on right) on their wedding day. (Courtesy of Geraldine Robbins.)

"grew up together and were close" (figure 2.2).[15] Whether at the movies or attending Sunday school, the Robbins brothers were always together. One of Roland's major interests as a child, like that of so many of his contemporaries, was baseball. "He played shortstop," recalled his wife, "and there was always a game going on somewhere."[16]

Although his interest in sports traveled well from city to city as his family moved, Robbins's transition from school to school was more problematic. He barely mentions his school years other than to state that "my formal education ended in 1924 after finishing one year of high

FIG.2.2. Roland (left) and brother Reginald Leonard
Robbins, ca. 1920. (Courtesy of Geraldine Robbins.)

school."[17] He later revealed his insecurity about his educational experience, explaining that

it was common practice for you to look for a job once you got out of grammar
school. . . . In my time, to finish grammar school was the equivalent of completing high school today. And to complete high school then was like getting
your first college degree today.[18]

Reflecting on the link between education and employment, he wrote
that "attitude meant everything—it was part of the job. A good attitude
and a disciplined attention to what you were doing went a long way. It
was like serving an apprenticeship, even if the job was becoming only an
office boy as I did."[19] This theme of the value of apprenticeship, on-the-
job training, and self-directed study would recur in much of Robbins's
later writing as he sought to establish his credentials in archaeology, but
it ran counter to the movement of archaeological training out of the
realm of craft apprenticeship and into the university.[20]

After leaving high school in 1924, Robbins found work as a clerk with R. G. Dun & Company, a credit reference bureau in Boston. He spent several years with this firm and went on to work for several Boston-area employment agencies, becoming manager of the newly formed Boston Reference Bureau in 1928. In 1929, the stock market crash and economic depression forced the company to close; Robbins ironically noted that "I couldn't find a new position for myself, let alone drum up positions for the Boston Reference Bureau to fill."[21] That same year, he suffered the loss of his mother, Lucy May, who died at the family's home in Somerville, Massachusetts.[22] Lucy's death appears to have precipitated her husband's decline and death two years later, leaving the unmarried twenty-three-year-old Robbins alone to find his way in the world.[23]

Like millions of unemployed Americans in the early 1930s, Robbins moved frequently, taking any job he could find. As a young adult, Robbins once again lacked the rootedness of an established home or stable job. He later wrote that "[I] took any means I could find to make enough to support myself. I rang hundreds of doorbells seeking odd jobs of cleaning cellars, washing windows, waxing floors, painting—you name it and I'd do your job for you. This way I got by and saved my personal dignity."[24] In 1932, Robbins headed from Boston to rural Rutland, Vermont, in search of work. Initially living out of his car, he found lodging and a part-time job as an attendant at a hiking shelter maintained by the Green Mountain Club. When no permanent jobs appeared, Robbins began to wash windows and houses for Rutland's elite.

While scrubbing the Clifford Funeral Home in 1932 he began writing "Vermont verse." The subject matter of his musing was eclectic and reflected his keen powers of observation of the world around him. He would later recall that his writing "kept [his] mind occupied . . . when I was alone and confused by the discouraging prospects for my future."[25] Robbins's poetry and verse writing served as an important outlet for his frustrations over his lack of steady employment, wandering lifestyle, and feelings of loneliness. His despair at his situation is clearly evident in the first lines of verse that he wrote: "When a fella's down and out and surely needs a friend, I ask to whom he can turn—on whom he can depend."[26]

Robbins submitted his work to local newspapers and had almost two dozen poems published.[27] The *Rutland Daily Herald's* editor, Howard L. Hindley, noted of one poem that "Roland Robbins has done a piece of genre work in his story of Gramp Fifield's funeral that either Walt Hard or Arthur Goodenough would have loved to do. In some of its grimmer implications, it suggests Mark Twain's pet horror—dallying with death, and its attributes."[28] While clearly pleased with his publishing successes, Robbins was quick to caution that the experience "didn't add a nickel to my income and I had the same problem of finding work to support myself."[29]

This support continued to come primarily through odd jobs until 1934, when a customer who owned the local Ford Motor dealership hired Robbins to sell cars on commission. That same year, in August, Robbins married Vermont native Geraldine Prior, and they set up house in a small apartment in Rutland. "When I first met Roland," Mrs. Robbins recalled, "he was sleeping in his car and working odd jobs; I guess today we would call him a homeless person."[30] He didn't have much in common with her brothers or sisters, she remembers, but he "was quickly adopted into my family; they were very fond of him."[31]

Disappointed with his meager sales commission income and facing the prospect of a cold Vermont winter, the two loaded up their used Chevrolet in October 1934 and headed back to Massachusetts. The newly-weds settled into a one-room apartment in Cambridge, where they lived for the first two years of their marriage. Robbins quickly established a small "but successful" window-cleaning and odd-jobs business, and expanded it to include interior painting and refinishing.[32] These "were still the depression years, and money was hard to come by," Mrs. Robbins remembered; however, "there was always some money coming in and some work to do."[33]

In 1936, through a "fortunate family situation," the Robbinses moved into "a newly-built Cape Cod cottage with more than an acre of land" (figure 2.3) in the town of Lincoln, Massachusetts.[34] Robbins's uncle, real estate agent Charles Davis, loaned the young couple the money to pay for the lot, and they were able to get a mortgage to build their first and only home.[35] Although it was "bleak and bare" at the beginning, Robbins loved the house and the stability that it represented.[36] According to his wife, "he never had any intentions of moving away, he had moved a lot as a child and never wanted to move again."[37] Robbins's business continued to grow, and he soon had "as much work as he cared to handle— since making money was not a big issue to him."[38] Settled into their new house, the couple started a family; son Richard (Dick) was born in 1937, daughter Jean in 1939, and daughter Bonita in 1944 (figure 2.4).[39]

With his young family, heavy work schedule, regular social engagements, and daily tennis games, Robbins had little time left to write po-

FIG. 2.3. Roland and Geraldine Robbins on the back porch of their new home on moving day, July 4, 1936. (Courtesy of Geraldine Robbins.)

etry. Yet, hoping that it would contribute to his financial support, he collected his earlier work in *Thru the Covered Bridge* and published it in 1938.[40] Robbins later wrote that "it was too personal to me when I was experiencing the trying times of the depression years to just discard it."[41] The collection was generally well received by critics.[42] The reviewer for the *Burlington Free Press* found fault with Robbins's poetic style but noted that he "seems to have caught the Vermont rural spirit in his verse, which emphasizes a certain atmosphere more than rhyming or metrical perfection."[43] Robbins wrote from the perspective of a quaint and irascible New England character and thus was the very essence of the quintessential self-reliant Yankee that had been under construction since the early twentieth century by writers such as Robert Frost and in regional publications such as *Yankee* magazine.

Both Frost and *Yankee* were participants in a new regionalist movement that was sweeping the country in the first decades of the twentieth century, one that increasingly identified the essence of New England in the northern states of Vermont, New Hampshire, and Maine.[44] It was in

FIG. 2.4. Robbins and children Dick (left), Bonita (center with Robbins), and Jean (right) visiting the grave of Major William Bradford, Plymouth, Mass., July 17, 1946. (Courtesy of Geraldine Robbins.)

North of Boston that Frost first embraced the persona of the Yankee farmer-poet and "celebrated the Yankee character and pastoral landscape of Old New England."[45] In his later work and in his public readings, the urban-born Frost got "Yankier and Yankier," becoming "New England's version of Will Rogers."[46] In the depths of the Depression, *Yankee* magazine "delivered its own version of Frostian New England to thousands of readers each month."[47] The magazine embraced the ideal of "authentic Yankees who refuse to blame their problems on capitalism or the environment and whose heritage of self reliance and tenacity suggested that the region might endure the depression."[48] In the same vein, the Yankee spirit and Vermont setting that Robbins tried to capture in his verse expressed a New England tradition of individualism and personal freedom that he would cherish and live by.[49] As Robbins turned to Thoreau in his later writing and public lectures, and he positioned himself as a "Thoreau Yankee," a native New Englander—handy, resourceful, inventive, and practical—who could legitimately discover Thoreau's Walden home or offer up a good yarn about the simple, rural life of his adopted state. Yet, like Frost, Robbins was not the poet farmer that his verse suggested, having himself grown up in an urban environment around Boston. But he was still an authentic Yankee. While not a simple Vermont farmer, Robbins was a self-reliant, tenacious man, who used his curiosity, energy, and drive to succeed.

"Roland was always busy with something," his widow remembered. Thus, when he had written "all the poems he had in him," he turned to other types of research and became an avid observer of the world around him.[50] Robbins began keeping detailed journals and prosaic records, regularly documenting the weather and chronicling the changes in season. Explaining this transition to research and writing, he related how the "venerable historical setting" of the towns of Concord and Lexington provided him with a rich source for satisfying his "innate curiosity about events that formed our American history."[51] It is likely that his interest in the past also grew out of his unsettled roots and desire to create a stable life for himself and his family. His ancestors' past and traditions were almost unknown to him; he later wrote that "for all my research, I know very little about my name. . . . By the time I got interested in my ancestry, my parents had died."[52]

Robbins began his first major research project in 1943 while painting the living room of a house in Concord. His customer recounted that he had served as one of the models for sculptor Daniel Chester French's famous statue of the Minute Man. His curiosity piqued, Robbins set off on a "long search for all the details about French and his famous statue at the Old North Bridge."[53] Over the next couple of years, Robbins researched and wrote *The Story of the Minute Man* (1945), a pamphlet on the history of the sculpture.[54] An important piece of twentieth-century art, the sculpture had become a shrine symbolizing the cause of American independence and freedom during the Second World War, appearing as the central image on war bonds.[55] Robbins spent many weekends using sources in the Concord Public Library and courthouse. According to journalist James Dodson, who interviewed Robbins for *Yankee* magazine in 1985, "most of his education . . . came from the basement of the Concord Public Library . . . rummag[ing] through the personal writings of Concord's greatest thinkers—Emerson, Alcott, Channing, and Thoreau."[56]

This first attempt at historical investigation, Robbins felt, established his "local reputation as a researcher." In reflecting on his work on French, he stated that he "felt overpowered by an urge to find out how a young man of Concord, who never before had been commissioned as a sculptor, had won the chance to design this memorial."[57] This declaration underscores Robbins's longing to discover how he himself could secure a chance to pursue a meaningful career with little experience or education. He would soon find the opportunity he sought in the excavation of Thoreau's house at Walden Pond and other hidden ruins of New England's past.

Although Robbins would always consider his Walden Pond excavations as his amateur work, the project gave him his first real taste of the excitement, satisfaction, and recognition that he could acquire through historical and archaeological exploration. Moreover, the enterprise offered a solution to his crisis of vocation that drew on his practical experience as a workingman and Yankee tinkerer. Robbins's new career searching for ruins would furnish him with the materials to build his own personal foundation, a solid basis on which he could establish a stable life. While his interest in and study of historical problems and questions originated with his work on the Minute Man statue, it was magnified and intensified during his quest for Thoreau's house site. The story of the excavation demonstrates the essential manner in which Robbins began to acquire his knowledge of historical archaeology, combining his own research and experimentation with the expertise of specialists in a wide range of areas including history, archaeology, and conservation. During his search at Walden, Robbins also established a lifelong interest in Thoreau that would inspire and sustain him throughout his controversial thirty-five-year career in archaeology.

While Robbins worked full-time at his odd-jobs business (figure 2.5), he continued to explore his interests in a variety of local and regional historical subjects. He was introduced to the continuing debate about the actual location of Thoreau's house while attending the centennial ceremony of Thoreau's sojourn to Walden Pond held on July 4, 1945. Following readings of Thoreau's work, presided over by local historian Allen French, a discussion ensued about the accuracy of the location of the memorial cairn started by Bronson Alcott and Mary Newbury Adams in 1872. Some older members pointed out that the location of the cairn did not agree with Thoreau's own description of the house site "on the side of a hill . . . and half a dozen rods from the pond."[58] Other audience members recalled that the cairn was previously closer to the pond and questioned Alcott's memory of the original house site. Several members pointed out that the cairn location agreed nicely with Thoreau's map of

FIG. 2.5. Robbins and daughter Jean take a break from window washing, October 1942. (Courtesy of Geraldine Robbins.)

Walden Pond, while others questioned whether it was even illustrated on the correct cove.[59]

Following a picnic lunch at the Cliffs, a favorite Thoreau haunt, French reportedly stopped Robbins and said that he was pleased to see him turn his interests to the problem of Thoreau's house.[60] Robbins recounted that

after such a verbal pat on the back as was given me by Mr. French—not too common an experience with me—I had no alternative. Besides, I had become unusually interested in the controversy. I made up my mind that I must try to establish the site of Thoreau's house.[61]

Several weeks after attending the centennial, Robbins received a note from a friend, who warned him that others were planning the same "hunt" and that he might have a "race" on his hands.[62] Clearly hoping that he would discover the site himself, Robbins wrote that this information "startled me into getting out my inadequate six-foot steel ruler the following evening and heading for the pond together with Mrs. Robbins."[63]

As Robbins approached the Walden site in 1945, he took with him an intuitive knowledge of the world around him and the ability to apply this knowledge to the demands of his research. He utilized an interest in history, a natural talent for meticulous documentation, and his everyday skills as a handyman. He familiarized himself with soil strata and with the use of artifacts and features for dating and site interpretation through on-the-job experience, consultation with other practitioners and experts in the field, and reading in history and archaeology. He also drew on his basic knowledge of carpentry, masonry, and surveying and his inventive mind to craft commonsense solutions to the puzzle at Walden.

During this first visit to the pond in August 1945, Robbins measured the distance from the shore to the cairn and site marker and found that it was over two hundred feet. This distance, he recorded, was "considerably beyond the 6 rods that Thoreau credits as the interval from his 'house' to the pond."[64] The initial measurements piqued Robbins's curiosity and prompted him to inquire further about the present cairn location and hut monument. Fred Hart, the park caretaker, told Robbins that he had placed the boulder in front of the cairn based on the testimony of "two old timers," Cy Clark and George Warren, and mounted the plaque on the stone in 1928. He also revealed that the early hut markers west of the cairn had been laid out in 1931 by "a fellow from the south."[65] Skeptical of the accuracy of the cairn's placement, Robbins searched his copy of *Walden* for references to the house's whereabouts, finding several allusions to its location on the shore. After comparing references to the house's location in *Walden* with those recorded in the *Journals*, Robbins decided that Thoreau's descriptions and measurements of the house in the former work were not entirely accurate. He then located several late-nineteenth-century images of Walden Pond taken by photographer Herbert Wendell Gleason that documented that the cairn had remained in the same position since at least 1899. Confident that the cairn remained on or near the original site, Robbins returned to the pond several times during August and September of 1945

FIG. 2.6. Robbins probing around the tree stump at the Thoreau house site, 1946. (Courtesy of the Roland Wells Robbins Collection, the Thoreau Society, Lincoln, Mass., and the Thoreau Institute at Walden Woods.)

to match contemporary descriptions by Channing and Thoreau with the current landscape at the site.[66]

During one of these visual inspections, he located some brick fragments embedded in the pathway that led to the cairn with the help of his "prodding rod" (figure 2.6).[67] When additional searching failed to turn up further evidence, Robbins studied Thoreau's 1846 map of the pond for several evenings but gleaned no new evidence.[68] Realizing that Thoreau had written *Walden* after leaving the pond, Robbins concluded that there was "no need of my seeking the answer from Henry Thoreau's writings alone. I wrote to Aaron Bagg saying that it seemed to me a waste of time to expect that Henry Thoreau's recorded references to his house and its location would lead me to the solution."[69] Commenting on the work ahead, he noted dramatically that "this has got to be done the hard way. I'm going to start from scratch."[70]

In October 1945, he applied to the Middlesex county commissioners for permission to excavate and began digging in the area of the previously identified brick fragments. He noted in his log that he found one hundred fragments of old brick about 13 feet from the cairn and about 2 to 7 inches below the surface.[71] Robbins took a sample of these bricks to the Northeast Brick Company in North Cambridge for dating.[72] A brickyard employee, Mr. Carleton, identified the pieces as "old water struck, hand-made brick considerably older that one hundred years."[73] While this did not prove that the bricks came from Thoreau's house, Robbins hoped that they were part of the "one thousand second-hand brick" mentioned in *Walden.*[74]

Robbins dug several large excavation holes in search of the house; one produced 1,155 brick fragments and the first traces of mortar and plaster.[75] The next excavation area, containing more artifactual evidence of the house, lay adjacent to a large tree stump west of the cairn.[76] Curious about the age of this tree and its relationship to the cairn and house site, Robbins confirmed the tree's presence in several 1899 Gleason photographs.[77] He then contacted John Lambert of the Division of Forestry, who accompanied Robbins to the site in November 1945 to visually inspect the stump. Lambert counted seventy-five to seventy-six rings, estimating that the tree was about eighty to eighty-one years old when it died, and noted that it "probably . . . snapped off in the 1938 hurricane."[78] This confirmed Robbins's initial suspicion that the tree had covered and protected the brick and plaster evidence of the house for all but about ten years after the site was abandoned and the house's superstructure was removed.[79]

Digging on the northeast side of the stump, Robbins discovered brick, plaster, mortar, nails, and glass, at a depth of 8 to 21 inches, and also identified several "boulders" or large rocks at about 21 inches.[80] He then moved to a spot 6 feet east of the stump at the north end of the cairn. Continuing to find additional stone and brick with mortar and suspecting that he had located a foundation, he enlarged the excavation hole.[81] On November 12, 1945, Robbins recorded in his log that he "uncovered the foundation of the house's chimney" (figure 2.7).[82] The square base of stone and brick pieces measured approximately 4 feet 8 inches north-south by 5 feet east-west. Thoreau, Robbins discovered, had noted in *Walden* that "I laid the foundation of a chimney at one end bringing two cartloads of stones up the hill from the pond in my arms."[83] After showing the chimney feature to several witnesses, including local Thoreauvians Wallace B. Conant, Mr. and Mrs. Allen French, and Mrs. Caleb

FIG. 2.7. Robbins standing in chimney base excavation, November 1945. Robbins had Thoreauvian Wallace B. Conant (left of Robbins) airbrushed out of this photo prior to its use in *Discovery at Walden*. (Courtesy of the Roland Wells Robbins Collection, the Thoreau Society, Lincoln, Mass., and the Thoreau Institute at Walden Woods.)

Wheeler, Robbins cleaned and mapped the foundation, and hired a professional photographer to document the chimney base.[84]

During the winter, Robbins focused on learning more about the chimney, searching for sketches of the cabin printed in early versions of *Walden* and in Thoreau biographies that would give some hint of the chimney's placement and orientation. He also studied the construction of the chimney at the Thoreau family's "Texas" house in the village of Concord, and found the use of fieldstones mortared and filled with small brick fragments identical to that of the chimney at the Walden house. Robbins noted that the original Ticknor and Fields printing of *Walden* (1854) showed "the house facing east or southeast, also the chimney is inside the house in this picture."[85] He also checked the compass orientation of the chimney foundation with Thoreau's 1846 map of Walden Pond and found that "they lined up with one another quite perfectly."[86]

Robbins next began looking for the cellar, excavating a hole at the northeast corner of the cairn; he noted that "the soil seemed to me to be in a virgin condition . . . a white and fine sand soil which had some gravel in it."[87] Robbins's last excavation area of 1945 was along the east side of the chimney foundation, where he "dug for signs of post holes."[88] He found no evidence of posts, but at 6 inches below the surface he discovered thirty-one nail fragments and an ash deposit.

In early January, Robbins began discussions with several people, including architects Thomas Mott Shaw and Andrew F. Hepburn, about an appropriate monument for the house site.[89] Both men were principals in the firm of Perry, Shaw, and Hepburn of Boston, the architects hired by John D. Rockefeller Jr. to direct the Williamsburg restoration. Robbins also researched the development and dating of cut and wire nails and scrutinized the papers of noted author and antiquarian Thomas Wentworth Higginson for a reference to Thoreau's cellar with "a pine tree of ten year's growth in the middle."[90] He finally found this reference in a letter written in 1867 and speculated that the pine tree mentioned by Higginson might be the tree stump near the cairn. Robbins noted that

Bronson Alcott and Mrs. Adams are credited with establishing the cairn in 1872, only 5 years after Higginson made his hike to the pond, and early pictures show the tree that yielded my booty growing close to the cairn, it makes Higginson's observation quite accurate.[91]

Throughout the late winter and early spring Robbins analyzed the artifactual, documentary, and excavation information from the previous season's digging as he began to plan his work for the spring of 1946.

Robbins resumed excavations in the spring, digging to the west and south of the vicinity of the chimney foundation. There he uncovered additional features including the northwest and southeast corner foundations of the cabin and the structure's cellar hole. He also concentrated on a grouping of boulders within the area of the earlier granite markers. Robbins speculated that this might be the spot of Thoreau's "outdoor fireplace," which he had used for cooking before finishing the house and chimney.[92] Additional digging in an area about 6 feet northwest of the chimney foundation produced numerous artifacts including bricks and nails. Robbins interpreted this area, "banked on three sides" and open on the side facing the house, as the site of Thoreau's woodshed.[93]

In addition to his ongoing research, Robbins prepared a book prospectus and continued his discussions with the architects about a "Walden memorial."[94] Shaw provided revised plans for a memorial that included

10, six ft. high, 8 in. sq., drilled with chain hooks and set-up on hut's site, granite markers, also large boulders to cover site of hut's chimney foundation, with inscription of 150 letters on center boulder.[95]

Robbins met with local Thoreauvians Mrs. Caleb Wheeler, Mr. Wallace Conant, and Mr. and Mrs. Allen French to show them Shaw's plan, and noted that this group and the Middlesex county commissioners were "enthused with it and felt a July 4th or July 13th dedication would be possible and an excellent idea."[96] While Robbins clearly felt prepared to memorialize the site, skeptics questioned whether he had actually found the house. Writing to Thoreau scholar Walter Harding, Wallace B. Conant privately complained that Robbins's book prospectus "speaks rather hastily of the two spots that we marked but could not possibly have been the right place. Bet. U & me, [*sic*] there are points about the "discovery" that don't match up."[97] Conant argued against immediate placement of any memorials or new markers.

In May, the county commissioners notified Robbins that they had revised the plans for the memorial drawn by Shaw. The new plan called for a series of granite posts that enclosed the house site area and the cairn without marking the footprint of the house itself, which they feared had not been absolutely identified.[98] Robbins and his local supporters found this suggestion completely unacceptable, recommending instead that the cairn remain the only monument. The opposing parties held several meetings to resolve the dispute, which Robbins blamed on park caretaker Fred Hart's resentment at his discovery; both sides agreed to give the Thoreau Society the opportunity to decide on the final plan.[99]

Meanwhile, Robbins attempted to verify his discovery through additional documentary research and confirmation from other archaeologists and specialists. He took the artifact collection from his excavations to Frederick Norton of the Massachusetts Institute of Technology for identification and dating. Professor Norton looked at the materials and reported that "it was impossible to place a definite age on such evidence. But he said it appeared to be old enough to fit the period when Thoreau built at Walden."[100] Late in June, Robbins returned to the pond with forester Jack Lambert to "determine the exact age of the tree stump" by cutting a cross section for tree ring dating.[101] Lambert determined that the pine tree was ninety-one years old, indicating that it had begun growing in 1855, eight years after Thoreau left the site and the house was moved from the pond.[102] Robbins attempted to confirm this date using Gleason's photographs of the pond, discovering several views of the pine tree in the late nineteenth century. He also returned to his study of Thoreau's original map of Walden Pond, noting that it indicated that "the 12 rods distance from the hut's southern end to [the] cove is identical with the distance I measured from cairn to cove."[103] In early July, Robbins visited Boston archaeologist Sidney Strickland, who "does a great deal of excavating work down around Plymouth."[104] Strickland confirmed that all the nails were cut and from the "period that Thoreau lived at Walden."[105] Robbins recorded in his notebook that Strickland "was convinced I had found the original chimney foundation."[106] Robbins also visited with a Mr. Orchard at the Peabody Museum to obtain "information for binding and preserving the plaster and mortar found at Walden."[107]

In July 1946 he returned to the house site and resumed excavations in the area of the woodshed; discovering a feature of stone and brick "that follows the pattern of the chimney foundation," he identified it as the southeast corner of the woodshed.[108] Robbins also reported that he had located two or three boulders, 4 feet northeast of the tree stump and 10 inches in the soil:

the way they fit together, coupled with the fact that their top surface was about 10″ below present ground level shows that a hole was dug in the soil to embed them when they were laid. This and the fact that they are in the position where the northwest corner of the hut would have been located tends to prove the boulders were placed and used for a foundation of one corner of the hut.[109]

Robbins next searched in earnest for the house's 6-by-6-foot cellar hole. "Tunneling" under the cairn in search of the cellar, he identified "what appeared to be a boulder foundation" that went 2 feet into the ground, but he failed to find evidence for the cellar.[110] Upon further reflection, Robbins realized that the small stone foundation was located almost exactly in the center of the house. He returned to Joseph Hosmer's published account of his visit to the house in September 1845 and found that Hosmer referred to a "king-post . . . extending from the bottom of the cellar to the ridge-pole."[111] While the boulder foundation was not in the bottom of the cellar, Robbins speculated that it had been used to support this king post, and that Hosmer may simply have forgotten its exact position.[112] If this was the foundation of the king post, Robbins speculated, then "the 6' × 6' cellar hole should be found between the center of the hut site and the position of its door," suggesting to him that the rear of the cairn would have to be moved.[113]

Robbins received permission from the Middlesex county commissioners to move the rear of the cairn and excavate the area.[114] In August, he began to disassemble the cairn and discovered over thirty stones with inscriptions dating from the 1870s and 1880s at the bottom of the pile. These stones, he later learned through documentary research, had been placed by several groups of early pilgrims to the site.[115] Robbins was interested in the cairn both as a monument to Thoreau that provided a direct link through Alcott and others and, like historical signs and monuments, as a marker of the exact site of the house. It would become his job, as he saw it, to improve on markers that recorded the approximate locations of historical sites by discovering the actual physical ruins, which would provide a tangible link with a past event or personage. Even more than the cairn, Robbins's work provided a visible, physical foundation for the site, one that commemorated the past and yet was rooted in the present.

Beginning excavations under the cairn, Robbins and friend Anton Kovar relocated the supposed king post foundation stones and began to dig in the cellar area.[116] Here he found "old nails and pieces of plaster as well as odd pieces of glass. . . . The soil we dug out definitely was a mixture of different grades of sand and loam."[117] The excavation was conducted with the help of members of the local community and the Thoreau Society, including secretary Walter Harding. This part of the cellar hole was dug to approximately four feet below ground surface and yielded primarily cut nails. Before Robbins backfilled the cellar, Walter Harding prepared a statement about the discovery for those present to sign and sealed it in a bottle, and they placed it in the bottom of the hole.[118]

Excavation of the cellar hole continued after more of the cairn's stones were moved; this new digging uncovered a deposit of several large pieces of plaster along the cellar's southern edge measuring almost seven feet long, one foot thick, and three feet wide.[119] Upon finishing the work in this area, Robbins speculated that the location of the plaster just outside the cabin door indicated that the plaster feature represented either a disposal or preparation area used by Thoreau when he plastered the inside of the house in November 1845.[120] The plaster deposit also established the approximate location of the house's southeast corner in that it had to have been outside the already finished house. Cut nails sealed below the plaster, Robbins noted, were likely disposed of by Thoreau when he was working on the building.[121] Robbins reported that artifactual evidence from the cellar hole included plaster, glass, brick, crockery or pottery (stoneware and redware), and nails, all found about two feet below the upper "humus deposit." He stated that "wood ashes were also found. Three or four feet beneath the 2′ level of the cellar-hole, fill soil was found" that contained no artifacts.[122] Robbins speculated that this clean fill was deposited first and that the upper fill, containing a mixture of old and new artifacts, slowly filled the hole after the house was moved.

Following his work on the cellar, Robbins filled and leveled the site area and made measurements to prepare his final maps.[123] His work on the project during the remainder of 1946 and early 1947 focused mainly on historical research, including investigations on the inscribed stones that he found at the bottom of the cairn and the location of the Thoreau house after it was moved from Walden.[124] With Robbins's work on the site complete, the construction of the monument marking the house and the reconstruction of the cairn proceeded. The final monument design was based on Shaw's plan for a series of granite posts linked by chains outlining the house footprint; a large flat stone was used to mark the chimney (figure 2.8).

Robbins's work at the Thoreau house site was, in his own mind, a completely amateur undertaking. The investigation was creative and resourceful because of its integration of historical research and excavation data, including features and artifacts, and for its overall level of documentation.[125] His research program was remarkably similar to that reported by historical archaeology pioneer Reginald Pelham Bolton in his 1923 description of his and William L. Calver's excavations in New York. Their description illustrates the remarkable similarity between their approach and Robbins's work at Walden.

The method of discovery is by the use of old maps and historical books locating some old site . . . , then by searching the surface for indications . . . , and by prodding the soil with a light steel rod, . . . we attain a considerable degree of expertness in deciding the character of objects below the sod, then the shovel is brought into play exposing the buried layer or deposit, and in the sifter even such small objects are caught. . . .[126]

FIG. 2.8. Ray Harris (left) and Robbins erecting Thoreau House Memorial designed by T. Mott Shaw, March 29, 1948. (Courtesy of the Walter Harding Collection, the Thoreau Society, Lincoln, Mass., and the Thoreau Institute at Walden Woods.)

While Robbins did not excavate and record his work systematically in the sense of the grid-oriented testing that Harrington employed at Jamestown, or in modern terms, he did make decisions based on both documentary evidence and thorough testing with his steel "prodding" rod. As detailed in his daily logs, he used a wide range of documentary sources, including Thoreau's journals; the numerous editions of *Walden;* period letters and newspaper reports; photographs, particularly Gleason's; period maps; and interviews. His study of the Minute Man statue had prepared him for the documentary research required for the Walden project, and he quickly became skilled at interrogating the documents and weaving multiple strands of evidence together to support a theory. Rarely trusting a single source, Robbins used the documents in combination with physical evidence to locate Thoreau's house at Walden. Not one to leave any stone unturned, he followed up on all leads, whether early accounts of the house's location, descriptions of the building itself, or information about the cairn and its relationship to the original house. As Harrington did with his "Historic Orientation Reports" from Jamestown, Robbins made excellent use of his written/archival data in terms of choosing where to excavate. With information provided by several contemporary descriptions of the house and Thoreau's map of the pond, he used the location of the chimney and of pier features at the northwest corner to direct his future excavations.

Robbins utilized general horizontal controls, particularly for locating artifacts and features, such as the chimney and corner posts. He excavated vaguely by natural stratigraphic layers, although his records are less detailed in this regard. He mapped his excavation areas and features such as the chimney foundation using triangulation based on fixed points: the pine tree stump, for example, or granite markers, or the brass plaque mounted on the cairn (figure 2.9). In addition to his detailed sketch maps, Robbins took hundreds of photographs to document his work at the site.

While Robbins made numerous efforts to have the artifacts from the dig identified by various experts, he clearly saw them as less important than the actual foundations. As discussed in the previous chapter, this preference for foundations over artifacts was still quite typical in historical archaeology, as witnessed by the early Jamestown and Williamsburg excavations. Robbins was clear about this approach, noting that he "did not dig for artifacts . . . but for ruins."[127] At Jamestown, Harrington has noted that the "recovery of artifacts was not ignored, but it was incidental to the major objective" of locating foundations and buildings. In time, the discipline of historical archaeology would come to reject this hunt for foundations and embrace the pursuit of a suite of evidence—artifacts, features, and their contextual relationships—for the study and interpretation of culture.[128] To his credit, Robbins carefully collected and studied the materials that he recovered from his excavations at Walden, storing them in numbered envelopes that were referenced to his specific excavation locations and recorded in his daily logs.[129] While the horizontal provenience of the artifacts is relatively clear from Robbins's records, particularly his sketch maps, direct references to the depth of artifacts and their relationships to the various soil layers are less consistent. However, his daily logbooks contain the depth of selected artifacts and artifact groups and their general soil association. Recent reanalysis and plotting of this data using GIS software demonstrates that Robbins's level of documentation provides enough information to accurately place most artifacts and features in their correct horizontal position and spatial relationships across the site, and in some cases to discern the vertical or stratigraphic position of these materials.[130]

Before finishing fieldwork at the site, Robbins had attempted to sell the story of the discovery to numerous magazines, including *Atlantic Monthly* and *Life*, to raise money to cover his expenses for the project.[131]

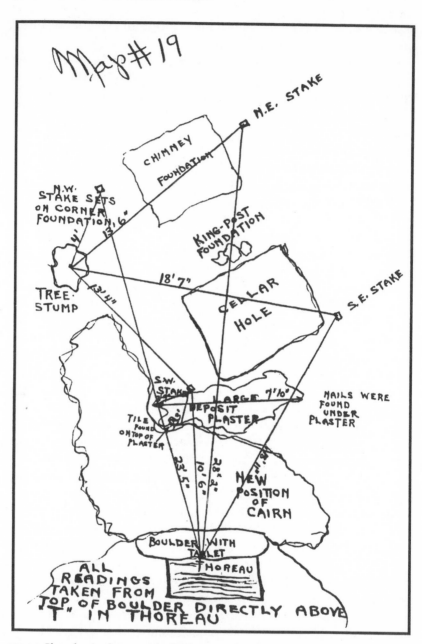

FIG. 2.9. Plan of major features at the Walden excavation, showing triangulation measurements. (From "#3 Thoreau Hut Notes," Map #19, Sept. 1946.) (Courtesy of the Roland Wells Robbins Collection, the Thoreau Society, Lincoln, Mass., and the Thoreau Institute at Walden Woods.)

Still earning his living through his odd-jobs business, he reported to Walter Harding that

I spent much money I didn't have on the work, and while I find myself in an embarrassing financial position at present, I believe that in the long run it will prove a most satisfactory investment. Let me assure you that I didn't enter into this search for the financial returns it might reward but rather because of my sincere interest in trying to reconstruct these problems.[132]

With no response from these publishers and his project almost finished, Robbins decided to produce his own book on the project in an attempt to generate some financial reimbursement from the work.[133] The resulting *Discovery at Walden* is a lively, detective story–like account of his experience that presents an engaging summary of the work and also reveals Robbins's personal insecurity about his future (figure 2.10).[134]

Robbins guarded his claim to the discovery of the house site, controlling who saw his fieldwork at Walden and maintaining a level of secrecy that in some ways worked against him. He noted that he "did not uncover the entire formation but will when the proper witnesses are present."[135] Some members of the Thoreau Society, for instance, remained unconvinced of Robbins's discoveries, particularly because of his unwillingness to let them view the diggings while the work was underway.[136] Early in the project, he refused to let Walter Harding look at his excavations, and later that year recorded in his field journal that "I told [Mr. Rogers] of my results at Walden Pond (but didn't reveal the foundations location)."[137] In recalling the incident, Harding remembered that Robbins was reluctant to allow him to see the site because he "was always very suspicious of any college teachers—he had one particularly unfortunate experience."[138] It seems that Robbins had told one of his window-washing customers, H. H. Blanchard of the Tufts University English Department, about his discovery. Blanchard, recalled Harding, was "one of those real stuffed shirt Ph.D.s who felt that no one without a Ph.D. was worthy to be in his presence."[139] Blanchard "belittled Roland's discovery" and, adding insult to injury, provided information on the discovery to the newspaper without telling Robbins.[140] Robbins felt betrayed, Harding recalled. He had wanted to keep control of the information and the situation; after all, "this was Roland's secret, not H. H. Blanchard's."[141]

It is clear from Robbins's earliest writing that he had a rather low opinion of academics, one that he would hold throughout his career. His

FIG. 2.10. Geraldine Robbins reading *Discovery at Walden* with
Roland looking on, ca. 1947. (Courtesy of the Roland Wells Robbins Col-
lection, the Thoreau Society, Lincoln, Mass., and the Thoreau Institute at
Walden Woods.)

verse "The Lecturer" (1938) is particularly interesting because it chroni-
cles Robbins's early working-class disdain for academics and presents it
in a quaint rural Yankee tale.

> Professor Knowall came to town
> And gave a lecture on
> The planting of the 'taters and
> The growing of the corn.
>
> He went ahead and told us how
> The milking should be done

And said we shouldn't scare the cows
Or try to make them run.

He swung and banged his dainty hands
To bring his ideas out
And used a lot of college words
We never heard about.

And ended up by telling how
To gather in the hay.
Then asked if there was anyone
Who had a word to say.

Sam Fifield stirred and looked about.
Then slowly he arose
And said, "I'd like to say a word
'Fore meeting's brought to close.

I sort of take it from your talk
That all we need to do
Is scratch about the soil a bit
And plant a seed or two.

Then sit back in our easy chairs
And watch it as it grows,
And count the profits that we'll make
From all the dif'rent rows.

You've even got the gumption, friend
To try and tell us how
To feed and raise our cattle—when
I doubt you've milked a cow.

I've done successful farming now
For more than forty years
So I don't think I need to know
You city folks ideas.

I find to get the best of life
You've got to work and plod—
And that alone ain't good enuff
Unless you work with God.

When your ideas can better that
And prove a finer way.
Come back, and I will listen then
To what you have to say.[142]

This early work expresses Robbins's hostility and contempt for academics well before the Blanchard incident. Still, Blanchard's insult and betrayal were doubly troubling to Robbins, as Blanchard was one of the very window-washing customers that he would gladly have forsaken in favor of a new professional career. Robbins's depiction of the "literary scholars" at the 1945 Thoreau Centennial meeting is a clear piece of sarcasm directed at Blanchard and his kind. Robbins comments that he

was impressed by the gray and intellectual heads that predominated among those in attendance. I, with all my 37 years, felt conscious of stepping from my generation into one I was not in a literary way prepared for. Here I was among the "Big League" of the literary world. Prominent professors of literature, as well as authors of note, were paying their respects to this site.[143]

Robbins's negative experiences with academics at Walden certainly colored his later relations with university professors, particularly those in archaeology; he remained forever distrustful of the academy and its members.

Robbins made no excuses for his careful handling of news about the discovery, stating that "many are they who want to know the secret and have gone out to Walden Pond to seek it. This is in vain as I took special precautions to conceal my work until plans were formulated to preserve it."[144] The plans he refers to included both his own publication on the discovery and the creation of a Thoreau memorial or shrine at the house site. In recording the discovery of Thoreau's house in his field notebook, Robbins noted that "Mr. Conant said it would prove to be one of the world's greatest shrines," and penciled into the margin, "*Let's hope so.*"[145]

Robbins, however, desired to do more than simply earn a living by unearthing ruins and re-creating buildings, explaining that "by profession I operate a small and successful window cleaning and painting business but by heart I live with the unanswered questions to the historical past."[146] He also used this heartfelt interest in the past to engage the public in the process of research and the excitement of discovery, albeit sometimes with an eye to financial gain. His animated style in *Discovery at Walden,* clearly drawing on both his earlier foray into poetry and quaint verse and his historical inquiry into the Minute Man statue, captivated his readers. The title page of *Discovery at Walden* promotes Robbins as the discoverer of Thoreau's Walden house. It also announces, like a supermarket tabloid, that the book contains the "*Exclusive* Photographs of

Thoreau's Chimney Foundation" (emphasis added).[147] Perhaps the book's most engaging feature is the presentation of a number of almost unbelievable coincidences, such as Robbins's moving into his Lincoln house on July 4, the day that Thoreau moved into his Walden house; the visit of a young man named Henry David Thoreau Jr., "a distant relative of Henry David Thoreau," to the site on the day Robbins discovered the first evidence of the house; and the discovery of the chimney foundation exactly one hundred years to the day after the building had been finished.[148] While adding mystery and excitement to the narrative, the many coincidences serve both to expand the storyline and to reinforce that Robbins was the true discoverer of Thoreau's house and certainly the right man for the job. It was, he seems to suggest, his destiny.

The book sold well, received good reviews from the press and the public, and created demand for Robbins as a lecturer.[149] Robbins distributed many review copies and received reactions from readers in all walks of life. Thoreau Society secretary Walter Harding wrote to him that "you did a superb piece of work. As for criticisms, I actually cannot find a single error in it—and I think that it is the first book on Thoreau that I've read that I could honestly say that about."[150] The book, he noted, is a "careful recording of each step in his [Robbins's] labors, scholarly in the best sense of the word, and as fascinating as a detective story."[151] Reviewers found *Discovery at Walden* to be a compelling and unique narrative. Clayton Hoagland of the *New York Sun* wrote that "*Discovery at Walden* has added an unusual chapter to the history of American literature of the nineteenth century. . . . [the] photographs are unique in the field of what I should call American literary archaeology."[152] A review in the *New England Quarterly,* noting the importance of Robbins's identification of the cabin location, also explained that

there are further reasons . . . for welcoming this little book—not the least being its story of the quest. . . . The story of the triumphant quest is as good as a detective yarn. . . . Robbins . . . tells his story with shrewd, homespun, naively humorous quaintness.[153]

Robbins employed the same literary devices that he had used in his book of Vermont poetry, styling himself as a tenacious, commonsense "Thoreau Yankee" who succeeded through hard work where others had failed. As he said to Walter Harding, "I know better than to try and compete with the eloquence that comes from the pen of a true Thoreau student. I will attempt to write the story in a view of Yankee humor and common sense. These are my only qualifications."[154]

The Walden excavations also propelled Robbins into the lecture circuit. "Walter Harding says he has been urging you to go on the lecture platform with pictures and relics of the Thoreau discovery," wrote local Thoreauvian W. B. Conant. "An excellent idea!" Conant continued, "I believe that by next season women's clubs, etc. will be receptive to such a feature and trust you will consider it well. Your personality and pleasing address (manner and form) commend you to the most exacting listener."[155] With the prodding of his associates, Robbins quickly found his voice for public presentations. He formalized his *Discovery at Walden* slide lecture, prepared a brochure to advertise it to interested parties, and joined the lecture circuit.[156] He wrote that his first lecture was "a vivid, humorous, and entertaining account by a New England Yankee of his unusual experiences and the amazing coincidences that accompanied his work at Walden."[157] Thoreau scholar Walter Harding commended Robbins, writing that

you have admirably succeeded in walking that hair-line of satisfying the most meticulous scholar and at the same time using a human approach which will arouse the interest of the man in the street who knows no more about Thoreau than that he was a fixture in the annals of American literature.[158]

Robbins's presentation of the Walden excavation placed him within view of many of the region's historical and patriotic societies and museums, who were attracted to his historic-sites excavation skills, New England Yankee persona, and self-confident demeanor.

The Walden project was Robbins's answer to a calling that came from deep within himself. It was at Walden Pond that he first realized that history and archaeology could fulfill his desire to establish a meaningful professional career. Geraldine Robbins remembers that "as he was doing window washing, and house painting, and all that, he never expected it to be his profession for life; this was always a stopgap."[159] He sought to be more, he said, than an "expert at washing other people's windows and renovating other people's houses."[160] At Walden, he began to formulate the answer to the question that had drawn him to Daniel Chester French's sculpture of the Minute Man. How could he secure a chance to pursue a meaningful career with little experience or education? Working amidst Thoreau's chimney foundation, he experienced for the first time the power of physical remains to captivate both his imagination and the imagination of those around him. Although Robbins's entry into this work created feelings of anxiety and financial insecurity, it also held immense promise for the future; in his mind there was no turning back.

While Robbins always considered his Walden excavations as his amateur work, the project set the pattern for his future career in historic-sites archaeology and restoration. He applied his intuitive knowledge of the world to the task at hand, utilizing an interest in history, a natural talent for meticulously documenting the world around him, and his everyday skills as a handyman. During this first excavation, he depended heavily on his practical workman's knowledge of materials, tools, and crafts embracing far more than painting houses or washing windows, and on his proficiency in problem solving. In addition, he studied and became familiar with soil strata and explored the use of artifacts and features for dating and site interpretation. Much of what he learned at Walden was acquired through on-the-job experience, through discussions with other archaeologists and experts, and through reading in history and archaeology. Robbins thus used his basic knowledge of carpentry, masonry, and surveying and his inventive mind to craft commonsense solutions to the puzzle that he endeavored to solve at Walden.

After his fieldwork at Walden, Robbins crafted his trademark detective-story approach to writing about his work, a formula that would be adopted by Ivor Noël Hume and James Deetz in the 1960s, and he first successfully experimented with his public speaking skills. But a professional career required more than one dig. While the Walden excavation captured his imagination, created a lifelong interest in Thoreau, and launched him on the road to historic-sites archaeology, it was at the Saugus Iron Works that Robbins would firmly lay the groundwork for a life dedicated to identifying and restoring the ruins of New England's past.

CHAPTER 3

Forging a New Career

Excavating the Ironworks Sites of New England

Following his work at Walden, Robbins vigorously promoted the discovery of Thoreau's house site. He lectured about his remarkable find to civic organizations and local and regional preservation and historical societies, groups that were increasingly interested in the development of archaeological sites as monuments to early New England. Robbins's enthusiastic lectures on his work at Walden, and his humorous and quaint lecture style in the persona of the archetypal New England Yankee, captured the imagination of these eager preservationist groups, who solicited him to visit their sites. His lectures and publication on the Walden excavation and his decisive self-promotion led directly to Robbins's participation in historical archaeology projects at other sites in the eastern United States.

Although historical archaeology did not emerge "as an organized and established field between 1946 and 1960," it did become much more widely practiced during this time.[1] A heightened awareness of historic sites developed among both archaeologists and historians, and the practice of historical archaeology underwent a slow refinement of methods and technique. Investigations took on a greater interest in the careful study and interpretation of artifacts, particularly their stratigraphic relationships and context, and the production of more thorough, albeit largely descriptive, publications. Excavation techniques improved and stratigraphic controls were borrowed from prehistoric archaeology, resulting in systematic proveniencing of artifacts using site grids and careful vertical control within layers and features. Yet, even with increasing interest in historical archaeology, the field remained firmly grounded in the restoration and preservation approach through the late 1950s. As a profession, it was still largely unorganized and struggling to identify its intellectual foundations.

Historical archaeologists practicing in the late 1940s also paid little attention to industrial sites, allowing Robbins to perform pioneering work at a series of important industrial and commercial sites. From the late 1940s to early 1960s, he investigated the Saugus Iron Works in Saugus, Massachusetts; the John Winthrop Jr. Blast Furnace in Quincy, Massachusetts; the Dover Union Iron Company in Dover, Massachusetts; Sterling Blast Furnace in New York; and the Philipsburg Manor Upper Mills in Tarrytown, New York, working for preservation organizations that sought to develop and enhance their properties through historical restoration, reconstruction, and monument building.[2]

As in the late nineteenth and early twentieth centuries, preservation after World War II was driven by national insecurities and a need to protect and promote American values and strengths. The postwar period was an age of anxiety, "a time when concerns about national security, swift social change, and a profound sense of historical discontinuity troubled people deeply."[3] Historian Michael Wallace has written that "the populist openings of the thirties were checked and reversed . . . the meaning of 'historical' was narrowed . . . [and] the bourgeoisie set out to uproot 'un-Americanism' and celebrate . . . 'the American Way of Life.'"[4] Historical museums and sites around the country reacted to this growing angst and began to market themselves as sources of patriotic inspiration and national pride and as keepers of the legends of early America. Many of these organizations tried to educate the public through new research initiatives and revised interpretative displays, while at the same time fulfilling their "desire to preserve oases of the pastoral, pre-industrial past at a time of startling technological and urban change."[5] Other groups "fetishized history," glorifying American exceptionalism and praising technological and industrial progress.[6]

The American Iron and Steel Institute, for example, underwrote the Saugus Iron Works restoration in part to create a symbol of the industry's important contribution to the past and present growth of the country. In this context, the Saugus project was wedged between the tradition-oriented, antimodern values of the early preservation movement and the burgeoning commercial utilization of the past. This so-called "Corporate Roots movement" had its own agenda, one frequently at odds with the goals and desires of preservation professionals.[7] Robbins was able to assist preservation organizations through his restoration-focused archaeology, but he also experienced firsthand the inevitable conflicts and tensions inherent in these relationships.

· The often complex, varying objectives and lack of experience of restoration-minded organizations and their sponsors made planning and implementing excavations difficult and required Robbins to do far more than excavate. At Saugus, for instance, he served simultaneously as a member of the restoration planning committee, primary archaeologist, exhibit planner, site interpreter, museum curator, landscaper and landscape restorer, maintenance chief, and often day-to-day manager of the site. This multitude of responsibilities provided Robbins with daily challenges and stresses, limiting his time and reducing his ability to concentrate on the archaeology at hand.

The mixed messages that Robbins received from Saugus's executives— J. Sanger Attwill, the president of the First Ironworks Association; Quincy Bent, the chairman of the Joint Reconstruction Committee; Walter S. Tower, the president of the American Iron and Steel Institute; and Conover Fitch, project architect for Perry, Shaw, Hepburn, Kehoe and Dean— caused ongoing conflict over both archaeological and nonarchaeological concerns. The schizophrenic management of the Saugus project eventually brought Robbins to the brink of a nervous breakdown. Nevertheless, the experience broadened his understanding of history and archaeology, and he gained important insights into managing archaeological projects within the setting of institutional constraints and monetary pressures.[8] Building on his previous business experience, he acquired management skills at Saugus that enabled him to develop into a consummate professional consultant. At the same time, however, he began to emerge in the eyes of academic archaeologists as an opportunistic exploiter of the past. Within archaeology in general at this time, historical archaeologists were extremely hard to come by, and few academic archaeologists were interested in historic sites or available to do consulting work for historical societies and house museums. Thus, Robbins's interest in historical sites and monuments and his availability for consulting jobs made him a natural choice for these organizations. Ironically, the very act of engaging in this consulting work eventually resulted in Robbins's career and credentials becoming more suspect to members of the academy.

The Saugus Iron Works project illustrates Robbins's developing research and excavation approach within the context of a major reconstruction-oriented project, one typical of the preservation activities conceived of and carried out in New England during this period. Furthermore, it marks his entry into industrial archaeology, particularly sites related to the evolution of the iron industry in New England and the Northeast. Robbins went on to excavate numerous early industrial sites in the Northeast using a thoughtful approach that, in retrospect, embodied many characteristics of modern industrial archaeology practice. Archaeologist Marley R. Brown III commented in 1978 that "although Robbins's dependence on heavy equipment in his excavations has been a source of controversy among professional archaeologists, he is one of the leading authorities on seventeenth- and eighteenth-century industrial sites in New England."[9] Of the sixty archaeological projects that Robbins completed during his career, thirty-two were industrial sites; of these, twenty were iron-industry complexes. Robbins's work at the Saugus Iron Works provides a context for examining his passion for and approach to excavating industrial sites.[10] The Saugus Iron Works project provided Robbins with the opportunity to engage in historical archaeology as a professional, one that he quickly recognized, and it demonstrates how his career developed after Walden.

The Saugus Iron Works was established in about 1646 by a group of English investors known as the "Company of Undertakers of the Iron Works in New England." John Winthrop Jr., son of the Massachusetts Bay Colony's governor, was instrumental in forming the company and planning the ironworks at Saugus. As the Great Migration of the 1630s came to an end, the Massachusetts Bay Colony found that iron products were becoming scarcer and more expensive. A 1641 ordinance from the colony's General Court encouraged the search for mineral deposits that could be used for ironmaking. Propelled by the need for iron products and encouraged by the discovery of iron ore deposits in the Saugus area, Winthrop assembled a team of skilled English ironworkers to construct a series of ironworks in the colony. The first ironworks plant built by the Company of Undertakers, known as the Braintree Works, was begun in 1643 and was also excavated by Roland Robbins (John Wintrhop Jr. Blast Furnace, Quincy, Mass.). Several years later, the company built the Lynn Works at Saugus (the Saugus Iron Works), and this facility continued in production until circa 1668. The Saugus Iron Works complex included the blast furnace, forge, rolling mill, and a collection of worker's dwellings. The Saugus Iron Works marked the first sustained operation of a fully integrated ironworks in North America and, along with the Braintree Works, served as a prime training ground for skilled ironworkers in colonial America.

As Saugus's promotional literature would later boast, the ironworks reconstruction was intended as both a shrine to the iron and steel industry and as a measure of the industry's progress. In 1948, the First Iron Works Association of Saugus, Massachusetts, aware of Robbins's recent successes at Walden, hired him to excavate the ironworks site. The president of the association, J. Sanger Attwill, invited Robbins to participate in an "Antique Treasure hunt" to locate the site's iron-making components.[11] Robbins was initially engaged for a trial project, but became "so successful" at finding the iron-furnace ruins during the first few weeks that he was retained on a full-time basis.[12] Working with a crew of day laborers and heavy mechanical equipment, Robbins built on his experiences gained at Walden, developing and refining his nascent archaeological skills.

By the time of Robbins's initial involvement in the Saugus project, the ironworks property had a long and complex history within the historic preservation movement. Incorporated in 1943, the First Iron Works Association was actually the result of preservation efforts begun around the turn of the twentieth century.[13] While the seventeenth-century Iron Works House had survived, the remainder of the industrial complex was buried deep beneath the ground and forgotten. The Iron Works House was an important shrine that seemed to interest every preservation group and organization at one time or another except the Rockefellers, providing a veritable who's who of early preservation figures. SPNEA founder William Sumner Appleton acted as a historic-property broker when the house came on the market in 1911.[14] After negotiating with Henry Clay Frick, Andrew Carnegie, and the local Daughters and Sons of the American Revolution (DAR and SAR) chapters, Appleton interested noted antiquarian Wallace Nutting in purchasing the house in 1915.[15] Nutting restored the structure and used the building to display his collection of antiques and reproduction furniture.[16] The property was again sold in 1920 and passed through several owners before being purchased by Boston antiques dealer Philip A. Rosenberg in 1925. Rosenberg subsequently promised local DAR leader M. Louise Hawkes that "he would sell the house only to the Daughters of the American Revolution or to the Town of Saugus."[17] Negotiations between Rosenburg, the DAR, and the town to purchase the house in 1930 and again in 1941 failed to reach an agreement.[18] In 1935, Miss Hawkes successfully purchased the adjacent ironworks parcel, containing the buried remains of the early ironworks complex, and turned it over to the Parson Roby Chapter of the DAR.[19]

With the failure of the town and Rosenburg to reach an agreement, he sold the house to the Alumni Association of the Henry Ford Trade School in 1941. Their plan to move the structure to Ford's developing Greenfield Village in Dearborn, Michigan, resulted in outrage on the part of the community.[20] When local fund-raising to purchase the house failed, Appleton created a nonprofit corporation to acquire the house and run the property. In 1943, a major fund drive, pitched "To lovers of Old New England," raised the money necessary to purchase the house and adjacent ironworks parcel, and the First Iron Works Association officially assumed operation of the property.[21]

In 1948, J. Sanger Attwill, then president of the Lynn Historical Society and an early supporter of the ironworks project, became the association's second president. His local business of reproducing and restoring period furniture provided an excellent network for fund-raising and support. Among the organization's board of directors was the well-heeled and influential preservationist Louise du Pont Crowninshield. Mrs. Crowninshield, a founder of the National Trust for Historic Preservation, was both a financial contributor and fund-raiser for the project, and it was she who in 1944 approached Quincy Bent, a vice president of Bethlehem Steel Corporation, for money.[22] Bent visited the site in 1947 and, while generally unimpressed with the Iron Works House itself, was very excited by the nearby slag pile and the potential of the site to contain original ironworks ruins.[23]

In 1945, the First Iron Works Association formed a Reconstruction Committee of knowledgeable individuals who, like Bent, had recognized the great potential of the site.[24] With the forceful and well-connected Bent now taking the lead, the Reconstruction Committee approached the officers of the American Iron and Steel Institute for financial support. The institute, however, would not fund the project without some tangible evidence that remains of the ironworks actually existed on the site. Therefore, in the summer of 1948, Attwill approached Roland Robbins, whom he had seen lecture on his Walden discovery, about a brief exploratory dig at Saugus.[25] Robbins, between seasons for window washing and painting, readily agreed to begin digging in the fall of 1948.

Neither industrial archaeology nor even much of a historical interest in industrial sites existed in North America as the First Iron Works Association began to reconstruct the ironworks complex. Although not formally established in this country until the 1950s, industrial archaeology had a long tradition as an avocational pursuit in England.[26] Several studies on industrial sites would be published in the United States by the late 1960s, but it was not until the late 1970s that industrial archaeology "made itself known in the university curriculum."[27] Like historic-sites archaeology several decades earlier, the new subdiscipline became somewhat controversial in the United States, generating a "great debate over its value, direction, and service."[28] The journal *Historical Archaeology* published several articles in the late 1960s that debated the proper place for industrial archaeology within the discipline of historical archaeology and argued for the need to professionalize its practice.[29] Archaeologist Vincent Foley wrote that it was "only reasonable that a person interested in the history of a particular technology or trade, who desires to call himself an archaeologist . . . justify it [his or her research goals] with the addition of his background and degrees in archaeology."[30]

Of course, Roland Robbins had little background and no degree in industrial or any other type of archaeology when he arrived at Saugus in 1948, nor any prospects to get a degree given the lack of interest in industrial and historical archaeology by academic archaeologists. What Robbins did possess was a visual acuity for unraveling industrial sites that was linked to his interest in how these sites had worked and how people had used them. His early years set the stage for his career in historical and industrial archaeology in that he personally experienced a longing for roots in the community and a sense of place, and cultivated his natural abilities to read the clues of the past in the landscape of the present.

Robbins's interest in industrial sites can best be understood within the long-standing tradition of Yankee tinkerers. His preoccupation with these sites stemmed from his roots as a laborer and from his innate Yankee curiosity in how things worked, particularly mechanical devices and processes. He had, his widow recalled, quite an inventive mind and was endowed with a commonsense approach to problems. Mrs. Robbins recalled that he was always "thinking up things—mostly either electric or mechanical."[31] Robbins would even go so far as to patent them but would "immediately lose interest as soon as they were done. He was interested in the process."[32] Robbins's work at industrial sites was also informed by his excellent visual skills: "he was very astute visually . . . he saw so much, not just in detail, but in terms of landscape and relationships of landscape."[33] Archaeologist Paul Heberling recalled a visit that he and Robbins made to the Greenwood Furnace in western Pennsylvania: "He just walked around and looked at the terrain. He would see something and get out his probe rod to confirm his suspicions. In this way, he figured out the entire setup." "He had such an astute, alert awareness of iron complexes," Heberling continued, "that he immediately recognized what he had."[34]

Reflecting on his years of collaboration with Robbins, author Evan Jones commented that Robbins, unlike his later anthropological colleagues, was not particularly interested in the lives of the people at the sites that he excavated. "He was interested in the problem," Jones recalled. "He may have considered how a miller did something or made something, but only in the context of trying to figure out the mechanical setup and the archaeological problem at hand."[35] Jones's recollection reflects very accurately how Robbins came to approach the Saugus site.

Association president Attwill first met with Robbins at the Iron Works on September 10, 1948, to brief him on the primary objectives of the initial work: locate and excavate the blast furnace foundations. Robbins's "testing [of] the soil by sinking holes" revealed that the land along the Saugus River was covered with as much as four feet of slag fill.[36] After four days of digging "numerous test holes," Robbins identified the stone foundation of the furnace "buried three feet deep and some fifty feet north of the slag heap."[37] His success so impressed the Reconstruction Committee that it agreed to finance his work for an additional six weeks.[38] By mid-October, he had identified the entire "outline of the furnace foundation, the heavy timbered base for the bellows, and the crucible cavity," as well as several wooden beams that he speculated had been part of the waterwheel and sluiceway (figure 3.1).[39] The furnace waterwheel, he reasoned, would lie north of the furnace under the Central Street roadway. His report on the 1948 excavations suggested that "future research and excavations should prove very fruitful . . . [and recommended a] concerted effort to concentrate on the [documentary] records . . . for a thorough study and analysis."[40]

The Reconstruction Committee, fortified by Robbins's success at finding ironworks ruins, once again approached the American Iron and Steel Institute for funding.[41] The institute agreed to finance additional archaeological work as part of a larger reconstruction project. The First Iron Works Association and the institute formed a Joint Reconstruction Committee to manage the project in 1949. It elected Quincy Bent as

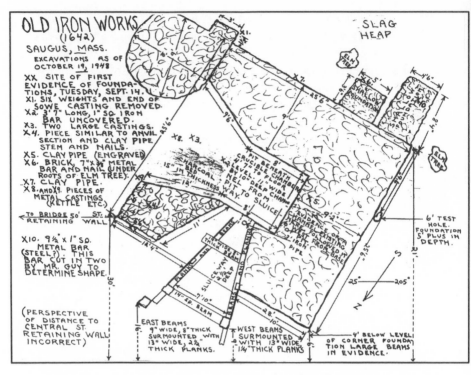

FIG. 3.1. Old Iron Works, Saugus, Mass., excavations as of October 19, 1948. (Courtesy of the Roland Wells Robbins Collection, the Thoreau Society, Lincoln, Mass., and the Thoreau Institute at Walden Woods.)

chairman and hired E. Neal Hartley of the Massachusetts Institute of Technology to begin a long-term historical research project on the ironworks. With the Joint Reconstruction Committee in place and the project historian on staff, Robbins and a team of local laborers began full-time excavations at the Saugus site in May 1949.[42]

Robbins immediately expanded the previous year's exploratory excavations at the furnace, identifying the furnace waterwheel's tailrace. By July, he had completely uncovered the furnace foundation and discovered evidence of the forge building. He also started a search along Central Street for the canal that had supplied water to power the furnace. His excavation strategy consisted largely of tracing out and following identified features and evaluating the landscape and topography. For example, testing north of the ironworks property resulted in the discovery of a series of watercourses for powering the operation that he then carefully followed downstream to identify associated features and buildings.

Finally, he traced all the watercourse features to the river, where he uncovered the dock or wharf area.

Robbins reported early in the project that "our museum is bulging with tons of various artifacts uncovered during past excavations." In addition to cataloging these "relics," he investigated conservation methods to preserve the site's many iron and wood artifacts.[43] Robbins also began sending samples of iron artifacts to laboratories at several steel companies; the Joint Reconstruction Committee hoped that chemical and physical analyses of these samples would provide information on the ironmaking process, result in the identification of raw material sources, and help to distinguish products made at Saugus.

Robbins next turned his attention to excavating the Bridge Street area, where almost immediately the digging identified two stone foundations and a "large circular affair" that appeared to be an anvil or hammer base (figure 3.2). At a depth of 34 inches, he found a "stump or block of a tree that measured 41 inches in diameter." "The theory at the moment," he recorded, "is that [it] is the base on which the hammer fell and the metal waste . . . was the accumulation of the impurities extracted from the iron by the hammer action."[44]

Several months later, Robbins and his men found a second anvil or hammer base near the first, also shrouded in metal waste. Robbins was excited about these discoveries, believing that the hammer bases were likely part of a refinery forge building with two forging hammers; a refinery forge used large, water-driven hammers to literally pound impurities out of the iron. This interpretation was strengthened when he found the five-hundred-pound head of a trip-hammer in the immediate vicinity of the bases (figure 3.3), along with uprights that supported the hammer beam, and evidence of two watercourses and several waterwheel pits.

In September 1950, Central Street was rerouted and Robbins began his search for the furnace waterwheel, which he believed was buried some 20 feet below the street's surface. Digging along the Central Street slope near the furnace, he identified a stone feature that had likely been the foundation or retaining wall for the furnace charging bridge (the bridge, running from the high ground above the ironworks to the top of the furnace, was used to load the furnace with fuel and ore) and discovered a disturbance in the ravine that proved to be the furnace watercourse. Using this watercourse as a lead, Robbins concentrated his energies on finding the furnace waterwheel pit. In early 1951, he identified

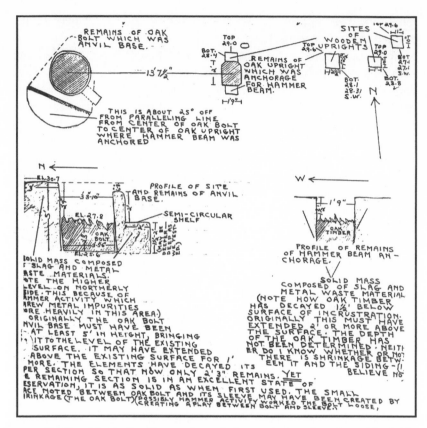

FIG. 3.2. Details and sketch of anvil base, anchorage for hammer beam, and wooden uprights, Bridge Street refinery. (From "Saugus Ironworks Daily Log—1950," 225c.) (Courtesy of the Roland Wells Robbins Collection, the Thoreau Society, Lincoln, Mass., and the Thoreau Institute at Walden Woods.)

waterwheel parts that led him to uncover the wheel pit and raceway. The degree of wood preservation was remarkable, and Robbins eventually found 40 percent of the original furnace waterwheel, the entire wheel pit, and a portion of the raceway (figure 3.4).[45]

During the rest of 1951 and 1952, Robbins followed the furnace watercourse to the river, where he discovered large logs that he interpreted as base sills and cribbing for the site's wharf or dock. While working in the dock area during 1952, he also completed limited excavations of the foundations of a forge operation along the furnace tailrace that he believed had belonged to colonial ironworker Joseph Jenks. Robbins's crew eventually identified three separate waterwheels that had powered various components of the operation, as well as Jenks's forge hearth. He

FIG. 3.3. Robbins shows 500-lb. iron hammer found at Saugus to schoolchildren. (Courtesy of the Roland Wells Robbins Collection, the Thoreau Society, Lincoln, Mass., and the Thoreau Institute at Walden Woods.)

spent the last months of 1952 and early 1953 working on an area containing two additional watercourses and wheel pits that he believed to be the rolling and slitting mill site; this operation would have been used to shape the iron into bar and rod stock for later manufacture into a variety of products.[46]

Robbins returned to excavate in the Central Street area in June 1953, running test trenches to "determine the extent of fill" and "pick up contours that existed there 3 centuries ago." This process of returning the landscape to its earlier appearance continued until July, when Quincy Bent ordered him to stop all work. Several days later, Robbins resigned. While his resignation appears to be rather abrupt, in actuality he had been increasingly unhappy with the management style of Bent and others and the direction of the reconstruction plans and process. Robbins felt that more work was necessary to fully understand and interpret the site, while the association was anxious to complete the restoration and

FIG. 3.4. Visitors looking at remains of furnace waterwheel and raceway. (Robbins stands in the waterwheel pit with remains of the original wheel.) (Courtesy of the Roland Wells Robbins Collection, the Thoreau Society, Lincoln, Mass., and the Thoreau Institute at Walden Woods.)

open it to the public. The tensions between Robbins and Bent and the Joint Reconstruction Committee and reconstruction architects that ran through the Saugus project had a negative effect on the overall archaeology program.

Robbins based his excavation decisions at Saugus on a dialogue with documentary evidence and on following features to determine building locations or activity areas.[47] Excavating roughly by natural strata or soil layers, he developed general vertical and horizontal provenience controls for artifacts within roughly defined test units and trenches. Robbins excavated many small units to determine the site's stratigraphy and identify ironworks foundations and features, prior to more extensive mechanical excavation.[48] He used these small initial units to determine what he thought to be the target level or original ironworks surfaces; mechanical equipment was generally used to remove the fill levels that Robbins deemed to be more recent from above these target strata. This type of heavy mechanical excavation was anathema to archaeologists trained in excavating prehistoric sites with their extremely fine-grained, hand excavation techniques. Although Robbins used the machines in a remarkably controlled fashion and was able to carefully uncover early surfaces and features, much of the stratigraphic control of artifacts above these "ironworks layers" was lost, thus limiting the ability of later archaeologists to explore the relationships between layers across the site.[49] Fortunately, his extensive plan and profile drawings provide quite accurate information on the locations of both features (such as foundation walls, wooden building posts, and waterways) and selected artifacts (such as the large forge hammerhead) as well as the stratigraphic profiles in these areas (figure 3.5).[50]

Throughout his career, Robbins consistently valued foundations over artifacts, declaring that he "did not dig for artifacts . . . but for ruins."[51] Although clearly of secondary concern to Robbins, as they were to many researchers of the period, he collected, provenienced, and curated artifacts during each of his excavations. He regularly used these artifacts at Saugus for feature interpretation and dating.[52] Not surprisingly, his Saugus collections were neither systematic nor completely representative in terms of modern sampling practice, and thus pose many challenges for current archaeologists. Artifacts from the excavation were generally stored with provenience or locational information, although this information and even some of the artifacts were lost during subsequent handling of the collection by the association and later by the National Park Service.[53]

The restoration goals of the Saugus project clearly drove the overall research, particularly the archaeology. Robbins frequently received conflicting messages from the multiheaded management team of the project. He worked with and for a host of individuals, and his position at Saugus was further complicated by his own multidimensional role in the organization. In actual practice, Robbins and his team provided draw-

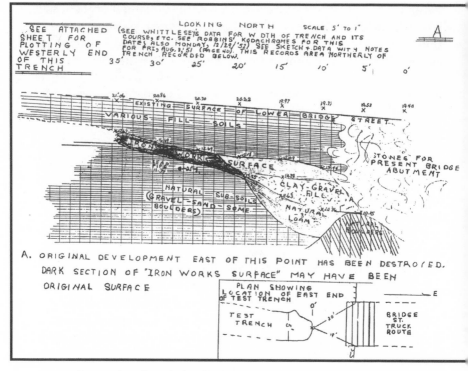

FIG. 3.5. Cross section of trench dug along Bridge Street to locate additional raceways. (From "Saugus Ironworks Daily Log—1952," 127a.) (Courtesy of the Roland Wells Robbins Collection, the Thoreau Society, Lincoln, Mass., and the Thoreau Institute at Walden Woods.)

ings and photographs of the archaeological evidence to the Joint Reconstruction Committee, which then worked with the architects. He was repeatedly frustrated by the architects' failure to talk directly with him about the evidence, a situation that often resulted in his having to uncover specific evidence a second or even third time to support his documentation of construction details. Writing to committee member Charles Harte about the restoration of the blast furnace, Robbins complained:

[they] have had the use of all of Hartley's, Bradford's, and my notes, as well as a complete set of our photographer's photographs, as well as material you sent them—and yet are at a loss as to certain details and elevations. What pray tell will they have to offer for the upper section of the furnace for which no evidence was uncovered?[54]

Later in the project, the architects regularly gave him draft copies of drawings, which he liberally marked up with changes, although his original comments and interpretation and later notes on drawings were not always heeded.[55]

From the very start of his full-time employment at Saugus, Robbins's approach to the excavations assumed an outwardly haphazard appearance, apparently lacking any organized plan. Although Marley Brown has commented that "in most cases, Robbins's testing proceeded on a rather random and limited basis, reflecting the location of utility trenches and other construction activity, rather than the application of any systematic sampling scheme," a closer look at Robbins's field notes and logs suggests that his work was far from random.[56] He attempted to follow the evidence in a logical sequence: for instance, beginning with the furnace complex and then defining its watercourse and the source for this water. As discussed above, his strategy consisted of tracing identified features and evaluating the landscape, through both testing and topographic clues.[57] While several areas were often under investigation at the same time, Robbins attempted to completely work through specific areas and features, striving to finish work in one area before moving on to another. However, issues of access to private property, design and construction demands of the architects, and severe weather conditions all hindered his attempts to carry out his work as systematically as he would have liked.[58] Robbins was frequently promised access to properties by the association's attorney, but after preparing for the work he would find that the situation was not properly resolved.[59] Lengthy delays in rerouting Central Street severely disrupted his plans for completing work on the furnace complex before moving to other areas.[60] Along Bridge Street, his excavations on several of the watercourses and the refinery complex were disrupted when attorneys discovered that they had not obtained permission to work in the street's right-of-way.[61] This delayed the recording of features related to the refinery building and forced Robbins to work on other areas.[62]

Robbins's work plans were also disrupted by the architects and builders who literally followed him across the site during the reconstruction process, prompting Brown to characterize Robbins's work as a "restore as you go" approach.[63] The architects frequently asked him to stop work in one area and move to another to answer a specific question or respond to a problem that had developed. Guidelines set by the Joint Reconstruction Committee also limited Robbins in that they directed him to "concentrate his activities on locating and exposing only the major features of the industrial complex of the Iron Works proper."[64] Although his ability to focus on specific archaeological areas and features would become increasingly impeded by the overwhelming demands of the managers and the complexity of the site, Robbins initially succeeded in organizing his work around the furnace. Summarizing his investigations in 1949, he wrote

my major problems were not the locating and excavating of buried foundations, but rather the association of these foundations one to the other and their
functions. This was necessary to determine the original pattern of the plant and
its layout.

While proud of his accomplishments, Robbins concluded that identifi-cation of the ruins was not enough. Sounding much like historical ar-chaeology pioneer J. C. Harrington in summarizing his approach at Jamestown, Robbins wrote that "the fact that many foundations and sites have been located does not indicate that my work with them is done. To locate foundations is one thing—to fit them and their intrica-cies into the over-all picture is another matter."[65]

Robbins's resignation in 1953 stemmed from his growing frustration with the project and the site's overwhelming intricacies.[66] Marley Brown writes that "it would appear that Robbins's resignation was triggered in part by an argument with Quincy Bent." Historian Stephen Carlson has likewise reported that, "increasingly, Robbins came into conflict with Quincy Bent over the extent of the remaining archaeological effort."[67] Robbins's decision to resign likely grew out of a variety of real or per-ceived obstacles, including his continuing frustration with the decisions of First Iron Works Association and Joint Reconstruction Committee members and architects, an extremely complex archaeological site, over-work caused by responsibility for many nonarchaeological issues, and the cumulative effects of these stresses on his physical and mental health.[68]

Robbins became disenchanted with First Iron Works president J. San-ger Attwill early in the project because of his failure to run a tight ship. Robbins's powerful personality and need for control and autonomy con-flicted with Attwill's equally autocratic style. Ironically, Robbins's own need for control resulted in his taking on a huge workload that nega-tively affected both his health and his archaeology projects. Although unhappy with many daily operational problems, he felt particularly dis-gusted by Attwill's repeated failure to pay his crew's meager salaries on time.[69] Robbins was also discouraged by what he felt was the architects' lack of interest in and ignorance of the archaeological evidence.

On several occasions, Robbins and other Joint Reconstruction Committee members questioned the quality of architectural work by staff at Perry, Shaw, Hepburn, Kehoe and Dean. For instance, Robbins recorded that

for the past 2 years the architects have had the opportunity to study the detail and features of the furnace . . . etc; and yet are confused and ignorant of desirable furnace foundation data.[70]

Several months later, surveyor John Bradford was instructed by architect Harrison Schock to provide his working drawings of excavations in the wharf area, but Robbins told Bradford to do "no such thing."[71] Robbins commented that

Schock . . . [does] not . . . understand the details of my business. . . . As such I do not intend to have Schock "decipher" and interpret something which is still in its preliminary state and very complex. Schock will receive a copy of my report on this area when it is prepared, and with other associates.[72]

Schock later complained to Bent that Robbins was not providing the needed data to the architects. Robbins responded to Bent

how can I be refusing him data if he doesn't ask for it. All my work has been with [Conover] Fitch. . . . Apparently Schock again has his rear in a sling and is going to try and use Robbins as a means of getting out of it.[73]

Following a meeting of the Joint Reconstruction Committee in 1952, Robbins reported that both he and Hartley had remained silent about problems with the reconstruction, noting that "this silence was our tribute to Fitch, who is a hellava nice fellow—and not personally responsible for the architects' errors."[74]

Problems also existed within the infrastructure of the Joint Reconstruction Committee, particularly the free hand given to chairman Quincy Bent by the American Iron and Steel Institute.[75] Robbins's conflict with Bent, himself a powerful personality, began early in the project and mounted quickly.[76] Bent made it clear to Robbins that he was in control in every regard; Robbins was their "digging technician." In one instance, Robbins was invited to present a lecture on the Saugus excavations to the Eastern States Archaeological Federation, and wrote to ask Bent if he should accept.[77] The tone of his salutation, "My dear Robbins," suggests Bent's dismissive attitude toward him. He went on to indicate that Robbins would need to get the "concurrance [*sic*] of Hartley and the Institute" to proceed with the lecture.[78] Despite problems with Bent, Robbins generally worked well with the staff of the American Iron and Steel Institute. Institute president Walter S. Tower supported Robbins's work and commended him for his extra efforts and outstanding achievements, while urging him to try to maintain a good working relationship with Bent.[79]

As a consequence of the enormous archaeological task and the problems associated with working for multiple project managers, Robbins drove himself "beyond all reasonable limits." His wife Geraldine reported to Quincy Bent that "in a desperate effort to keep going he went from doctor to doctor and specialist to specialist. The diagnosis in every case was the same—overwork."[80] Robbins came to realize the trouble himself, yet apparently did not see his need for control as part of the overall difficulty. He wrote to Quincy Bent that

as complex as my archaeological work was it presented no problem which would wear me out, both physically and mentally. But to mix this work with sundry duties ranging from overseer of all problems to caretaker of washrooms, interspersed with two museums to study and carefully prepare appropriate exhibits for, as well as public relations and goodwill, research which developed mediums for restoring our priceless artifacts, both metals and wood, annual meetings which necessitated careful planning and many late evenings, as well as numerous other time absorbing details, was more than my strength could contend with after dieting on it for five years.[81]

All these factors affected Robbins's physical and mental health.[82] The confrontation between Bent and Robbins over the Central Street excavations in July 1953 was the final straw. Robbins had dealt with the "human elements" and overwork for too long and was "completely worn out." He remained characteristically resilient about his trouble at Saugus: "of course there were certain human elements that saw to it that my life was unpleasant. But that happens wherever you go."[83]

Robbins was never completely satisfied with the accuracy of the finished reconstruction. In fact, some features he uncovered were ignored by the architects because they literally did not fit into their reconstruction plans. Marley Brown suggests that there was "little effective cooperation between the archaeologist, the historian, and the architects. This lack of communication is especially clear in the use of archaeological evidence by the architects in the course of drawing up plans."[84]

Despite the battles over final construction details, Robbins's evidence clearly played a large and critical part in guiding the reconstruction of the site. His excavations supplied excellent detail on the operation of the blast furnace area, identifying the furnace base, furnace bellows support timbers, furnace waterwheel, casting-shed uprights, charging-bridge footing, and casting beds, along with an amazing collection of hand tools, products, and waste materials related to the iron-making operation. The abundance of evidence for the furnace complex allowed for a high level of accuracy in the reconstruction of this area. For example, Robbins carefully documented the large intact section of the furnace waterwheel, down to the animal hair used to caulk the individual buckets of the wheel.

There does seem to have been some dispute and tension between Robbins, the reconstruction team, and English ironworks expert Dr. H. R. Schubert about both the crucible cavity and the layout of casting beds.[85] Schubert refused to accept Robbins's interpretations, reluctantly changing his mind only when shown the physical evidence. Following his visit, Robbins noted sarcastically that he "should have been brought over 3½ years ago. With his knowledge of English Iron Works there would have been no need of engaging an archaeologist to determine the basic pattern of the Saugus Iron Works."[86] Robbins felt concerned that Schubert was advocating for the use of seventeenth-century English ironworks examples as exact prototypes for the Saugus complex. He complained to colleague Charles Harte that

in many instances [my work] . . . clearly showed deviation from the conventional English or European iron works of that period. These deviations are probably some of America's earliest evidence of Yankee ingenuity. Certainly they show the adaptability of our early settlers.[87]

In another case, Robbins complained about recurring inaccuracies in the architectural drawing details for the furnace tailrace, recording that once again "incompetency on the part of the architects is responsible for wrong details and unnecessary work."[88]

Robbins identified the refinery forge building based on its multiple waterwheels, two hammer or anvil bases, the trip-hammer base and supports, a retaining wall, and associated artifacts including one of the trip-hammer heads, tools, and waste materials. The interpretation of the forge building proved controversial when Robbins discovered the second anvil base. He felt that the heavy buildup of slag and impurities around both anvil bases indicated that they were used with large water-powered trip-hammers. However, historian Hartley wrote that "other archaeological data, including the size of the forge building, watercourse outlines, and the assumed location of the fineries and chafery, plus the absence of documentary reference to a second hammer, made the actual use of two hammers highly questionable."[89] The final interpretation of the forge appears to have relied heavily on contemporary illustrations and plan drawings of English forges, such as John Smeaton's plan of the Kilnhurst Forge.

Even more ambiguous was another waterwheel pit and building location, which the Joint Reconstruction Committee interpreted as the rolling and slitting mill. Although Robbins recovered slit bar stock that he identified as coming from a rolling and slitting mill operation, he remained uncertain about the building's configuration due to a lack of specific architectural evidence, such as foundations or structural post-holes, and ultimately recommended caution regarding the reconstruction of this structure. In reviewing the documentation, archaeologist Marley Brown notes that "there was not enough structural evidence recovered to permit its use in designing the lay-out of the building."[90] The other team members felt that because the building was referred to in period documents and was in a location next to the refinery forge it must have been the rolling and slitting mill and that it should be rebuilt as such. Again, other than the evidence for the waterwheel pit, the final interpretation of the rolling and slitting mill structure relied almost exclusively on contemporary illustrations and plan drawings, such as those from Swedenborg's 1734 tract *De Ferro*.

Robbins also identified and partially excavated the Joseph Jenks forge site, including two or three waterwheel pits and a forge hearth base, built along the tailrace of the furnace; he was forced to abandon this work due to time constraints, and it was not included in the reconstruction. He also identified, excavated, and documented the dock area, including extensive wharf cribbing along the Saugus River.

At Saugus, Robbins attempted to "restore the contours," or literally to return the site to the original ground surface and configuration based on his reading of the early soil strata and evidence for building floors and surfaces.[91] The accuracy of his landscape interpretations has been rightly questioned, particularly given the lack of documentation explicitly explaining his methodology. Robbins would employ this technique at many later sites, and it was one that generated a great deal of rebuke from professional archaeologists. Of the process at Saugus, Brown noted that "Robbins engaged in a very extensive earth-moving operation . . . made up of back fill removal and grade or contour restoration. . . . [this] restoration of the landscape had both an additive and subtractive dimension."[92] A close reading of Robbins's records suggests that his decisions regarding the historic topographic configuration at Saugus were generally well reasoned and accurate, based as they were on soils data, a host of building-floor levels, watercourses and waterwheel pits, work-area surfaces such as the casting beds, and water levels in the Saugus River and pond above.[93] While Robbins seems to have done a fairly good job of reconfiguring the actual historic ground surface, the movement of soils around the site resulted in problematic mixing of soils and artifacts from various areas, along with the general destruction of potentially intact soil layers and artifacts from some portions of the site.

The artifacts amassed during the excavation represent an early and unparalleled collection of ironworks materials. Interestingly, little use was made of the extraordinary artifact collection in furnishing the reconstructed buildings. Tools and implements were chosen according to documentary records, particularly the inventories, and replicated from drawings in historical sources. In his review of Robbins's work at Saugus, archaeologist Eric Johnson has noted that notwithstanding the limitation of the artifact collections, in particular the lack of consistent provenience or locational information for portions of the collection, "they constitute a known archaeological resource with considerable research and interpretive value."[94] Johnson goes on to explain that the collections and related archives can be

used to address a wide range of research topics related to seventeenth-century industry. . . . [and] provide comparative materials to researchers investigating contemporary iron works in England or elsewhere in Europe and North America.[95]

Robbins's use of a host of special studies, particularly in regard to faunal remains (animal bone), tree ring dating and geoarchaeology, metals and materials analysis, and artifact conservation was very advanced for this period in historical archaeology and also provides important comparative data for future study. Interestingly, the discipline as a whole would not embrace the study of animal bone remains and geoarchaeology until at least the late 1970s and early 1980s, and the use of materials analysis and artifact conservation is still not standard within the discipline.[96]

Assessing Robbins's work, Johnson notes that he was "extraordinarily successful in uncovering and documenting the industrial complex at the Saugus Iron Works Site."[97] Although politics and neglect of evidence led to errors or questionable parts in the finished reconstruction, Robbins's work was essential for guiding the project, and he succeeded in translating his physical evidence and interpretation into a vision that strikingly captured this early industrial landscape. In this sense, Robbins's Saugus excavations provided the first accurate glimpses of the layout and operation of one of New England's and America's earliest industrial sites.

The ambitious restoration goals of the Saugus project compelled the association's managers to press Robbins to finish his work as fast as possible so that they could complete the physical reconstruction. Funding was not unlimited, and both the First Iron Works Association and the American Iron and Steel Institute had their own agendas for the finished complex. In large part, these goals arose out of the increasing use of the past, specifically historic sites, for political and commercial purposes. The application of tradition and nostalgia to marketing, whether for manufacturing, sales, or tourism, grew steadily following World War II. A huge rise in mobility, due to increased use of automobiles and the construction of the national interstate highway system, was expanding tourism and travel to historic sites. Ties between the past and the present were seen everywhere, particularly in New England.

The American Iron and Steel Institute promoted and celebrated the Iron Works's legends and traditions and the progress of American industry in the 1955 film *The Saugus Iron Works Restoration: A Shrine to Pioneers of American Industry.* Using the "Saugus Pot," long held to represent the first casting from the ironworks, as an example, the film's narrator explains that "tradition and fact are often worlds apart, so a spectroanalysis was made of both the iron in the pot and the iron found at the ironworks. Their chemical composition was found to be identical. Tradition was fact."[98] The message is clear: science and careful research could verify history, and the traditions of the past could successfully be linked to the realities of the present. The past and the present dissolve into one as the movie screen is filled with the image of several colonials sitting in front of the fireplace in the Ironmaster's House. "Before this very fireplace," the narrator explains, "New England's earliest settlers dreamed of the day that America would meet its own needs for iron."[99]

The Cold War threat of the early 1950s was taken seriously, and the production of materials for the resulting military buildup was extraordinary. The process of selling America's might and strength in the world was in full swing; a link to the past that embraced the tradition of American independence and industrial progress provided an excellent justification for this militarism. The use of historic sites and symbols to support democratic beliefs and the war against communism, in both public and private agencies, became quite common.[100] In fact, Robbins himself took part in the campaign to root out communism within the United States, serving on several grand-jury cases that he characterized as "Un-American Activity Investigations." In September 1951, he reported with some satisfaction that his grand jury had indicted two local professors on charges of "conspiracy and advocating the violent overthrow of the government of the United States."[101]

Uncertain about their future, explains historian Barbara Clark Smith, "Americans exhibited both a sense of celebration and a sense of defensiveness about their country, its values, and its history."[102] For instance, John D. Rockefeller III thought that Colonial Williamsburg should be "a significant and constructive force and factor in our world today." Similarly, programs to enhance the "teaching of American history and heritage . . . in the ideological war against communism" were created for the New York State Regents.[103] In a speech in Saugus in 1952, Senator Robert A. Taft (R-Ohio) remarked:

Here on this spot . . . was the "Cradle of American Industry" . . . which is the lifeblood of not only our economy, but of the survival of the entire free world. And it was created by no Socialistic State. When Gov. John Winthrop . . . went to London . . . to interest British capital in the foundation of an iron business, he did not offer them cradle to the grave security, he presented them, rather, with an opportunity to invest their savings with the hope of earning a fair return. . . . Here was born an industry which today is the very core of our economy. It was founded by free men, it has been carried on under the American system, and, more than anything else, it has preserved the American way of life.[104]

The same themes of progress, patriotism, and national security echo throughout the 1955 Saugus film. "The Saugus Iron Works of 1650," the narrator explains, "is a prime example of the industrial pioneering that made America what it is today."[105] "The spirit of Saugus and the skills of Saugus men," he continues, "passed from father to son, from skilled workman to apprentice and helped to win the war of independence."[106] As the film reaches its end, the narrator reminds viewers that

> the ironworks at Saugus is no monument to a dead past, it is a reminder of the great advances which the iron and steel industry has made and will continue to make, helping to provide the sinews of our national security and the basis for our unmatched standard of living.[107]

The military buildup of the Cold War era was accompanied by a corresponding surge of civilian production, and progress and technology loomed large in advertising appeals.[108] "The great centers of iron and steel production which serve America today," the film's narrator explains, "represent the evolution and expansion of the industry from the early days of Saugus. Today, Saugus is not only a shrine but a measure of progress as well."[109]

Industrial sites like Saugus as well as domestic sites conveyed many messages, and they had great commercial potential. "The conversion of historic houses into shrines often had promotional [tourism] overtones," argues historian Michael Wallace.[110] In 1960, the New York State Joint Legislative Committee on Preservation and Restoration of Historic Sites reported that "tourism has become big business . . . and historic sites more and more are luring the tourist."[111] Heritage and patriotism became the bywords of travel literature and promotional campaigns run by state and regional economic development committees, and historic-sites visitation skyrocketed.[112]

The 1958 *Yankee Homecoming* guidebook is a fascinating example of the heritage-tourism marketing strategy in New England, one that engages the Yankee identity embraced by Roland Robbins. This official homecoming guide, authored by New England's own "Jack Frost," advertises the event as a chance for people from all over the country to "make a pilgrimage to New England, the section of our country that is second to none in the establishment of our Government and in its preservation and growth."[113] The idea, notes the author, grew from "an awareness . . . that thousands of Yankees had migrated to the west during the 1800s and that their descendants . . . should return to the old homesteads, villages, and towns to see for themselves where grandparents . . . had lived." As the idea grew, Frost continues, it became a "crusade to share with others the many historical landmarks still standing . . . the hallowed ground where the Patriots trod and worshiped, where freedom's battles were fought and won, and where our government had its beginnings."[114]

Celebrating the spirit of the hardworking and independent-minded Yankee, the events and tours of the Homecoming directly connected the successes of early New England pioneers with modern industrial capitalism. For the Homecoming Council, "Yankee" could be broadly defined: it "is not a race, religion or geographical destination . . . it is a creed . . . a belief in American ingenuity, free enterprise, and respect for another's rights, property and personal liberty."[115] Seeking to launch "New England's Patriotic Rebirth," the council planned a wide variety of special events and created organized tours such as "New England Route '75: The Yankee Trail" and "The Yankee Free Enterprise Trail."[116] The Yankee Trail marked, its guidebook said, the "path of American Democracy which was blazed by New England pioneers and heroes . . . this hypothetical route . . . threads its way through Yankee Shrine Towns."[117] Frost wrote approvingly that New England has "scores of 'Williamsburghs' [sic] except that they have always been here, just parts of our Living Yankee Past."[118]

The stops along the Yankee Trail, an agglomeration of villages, outdoor museums, and historic sites, ranged from Old Sturbridge Village to Mystic Seaport and Saugus, which the author notes as "the birthplace of America's iron and steel industry." The primary objective at Saugus, Frost writes, was to build as faithful and authentic a reproduction of the original as was humanly possible; the promise of authenticity was important for drawing visitors.[119] "This fidelity," Frost continues, "was made even more difficult because most of the reliable local records had long since disappeared. No plans or designs of this 17th century ironworks were available. The site was overgrown with brambles and its history with legends."[120] Robbins was very proud of his work untangling Saugus from the thick brambles and conflicting legends that had ensnared it for centuries, particularly because it provided, he said, "some of America's earliest evidence of Yankee ingenuity."[121] Yet, as discussed above, Robbins was not completely satisfied with the authenticity and accuracy of the finished restoration. His experiences at Saugus made him wary of the personalities, power, and influence of outside funding sources and their control of restoration and preservation decisions.

While often apprehensive of and irritated with the organizations for which he worked, however, Robbins did not stop pursuing other, similar archaeological projects. To do so would have limited his ability to earn a living at archaeology and would have impacted his self-styled mission of creating tangible reminders of New England's Yankee past, goals that provided a firm foundation and rootedness for him and a legacy for the future. In fact, by the mid-1950s he was embracing and encouraging the participation of the commercial world in preservation and history, formulating his own ideas for integrating archaeology into popular culture:

General Mills and similar commercial organizations spend millions annually on the Lone Ranger, Space Cadet, etc. The comic books are turning to stories on American History and Pioneering. And Davy Crockett lives again! I believe that the stuff I uncover can be just as fascinating. The factual material I find may not be good for public consumption, but when it is properly mixed with "legend," it is quite edible. Someday—and I hope that it will be in my day—the commercial organizations will swing to using data based on my kind of work. And when they do they will wonder why they hadn't thought of it earlier![122]

Interestingly, Robbins's ideas for making archaeology accessible to the public sound surprisingly like those of the early prehistorian Adolph F. Bandelier, who in the 1880s wrote that "by clothing sober fact in the garb of romance I have hoped to make the 'Truth about the Pueblo Indians' more accessible and perhaps more acceptable to the public in general."[123] Yet, Bandelier, Robbins, and even Ivor Noël Hume were decades ahead of the public archaeology movement of the 1980s and 1990s. While Robbins was a pioneer in delivering historical archaeology to the public, his early embrace of public history and archaeology once again pitted him against his academic brethren.

Robbins realized both the educational and the economic implications of public history and archaeology, and he also took them personally: he "thought wistfully about individualism, self-reliance, and other verities associated with the colonial period and the early republic."[124] It was not just the threats of the rapidly changing twentieth-century world that worried Robbins but also the daily personal and economic perils of his chosen career. Instead of brooding over these anxieties, however, he put them to work with extraordinary determination, remarkable energy, and a clear passion for the work that he was doing.

Robbins's energy and passionate embrace of life showed in everything he did: his odd-jobs business, his family, his research, and his tennis game. Geraldine Robbins, reminiscing about her husband's approach to tennis, noted that "he had an awkward style because he never took any lessons." He just "picked up a tennis racquet and whacked away. . . . He would just start swinging, like it was a baseball bat. He frequently won— not on his skill, but on his energy. He could wear down his opponents by tiring them out."[125] Robbins marshaled a great deal of concentration and energy for those things, like tennis, for which he held a passion.[126] His deep ardor for historical and archaeological research provided the impetus for devoting huge amounts of time and energy to his work, which subsequently enabled him to succeed in uncovering historic sites across New England against great odds. This force of personality also sustained him as he carried out the multiple job responsibilities foisted upon him by the organizations for whom he worked and during his many pitted battles with these same preservation organizations, and, as in his tennis game, he often used his phenomenal energy to simply wear down his opponents. However, as he discovered at Saugus, sustaining this approach eventually took its toll.

At Saugus, Robbins learned a great deal about himself and the evolving worlds of historic preservation and historical and industrial archaeology, and it was here that he came to understand the tremendous appeal of historic sites for the general public. For the first postwar decade or so, Robbins's research approaches and methods reflected general trends in historical archaeology, and set the standard for techniques and methods in the world of industrial archaeology. Increased federal involvement and the developing tourism and heritage enterprises resulted in the expansion of the practice of historical archaeology between the end of World War II and the early 1960s, and Robbins was ideally positioned to take advantage of these trends. The particularistic restoration approach, linked to the historic preservation movement and its desire to fortify tradition and reinforce legend, remained at the forefront of historical archaeology throughout the period. While historical archaeology and practitioners like Robbins focused on ruins, the anthropological archaeology of prehistorians concentrated its efforts on developing methodological standards and acquiring "data to expand our understanding of past cultures and long term processes of change."[127] Preoccupied with professionalizing their own world, anthropological archaeologists had little time for or interest in studying the remains of the past three hundred years.

The growing need for historical archaeology in the postwar era first became apparent in 1946 at the "Conference on the Use of Resources in Historical Areas Administered by the National Park Service."[128] J. C. Harrington has written that

many of today's historical archaeologists would be surprised, if not shocked, at the direction that this high level conference took, but it was only symptomatic of what professional people, including most archaeologists, conceived as the role of our discipline.[129]

In addition to figuring out its proper role and function, the biggest problem that faced historical archaeology, the group quickly decided, was the lack of trained personnel and training programs.[130] Although "the accumulation of data and collections, the large number of historic sites already excavated, and the recognition of the need for the training of 'specialists in the identification of historic objects' seemed to herald the emergence of a recognizable discipline in the immediate post war years," there was still little interest among anthropologists and prehistorians in what they derisively called "tin-can archaeology."[131]

By 1952, Harrington would identify two branches of historic-sites archaeology: *colonial archaeology,* involving sites related to the transplantation of an established culture to a "foreign territory," that is, the Colonial and Frontier periods in the United States, and *restoration archaeology,* including the "many projects in which building sites, military sites, and other remains are excavated for the purpose of locating structures exactly and obtaining information for their restoration."[132] Harrington's observations on restoration archaeology clearly reflect Robbins's situation at Saugus and later at Philipsburg Manor Upper Mills: "the problems of construction and restoration are so specialized that the archaeologist is not much more than a digging technician, and in most cases the conclusions and interpretations must be left to . . . specialists and architects."[133]

Historical archaeology witnessed a refinement in methods and technique during the immediate postwar period, and the projects completed illustrate the increasing interest in historic-sites archaeology on several fronts. These projects took a greater interest in the study of artifacts and their use for explanation and interpretation of human culture and daily life.[134] Excavation techniques were slowly being standardized, and refined stratigraphic controls were introduced and used in many projects.

Even with heightened interest in historical archaeology, however, the field was still unorganized and sought an intellectual identity. The National Park Service and other federal agencies had cut back on many of their programs during the war years, but slowly began new projects with the end of the war.[135] At the same time, the work of local historical and patriotic societies and associations, as well as municipal and state agencies, was revived and increasingly expanded. These groups "took on a new, active, and central role in post war historical archaeology."[136] In Virginia, for example, renewed interest in historical archaeology was spurred by the approach of the 350th anniversary of the founding of Jamestown in 1957.[137] The most significant of the projects was a renewed four-year research effort at Jamestown Island directed by John Cotter.[138] The project's archaeologists, Edward B. Jelks, B. Bruce Powell, Joel Shiner, and Louis R. Caywood, were all trained in prehistoric archaeology and "only Caywood had experience in the archeology of historic Anglo-American sites."[139] Yet even Caywood lacked formal training, and therefore, like Robbins, "the archaeologists learned on the job."[140] Unlike Robbins, however, these men had training in the techniques of prehistoric archaeology that were increasingly being used in historic-sites excavations; they had an appreciation and knowledge of the essential nature of artifact provenience and the importance of a systematic approach to recording this data.

Throughout the 1940s and 1950s, Colonial Williamsburg's "archaeological engineer," James K. Knight, continued the 1930s tradition of cross-trenching excavations to identify foundations. While successful for identifying foundations, this technique was very destructive to the archaeological record around the structure, particularly due to the loss of artifacts and their context. However, this approach changed with the appointment of Ivor Noël Hume as director of archaeology in 1957.[141] Noël Hume's background was in Roman-period excavations in England, where he was introduced to Sir Mortimer Wheeler's stratigraphic approach to excavation.[142] Like Robbins, he had no formal training in archaeology, but unlike Robbins, Noël Hume had completed a degree at St. Lawrence College in Kent, England.[143] Yet, his focus in school and following graduation was not archaeology but rather the theater. Noël Hume began his career in archaeology collecting artifacts along the Thames at low tide, selling his discoveries to the Guildhall Museum in London.[144] He ended up volunteering for the museum and working for the famous postmedieval archaeologist Adrian Oswald, eventually becoming a paid curator in 1949. It was through his on-the-job training and apprenticeship with Oswald that Noël Hume learned the fundamentals of archaeology.[145] Noël Hume's self-education got another boost with his marriage to Audrey Baines, a university graduate with a degree in classical archaeology.[146] His close work with Oswald and his "partnership" with his wife Audrey provided him with a level of training and resources—a solid foundation—that Robbins never received.

Upon arriving in Virginia, Noël Hume made a point of putting an end to Colonial Williamsburg's ongoing indifference to artifacts. Over the years, he developed a systematic approach to the excavation of historic sites using careful stratigraphic techniques to locate and record artifacts and features. He explained that there is "a lot more to archaeology than just digging up foundations with a gang of laborers with shovels."[147] Like Robbins, Noël Hume had an intense interest in presenting his findings to the public, one that grew out of his theatrical training. Also like Robbins, his popular appeal irked academics; their approach, he explained, was that "you did your research, you published it to your peers, and you weren't concerned with the public."[148] "Why are we being paid to save this stuff," he lamented, "if we don't show it to the public?"[149] Noël Hume suffered from many of the same complaints from academics as did Robbins: he was a self-trained archaeologist and an unapologetic showman. In fact, he applied his theatrical training to develop what has been called a "distinctly unacademic, unquestionably theatrical approach" to archaeology.[150] Yet, Noël Hume's prior training with Oswald and his ongoing partnership with Audrey, combined with the powerful and permanent institutional affiliation of Colonial Williamsburg, provided him with credentials and legitimacy that would always elude Robbins. Noël Hume has been credited with transforming the discipline of historical archaeology from "little more than a treasure hunt," a phase used by the president of the First Iron Works Association to characterize Robbins's initial work at Saugus, to "a rigorous scientific discipline."[151] The major difference between Noël Hume's and Robbins's work was the former's adoption of a consistently applied stratigraphic approach to excavation that drew on the system introduced by Sir Mortimer Wheeler.

One of Noël Hume's first digs in Virginia was at an eighteenth-century plantation on the York River known as Rosewell. Here he excavated a large refuse dump containing four distinct layers or strata, and, based on the cross section of soils, he developed a clear occupational sequence for the site, ranging from a Native American camp to a domestic plantation. Noël Hume's excavation at Rosewell has been called "the first sophisticated application of the stratigraphic method to a non-architectural feature in American historic sites archaeology."[152]

In addition to refining field techniques, the analysis of artifacts as evidence of human behavior and culture became increasingly important for interpretation in a historical archaeology that was more and more linked to the discipline of anthropology. An example of the application of more sophisticated levels of artifact analysis is James Deetz's work for Plimoth Plantation at Rocky Nook in Kingston, Massachusetts.[153] In 1959, Deetz excavated several structures that could be historically documented, using a series of test trenches.[154] Deetz's reports are important in "demonstrating further experimentation with dating techniques in historical archaeology."[155] He used Harrington's pipe stem dating technique for the analysis but found that it produced confusing results with multiple peaks.[156] Additional artifact analysis and excavation allowed Deetz to refine his interpretation to suggest two separate buildings on the site, one dating to the mid-seventeenth and the other to the early eighteenth century.

Although the field was slowly developing and refining its approach, the use of archaeology at historic sites was still quite unusual. Jamestown's J. C. Harrington expressed his surprise that historians were so slow to make use of "this obvious historical tool."[157] He advocated a close tie between archaeology and local history groups and societies, creating new opportunities for practitioners like Robbins.[158] Sounding a lot like Robbins in his later pronouncements on public involvement in archaeology, Harrington explained how a local history group could handle an archaeological project, noting that the most difficult item was arranging for the services of a trained archaeologist:

there are relatively few archaeologists with experience in this sort of work, and essentially none who have had the specialized academic training that would give them the necessary background. Most archaeological students in this country do their academic work in the general field of anthropology, having a course or so in archaeological methods and various courses on prehistoric cultures. Others receive highly specialized training in the Oriental and Classical fields, but none have academic training which qualifies them to excavate and interpret an early nineteenth-century frontier settlement, a Revolutionary War earthwork, a Colonial house site, or a seventeenth-century Jesuit mission site.[159]

During these early years, Harrington and the few other archaeologists interested in historic sites served as a sort of clearinghouse for historical archaeology, bringing together skilled practitioners and the organizations that sought their services. Through recommendations from these colleagues, Robbins obtained many of his projects.

It was his connections with Harrington and Harvard's J. O. Brew that took Robbins to Shadwell, Virginia, the birthplace of Thomas Jefferson, in 1954. Although located outside New England, this project illustrates Robbins's struggles with the goals of smaller historical organizations, and the focused use of archaeology for restoration and reconstruction. The Shadwell property, located on the south bank of the Rivanna River, was likely purchased by Peter Jefferson between 1736 and 1741. It was reportedly in the house that Peter and wife Jane Randolph built on this property that Thomas Jefferson was born on April 2, 1743. Peter and his family lived at the Randolph home of Tuckahoe from about 1745 to 1752, and returned to Shadwell in 1753. The family continued to live in the Shadwell house until it burned in 1770; Jefferson was by then building Monticello. The house seems to have been repaired and leased at some point following Jefferson's move to Monticello but was gone by the time that Downing Smith purchased the property in 1879.[160]

The Thomas Jefferson Birthplace Memorial Park Commission (TJBMPC) seemed ambivalent about archaeology at Shadwell from the start. The commission initially arranged to have NPS archaeologist Paul J. F. Schumacher search for the Jefferson house, and he excavated several trenches in the vicinity of two large foundations identified by architect Fiske Kimball in the 1930s and thought to be part of the Peter Jefferson home.[161] Unfortunately, Schumacher found little during his brief exploration project and concluded that "I do not believe that the Smith home site (the property's late nineteenth- and twentieth-century occupants) is the location of the Jefferson home site."[162] For some time, the TJBMPC considered proceeding with the reconstruction of Peter Jefferson's house without further archaeology.[163] However, at the urging of project architect Floyd Johnson the commission contacted Robbins about further exploring the site.[164]

Robbins visited the site and spent several days reviewing past reports, "becoming better acquainted with the terrain," and conducting a series of test probes and units.[165] His initial testing convinced him that evidence of the Peter Jefferson house could be found. He wrote to Floyd Johnson that

I am making recommendations for excavating the entire knoll. . . . The entire area should be shaved down by careful bulldozer operations. This work will reveal all disturbances [features] there. It will show the original layout of buildings, occupations by later generations, as well as reveal the location of all test pits and trenches dug by [previous] investigators. This work should not be undertaken—except by the most competent of specialists in this field. I am not implying that I am the man to do the work—but I must warn that if the work is undertaken by any other than a specialist in this extremely specialized work—the answers are lost for all time. It can *never* be done again. . . . I hope that nothing will be done with the area which we partially excavated to the east of the brick foundation. It may have been a refuse pit . . . [or] unlined cellars. . . . You fellows have got a rich bonanza! But it has got to be carefully minded.[166]

Johnson wrote to Robbins that the commission was "very much impressed with our recent find of artifacts" and might be interested in pursuing further excavations.[167]

Robbins returned to the site in 1955 and systematically tested the entire area with "small borings" to locate brick features or foundations, an approach analogous to modern shovel testing.[168] This approach provides a systematic look at the distribution of artifacts and helps in focusing more extensive excavations in areas of high artifact density that likely correlate with features like trash pits or foundations. After discussions with Johnson, Robbins decided to remove the plowzone (soil disturbed by plowing) by hand within a series of 10-foot grid squares rather than by bulldozer.[169] This excavation produced brick, mortar, window glass, ceramics, and hundreds of handmade nails, but failed to identify any major new foundations.[170] The distribution of artifacts was going to be critical, Robbins reasoned, because of the lack of extant brick foundations.

Although excited by Robbins's findings, the commission struggled with continuing financial issues related to the archaeological work. The additional excavation was an on-again, off-again proposition, but Robbins persevered and was able to identify several significant features at the site. The excavation of grid squares to the east and west of the "main house area," around two small brick cellars, produced distributions of artifacts that allowed him to "isolate the site of the main house from the brick cellar [Kimball's] to the west." Drawing on the soils and erosion data, feature excavations, and lack of chimney on Kimball's large brick cellar, Robbins was convinced that the main house was centered over these two small cellars.[171] With the submission of his 1955 report, plans were immediately formulated for the reconstruction of the Shadwell home.[172]

Robbins's work at Shadwell clearly demonstrates the increasing precision of his field techniques and research methodology, to a level that was not too different from that of his academic counterparts of the period. Through previous experience, exchanges with colleagues, and reading in the archaeological literature, Robbins discerned the need to approach shallow, plowzone sites such as Shadwell much differently from deep, stratified sites like Saugus. Precise horizontal and vertical excavation controls, Robbins asserted, were necessary to recover the scant artifacts from a shallow site and to determine the patterns of these materials.

Robbins's decisions to excavate at Shadwell were, as at Saugus, based on a dialogue with the documentary evidence, including the previous excavations of Kimball and Schumacher. Robbins excavated by natural strata and utilized precise and systematic horizontal controls by reestablishing and expanding Schumacher's 10-by-10-foot grid system over the entire ridge (figure 3.6). He systematically dug "small borings" or shovel tests across the grid that were designed to locate features and assess the site's stratigraphy.[173] He even engaged a local soil scientist to test his hypothesis regarding erosion at the site, data that proved critical to his eventual conclusion that the main house foundation had been destroyed by "salvage, plowing, and erosion."[174]

In addition to his methodological approach to the project, the level of documentation of Robbins's excavations at Shadwell unquestionably separates his work from that of his predecessor Kimball and even Schumacher.[175] His plan drawings and field notes provide precise information on the excavation of each 10-by-10-foot test unit, including soil descriptions, artifacts, and the location of features or disturbances.[176] Johnson remembers that Robbins "was meticulous in everything that he did, photographing, keeping records, cataloging, and it was not a slaphappy operation."[177]

Robbins recognized and documented soil changes and was certainly able to read and understand this evidence.[178] He recorded the identification of several postholes during the Shadwell project; commenting on an extant barn's post-in-ground construction, he correctly speculated that "if the Shadwell mansion had been supported on this kind of a structure, then the posthole evidence can be located."[179] Robbins also identified and recorded the previous test pits and trenches dug by Kimball and Schumacher.[180]

Plowzone soil removed from each 10-by-10-foot unit was carefully sorted by hand and then stockpiled for later screening (figure 3.7).[181] The

FIG. 3.6. Aerial photograph of the excavation of Peter Jefferson's house site, Shadwell, Va., showing the grid-oriented excavation units and systematic posthole excavations, 1955. (Courtesy of the Roland Wells Robbins Collection, the Thoreau Society, Lincoln, Mass., and the Thoreau Institute at Walden Woods.)

artifacts from the excavation were stored with clear horizontal provenience information; however, the vertical provenience was less reliable and consistent. Yet, Robbins's field notes indicate that he typically separated the artifacts into plowzone or feature fill contexts, and in several instances divided features by layer.[182] Artifacts were placed in a paper bag for each square marked with the square number, stake numbers, and date.[183] The artifacts from Shadwell were never systematically analyzed as part of Robbins's work; however, he used them for feature interpretation and dating.[184]

Robbins went to work on the report of his 1955 excavations at Shadwell as soon as he returned to his home. Like his Walden book, the Shadwell report is written in a conversational style that is organized chronologically. Robbins captivates the reader with his approach to the problems and "controversies" encountered while investigating the site.[185] Although this report is primarily descriptive, it goes well beyond Kimball's exclusively architectural approach, providing chapters on the previous archaeological studies, on preliminary historical research, and on

FIG. 3.7. Robbins (right) and laborers excavating topsoil from 10-ft. units at Shadwell, 1955. (Courtesy of the Roland Wells Robbins Collection, the Thoreau Society, Lincoln, Mass., and the Thoreau Institute at Walden Woods.)

excavations of test pits and grid squares, as well as a brief summary of the artifacts, conclusions, and recommendations.[186] J. C. Harrington wrote of Robbins's work and the report that "although I would not say that he has given absolute proof that the Peter Jefferson site was found, I think he has presented an excellent case."[187]

When compared with other projects of the period, some aspects of Robbins's work are quite advanced. For instance, he used artifact distribution data from excavation of the grid squares to "pin-point the sites of buildings," successfully delineating several activity areas.[188] Robbins's conclusions, particularly his reliance on comparative examples of early Virginia houses and the lack of chimneys at Shadwell, ultimately resulted in the misidentification of the main dwelling and outbuildings. However, his recommendations, including the need for additional historical research and complete analysis of the artifacts by an appropriate expert, such as C. Malcolm Watkins of the Smithsonian, demonstrate his concern with accurate interpretation of the site and appropriate treatment of both the artifacts and the records.[189] Most importantly, even though his interpretation was incorrect, his systematic methods of collecting and recording allow his data to be integrated with current research.

Recent reexcavation has determined that the main house is almost certainly associated with the large cellars identified by Kimball in 1941, and that Robbins's two small cellars and clay pit feature were probably related to a kitchen and slave quarter, respectively. Former Monticello archaeologist Susan Kern, who directed the most recent excavations at Shadwell, notes that Robbins successfully identified all the features within the areas that he had excavated and kept very meticulous records. Kern and her staff did not originally have a copy of Robbins's base map and grid. However, using the detailed provenience information on the original artifact field bags, they were able to almost completely reconstruct the grid and site layout.[190] Robbins's records have been useful in the reinterpretation of the site; his systematic collection and recording of the artifacts within a grid have allowed for a complete reanalysis of the materials, including the application of computer-aided artifact distribution mapping.[191]

The Shadwell project was fairly typical of the type of small restoration project that was the norm in historical archaeology during this period. Even as late as 1960, historical archaeology had "not truly emerged as an organized and established field" distinct from restoration constraints.[192] The National Park Service created the little institutional organization that existed, historians rejected any role, and anthropologists were still generally too busy with Native American sites to really care.[193] As demonstrated by Schumacher's work at Shadwell, NPS archaeologists were largely technicians, limited by the power of the restoration syndrome and forced to collect very specific types of data.[194] Archaeology within the academy was little better. As archaeologist Robert Schuyler has noted, "an archaeologist signed a contract, undertook an excavation at a particular historic site, wrote a report that usually was never published, and then returned to his overriding interest—prehistory."[195]

Even with these seemingly overwhelming difficulties, changes were clearly under way in historical archaeology, and Robbins felt their impact by the mid- to late 1950s. As the Shadwell project came to a close, he became interested in parlaying this work into a project at Monticello. He reported to colleague Evan Jones in 1955 that Mr. Hildreth of the Thomas Jefferson Memorial Foundation had asked him to present his slide talk on Shadwell to the annual meeting of the foundation, and he was clearly excited by the prospect. "Sure thing, said I. What the heck, those are the kind of boys I want to do business with."[196] In April 1956, Robbins did a preliminary survey at Monticello to locate the site of Jefferson's "nail-

ery."[197] Floyd Johnson appears to have been advocating on Robbins's be-
half, writing in January 1957 that "I have talked with both Mr. Hildreth
and Charles Bareham about your future at Monticello. Both are pulling
for you but it appears your profession is a jealous one and I gather doctor degrees go a long way when boards get down to make selections."[198]
Robbins's reply indicates his disappointment with the news, and expresses
his growing reservations about the academy and academic participation
in historic-sites archaeology:

I was glad to learn about the developments at Monticello. Undoubtedly the doctors degree will give the project academic dignity. But I doubt it will be too helpful with the problems confronting them. . . . Frankly, Floyd, I do not need the
Monticello work. I have more than a year's work before me. . . . But because of
the significance of the Monticello restoration, and because of my great admira-
tion for Thomas Jefferson, I want to see the excavations at the sites of Mr. Jefferson's dependency buildings properly located and *interpreted*.

Historic-sites archaeology is a very specialized field. There is no university in
the nation where it is taught. When it comes to practical experience in this field,
I know of no archaeologist, with or without a doctors degree, that has chalked
up as many important discoveries. The results speak for themselves. The work
at Monticello is no great challenge, it is routine. But the person handling it must
know what to look for.

Such a rejection would have completely discouraged someone with less
tenacity, but Robbins remained convinced of the value of his work and
his skills as a historic-sites archaeologist. "My work," he said, "just helps
to show what can be done with archaeology in the United States. . . .
We're a country that has grown too fast and been too careless of our
landmarks."[199] In this respect, he had the support of his friends and
colleagues—Brew and Harrington—and impressed his clients with the
quality of his work. Floyd Johnson remembered that Edward Kendrew
and Singleton Moorehead of Colonial Williamsburg "thought very highly
of Roland."[200] "He was a marvelous person to work with and very ener-
getic," Johnson continued.[201] "He seemed very professional to me," Johnson recalled. "Having watched the other archaeologist [Schumacher]
work, Robbins went at it just as if he had all the college."[202]

Although he was praised by most clients, Robbins's position in the
emerging fields of industrial and historical archaeology was often hurt
by his colorful description of himself as a treasure hunter or subter-
ranean detective.[203] He made statements that seemed to disparage the

scientific and academic pursuit of archaeology from the very first, often shunning the title of archaeologist. Yet, at the same time he employed a logical and scientific approach to his work and frequently engaged scientists from other fields in his projects. In these early years of his career, it seems, Robbins was concerned about misrepresenting himself by using a title that did not really apply.[204] He knew that archaeologists were generally university trained and that he was a high-school dropout learning his craft in the school of daily experience. However, he clearly recognized that the average degree-holding archaeologist was a prehistorian, not trained for or usually interested in historic sites. Historical archaeology was, according to Robert Schuyler, "simply a minor topic within general archaeology, not a subdiscipline or a separate field."[205] Although the study of historic-period sites and artifacts "was of low prestige and considered redundant . . . by most prehistorians," and industrial archaeology was virtually nonexistent in the United States, a gradual migration had begun toward the academy, a trend that Robbins encountered directly in his dealings with Monticello and one that would eventually push him aside—slowly undermining the career foundations that he had so carefully laid.[206]

CHAPTER 4

The Rudiments of a Scientific Approach

If Saugus served as Robbins's training ground, then the small projects that immediately followed, the John Winthrop Jr. Blast Furnace, the Dover Union Iron Company, and Shadwell, the Jefferson birthplace, were opportunities for him to refine and practice his new craft.[1] By the mid-1950s, with his use of grids for horizontal control, increasing attention to artifacts and their vertical position, feature identification and excavation, and application of special studies, Robbins was in some respects practicing state-of-the-art industrial and historical archaeology. Yet some aspects of his work, particularly his use of heavy equipment to excavate, his lack of attention to more recent soil layers and their artifacts, and his inconsistent proveniencing of artifacts, resulted in the loss and destruction of data and increasingly opened Robbins to criticism from his academic counterparts. His increasingly systematic work at Philipsburg Manor Upper Mills (PMUM) in North Tarrytown, New York, and particularly at the John Alden house site in Duxbury, Massachusetts, drew on his numerous contacts with archaeologists J. C. Harrington, J. O. Brew, Henry Hornblower II, Ivor and Audrey Noël Hume, and Maurice Robbins; his continuing study of the archaeological literature; and his expanding field experiences. At PMUM, Robbins contended with a large seventeenth- to nineteenth-century commercial and industrial site that had been extensively filled and then altered during previous restoration activities. He spent five years removing the previous reconstruction, excavating the original complex of buildings, and negotiating the administration maze of this important historical site. While he faced major problems with the complicated stratigraphy and features at the PMUM site and had an increasingly difficult relationship with the

Sleepy Hollow Restorations staff, Robbins succeeded in identifying much of the colonial mill complex, work that guided the mill reconstruction, manor house restoration, and landscape restoration.

At PMUM, Robbins expanded public participation in his work, developing an active public archaeology program that inspired his fellow Americans with the romance of archaeology and the ruins of the past. While anticipating the current vogue in public archaeology by four decades and mirroring Noël Hume's theatrical approach at Williamsburg, Robbins's populist approach created tension between himself and university professionals that would ultimately damage his career. As the academy drew the discipline under its wing, it began the slow professionalization process that sought to control and standardize archaeological knowledge. Increasingly, the field's "secrets" were restricted to those with a symbol of professional proficiency.[2] Robbins's unrestricted approach, sharing archaeology with the masses and suggesting that they could themselves be archaeologists, ran counter to all that was then held sacred in the professional culture.

Ironically, Robbins was also an early proponent of professionalizing the discipline; he particularly stressed the need to create a professional association of historical archaeologists. Aware of the need for more exchange among the few researchers then practicing historical archaeology, he proposed a forum on historic-sites work to J. C. Harrington in 1954.[3] Robbins wrote that "it would be well if at some time in the future we could call a seminar where by all of us could compare notes and reveal the results of our individual endeavors. I am sure that we would all benefit greatly by such meetings."[4] Harrington answered several days later:

you are absolutely right that the few of us working in this somewhat unusual field should get together on occasion and not only discuss our individual experiences but work out ways of making them available to others working on similar projects. . . . I have often thought an association would be desirable. . . . However there are far too many associations. . . . Furthermore, I have never felt that I had the time that it would take to help organize such a group and help carry it along in the formative years. This is certainly one subject that we should discuss, and I am sure you have undoubtedly given some thought to it.[5]

It would be another thirteen years before such an organization would be realized in the creation of the Society for Historical Archaeology.

As at Saugus, Robbins continued to labor for preservation organizations that were developing their properties through historical restoration, reconstruction, or monument building. The often complex and varying goals of these groups, ranging from educational interpretation to tourism, made planning and implementing the excavations difficult and required Robbins to do far more than excavate. While the smaller and less complicated digs, such as Shadwell and the John Alden House, allowed him to concentrate on the archaeology, the major venture at PMUM once again required him to wear many hats, and regularly brought him into conflict with museum personnel, their restoration-oriented goals, and the operational needs of these museum organizations.

At PMUM, Robbins also struggled to establish his status within the organizational culture of the institution. As a consultant, he sought to balance freedom and autonomy against a need to validate his identity and position within the organizational culture.[6] Robbins wanted both the freedom of an independent professional consultant and the security of the organization—a foundation for his career and financial stability. As demonstrated with his careful treatment and protection of the Walden discovery and his later struggles with the architects at Saugus, Robbins treated his archaeological finds as a form of intellectual property and insisted upon complete autonomy in his work. Having been a self-employed person for most of his life, his self-conception and personality were wrapped up in his image of the independent consulting professional. Robbins did not want to be treated like an employee, subject to the power of others. This is evident in the Saugus project and particularly in the PMUM excavation, where he functioned within a large-scale, institutional framework. He had to give up the freedom of private practice and risked becoming "a digging technician."[7] As became evident in his deteriorating relationship with the PMUM staff, Robbins did not want inexperienced colleagues—be they architects, curators, or administrators—to manipulate and use his discoveries and impinge on his intellectual freedom as a professional consultant. At the same time, however, he also did not want them to "do him out of" his vacation pay, a benefit traditionally reserved for paid staff employees. As so often happens, Robbins's economic self-interest became bound up with his professional identity. His expansive agendas at Saugus and Philipsburg Manor created a situation akin to an open-ended contract that conflicted with the financial constraints of his employers and set him up for charges of conflict of interest by other professionals.

As Robbins became increasingly absorbed in his new career of archaeological consulting, he slowly phased out his odd-jobs business. However, he retained many of the skills he had learned in business, particularly the importance of lining up new projects and potential clients. He initially relied heavily on word of mouth and personal contacts to obtain new archaeological projects, but quickly realized the need to advertise to reach the regional preservation community and create a large enough base to sustain his business. Using both his far-reaching lecture program network and a variety of direct mail approaches, he applied his business acumen and energy to the problem and worked out a successful promotional strategy. As professionals marketed their university degrees, Robbins traded on his practical field experience; he created his own visible symbols of competence and disseminated them through his public lectures, brochures, and eventually his 1959 book *Hidden America*.

Between the end of the Saugus project in 1953 and the start of the PMUM work in 1956, Robbins kept busy with several smaller projects including Shadwell and the Dover ironworks, lecturing, and prospecting for new consulting opportunities. During this period, he wrote hundreds of promotional letters to foundations, historical organizations, and industries looking for new projects and funding.[8] Whether writing to the Daughters of the American Revolution, the Carnegie Institution, the Ford Foundation, the National Trust for Historic Preservation, or the National Association of Manufacturers, Robbins energetically pitched his expertise and the importance of historic-sites archaeology: "there are many worthwhile investigations that have national significance and bearing upon our early history and our heritage which cannot be conducted because of inadequate finances."[9] He was quickly becoming aware of the profitable connections between commercial interests and nonprofit foundations for supporting his type of work.

When writing to manufacturers, for instance, Robbins emphasized the industrial sites that he had excavated and wrote that "industry today should know more of their past history."[10] Rejections, which Robbins received by the hundreds during his career, did not seem to dampen his enthusiasm or slow down his tenacious letter-writing campaign.[11] His correspondence and lecturing always seemed to provide a new connection and project, as when Helen D. Bullock, a historian at the National Trust for Historic Preservation, wrote back that "we not infrequently have occasion to recommend archaeological examinations and would welcome the opportunity of forwarding your name."[12] However, this aggressive marketing and self-promotion eventually worked against Robbins as the discipline professionalized.

As they did with Noël Hume, academic professionals complained about Robbins's salesmanship and self-promotion as blatantly amateur and took exception to his entrepreneurial orientation, yet their lament may have been anything but altruistic.[13] Robbins's friend and colleague Paul Heberling, a university-based archaeologist, remarked of Robbins's promotional activities that "you just don't do that sort of thing if you are a scientist."[14] Heberling's observation reinforces the passive, noneconomic, and homogeneous professional veneer of the academy that is generally accepted by the public.[15] In Robbins's situation, without the security and support of an educational affiliation or permanent position, he had little choice but to promote his work and his accomplishments for himself.[16]

Although it rankled his academic colleagues, Robbins's promotional strategy yielded opportunities to participate in significant projects throughout the region. One of the more important of these projects was the Rockefeller-funded PMUM site in Sleepy Hollow (formerly North Tarrytown), New York.[17] John D. Rockefeller Jr. had become involved in the PMUM project in 1940, when the Historical Society of the Tarrytowns requested money to turn the Philipse Castle or Philipsburg Manor house into a "historic shrine."[18] Society president Hugh Grant Rowell argued that "the Tarrytowns, with the story of the North, are just as rich in lore [as St. Augustine and Williamsburg], and, in my opinion have a richer historic background than either of the other communities."[19] Rockefeller initially donated the money needed to purchase the property, which sat below Kykuit, his Pocantico Hills estate, and to complete repairs to make the house suitable as a headquarters for the society.[20] As the project progressed, members of the Rockefeller-funded Colonial Williamsburg architectural staff were called in to record changes made to the house.[21] The continued lobbying effort of the society's president along with the Colonial Williamsburg architect's report to Rockefeller convinced him to fund a major restoration of Philipse Castle beginning in 1941. While Colonial Williamsburg staff provided advice on the project, they were not involved in the day-to-day restoration process. When Colonial Williamsburg architects Rutherford Goodwin and Singleton Moorehead visited the site in 1942, they were not happy with what they saw, particularly the quality of the archaeology.[22] Although "the Williamsburg professionals did not like working with an amateur approach, nor . . . [like to] see their patron's funds used in such a way," they remained involved in upgrading the site's interpretation to visitors, drawing on the experiences of the Williamsburg operation.[23]

In 1952, the newly formed Sleepy Hollow Restorations (SHR) board of directors again brought in several Colonial Williamsburg staff members to assist in "increasing the educational merit and significance of these restorations while carrying forward their established traditions."[24] One of their new initiatives, a thorough research program to reevaluate the previous restoration and the site's interpretation, resulted in Robbins's employment as consulting archaeologist.

Robbins's unsolicited letter of inquiry to director Dr. Harold Dean Cater in 1956 began the process that ultimately landed him the job. "If . . . my services could be beneficial with your work of restoring the old grist mill," he wrote positively, "I would like to hear from you."[25] Robbins was clearly aware of Rockefeller's association with the site, having visited the impressive operation at Colonial Williamsburg on several occasions during his Saugus and Shadwell projects, and was no doubt excited about the SHR's vision to create a northern version of Virginia's colonial capital.

Robbins first visited Philipse Manor in July 1956, and his meeting with Cater and Robert G. Wheeler, the director of research, was a clear success. Wheeler wrote to Robbins that he felt "bursting with enthusiasm and the desire to follow up our talks."[26] Robbins scheduled preliminary testing in late summer, writing to Wheeler that "I think that the first thing we should do would be to go over all the pertinent material you have . . . about the Philipse family occupation and development of the site. This would give us a pattern to start with."[27]

Robbins discovered that the Philipsburg Manor Upper Mills site had been built in the 1680s by Dutch merchant and businessman Frederick Philipse. Philipse had settled in New Amsterdam by 1650, working as a carpenter. As the colony expanded, Philipse became involved in trade and mercantile activities. In 1662, he married Margaret Hardenbrook de Vries, a widow who was also active in trade and shipping. By 1674, Philipse was listed as one of the richest men in the New York colony, controlling a commercial empire that extended to the West Indies, Europe, and the Indian Ocean, and included several thousands of acres along the Hudson River. Philipse built two major settlements along the Hudson to serve his commercial operations: Philipse Manor Hall in what is now Yonkers and Philipsburg Manor Upper Mills near present day Sleepy Hollow, New York. The Upper Mills was to contain a gristmill and serve as a provisioning plantation for Philipse's Atlantic trade enterprise. Tenants and enslaved Africans at both settlements raised grains, particularly wheat, built the buildings, and provided general labor for the mercantile and provisioning operations. Historical evidence suggests that the mill and dam at the Upper Mills was in place by about 1684. Frederick's son Adolph inherited the Upper Mills estate in the early eighteenth century and continued to build on his father's successes. About 1750, the site became the property Frederick Philipse II (and later his son Frederick III). The Philipse family fled to England at the time of the Revolution, and the property was sold to the Beekman family who owned it until 1850, when it became the country home of New York mayor Ambrose Kingsland. The manor house was expanded and remodelled several times, and the mill was rebuilt multiple times as well; a mill and dam existed into the mid-nineteenth century. When Robbins approached the site in the late 1950s, it contained a mill and dam reconstructed in the early 1940s.[28]

Robbins faced major obstacles with the PMUM excavations (figure 4.1), particularly the complicated stratigraphy, heavily disturbed by previous excavations and early-twentieth-century landscaping, and an often problematic relationship with the SHR staff members. Although his excavation approach clearly resulted in a loss of important data, a review of the project suggests that his work was more systematic and thoroughly documented than has been previously understood.[29] For instance, Robbins used trench and unit excavations to determine the previous shorelines of the tidal Pocantico River and to establish the original spatial orientation of the complex, performed a shovel test survey to determine areas of archaeological interest on portions of the property, and engaged a variety of consultants to perform special studies including faunal analysis and geoarchaeology.

Robbins called the PMUM site a "deep" excavation, one that required the use of heavy machinery to expose and remove thick "fill" deposits that had built up over the colonial evidence. As discussed for Shadwell, Robbins was distinguishing between thin plowzone and deeply buried, stratified sites. He approached each of these site types differently in terms of his excavation methods, and he became convinced that deep sites, in most instances industrial or commercial complexes, could be efficiently approached only with the assistance of mechanical equipment. For example, after establishing the stratigraphic sequences across the PMUM site, Robbins had the machine remove the "modern" nineteenth- and twentieth-century soils, leaving a buffer or interface over the colo-

FIG. 4.1. River yard excavations with log cribbing in foreground, Philipsburg Manor house (Sleepy Hollow, N.Y.) in background on right, 1960. (Courtesy of the Roland Wells Robbins Collection, the Thoreau Society, Lincoln, Mass., and the Thoreau Institute at Walden Woods.)

nial strata or "contact surface." This interface was then removed by hand troweling and shoveling to expose early deposits and features such as foundations. "Deep excavations," Robbins explained,

can only be done with heavy equipment. But preceding that there is always a laborer with a shovel who is digging down to determine how much fill remains . . . and I'll investigate it and find that it's a fill depth and we will shave it down to within a foot of the bottom of the trench. . . . It's taken down very gradually with the various levels being analyzed as the excavations take place.[30]

This methodology was problematic in that Robbins rarely removed and recorded the entire stratigraphic sequence in a systematic or consistent manner.[31] Although he ended up with the early colonial deposits and artifacts that he sought, he destroyed important contextual information when removing the overlying and more recent fill sequences. These later deposits held keys to relative dating and to the relationships of later activities to the early Philipse complex. Thus, the vertical provenience of artifacts is problematic in many portions of the site and requires interpolation using Robbins's extensive records and photographs.[32]

Robbins's initial approach to the excavation of the PMUM site was one that combined a review of historical research and previous archaeology with a limited field survey. A program of historical research, coordinated by Wheeler, was carried out concurrently with the archaeological investigations. This effort provided a constant flow of historical information on the configuration of the property that assisted Robbins in selecting areas for excavation and helped later with interpretation.[33]

While the site was in Robbins's words a "complicated mess," his initial survey of the property was informed by both the results of the previous archaeological excavations and ongoing historical research. For instance, he used a mid-nineteenth-century map of the property to identify period structures, scaling the map based on surviving buildings and landscape features. Robbins's first survey effort at PMUM consisted of probe-rod testing to relocate several previously identified foundations. This work was expanded to include mechanical test trenching and hand-excavated "test holes" to identify cultural and natural deposits and features, assess the impact of the previous archaeology and restoration work, and establish the site's stratigraphic sequence (figure 4.2).[34] The initial survey program was intended to evaluate the potential for finding significant new information about the early mill and adjacent manor house, and to establish the value of a more extensive excavation. The deep mechanically dug trenches furnished Robbins with excellent stratigraphic cross sections of the property, identifying evidence of seventeenth- and eighteenth-century activity buried beneath multiple layers of nineteenth- and twentieth-century fill and confirming his suspicions about the complex nature of the site. In the area north of the reconstructed mill (1941) and south of the PMUM house, Robbins identified timber evidence in a trench that "went to a depth of 87″ near its northerly end—and still it was fill."[35] The upper fill of the trench was rich in colonial artifacts, including "whole Dutch bricks . . . early earthenware, metal pieces, and lots of shell."[36]

Robbins reported to Cater and Wheeler that the preliminary work was "most successful—and it showed that major excavations should now take place."[37] Wheeler submitted a plan and budget to Cater for a two-year program, noting that the "preliminary study . . . recommended that a thorough archaeological study be conducted of the entire Philipse Castle lands."[38] The members of the board seemed to favor proceeding with the program; however, they wanted to present an outline to John D.

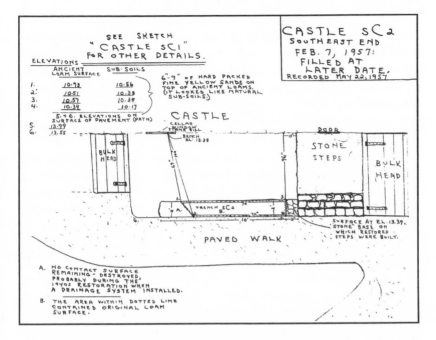

FIG. 4.2. Plan of trench sC2, February 7, 1957. (Courtesy of the Roland Wells Robbins Collection, the Thoreau Society, Lincoln, Mass., and the Thoreau Institute at Walden Woods.)

Rockefeller Jr. regarding the work and its financing.[39] With no official decision in sight Wheeler wrote to Cater that

Mr. Robbins has received a number of inquiries regarding his availability for similar explorations in New Jersey, North Carolina, and Pennsylvania. Naturally he feels that he has a definite obligation to continue his work at Philipse Castle, and he wishes to do so. He cannot make plans ahead, however, on the basis of the general work decision reached in the December conversation.[40]

Wheeler utilized the demand, or perception of demand, for Robbins's professional services as leverage to force the SHR management to act on his and Robbins's recommendation to expand the archaeological research program.[41] Several days later, Robbins enthusiastically noted in his daily log that "there was no question about the two year archaeological program going through!"[42] With an extended work program approved, the digging proceeded apace.

As he enlarged the excavations in the second and third years, Robbins expanded his system of test trenches, test units, and small "spot check-ing holes" or shovel tests, and began larger-scale mechanical excavation. For instance, he systematically investigated several areas to the west and north of the manor house using a small unit testing method consisting of systematically spaced 2-by-2-foot test units (figures 4.3 and 4.4). After the dismantling of the 1941 mill reconstruction, work focused on the var-ious early mill foundations, the millpond, the docks around the mill, and finally the sequence of early stone and wooden milldams (Figure 4.5).

Robbins initially maintained systematic horizontal control over the excavations by plotting test units relative to fixed points, such as the manor house. His early survey work consisted primarily of test trenches and units that were recorded in field notes and plotted on the general plan of the restoration using simple triangulation methods.[43] In the fall of 1957, Robbins and surveyor Hank Fridy laid out "a master grid" (fig-ure 4.6) that consisted of ninety-nine units or sections, each measuring 80 by 120 feet.[44]

As mentioned above, Robbins's vertical control over the site was less systematic than the horizontal control. He excavated roughly by natural strata and maintained vertical control generally by measuring with a transit from an established datum, referencing soil levels to fixed points, and digging spot checks to verify the stratigraphic profile (figure 4.7). He recorded the vertical data for the excavations in daily field notes and in-cluded elevations for the present surface and natural subsoils, as well as a description of "early surfaces" or "contact surfaces" with artifacts. Rob-bins utilized archaeological jargon acquired through his reading and from contacts with professionals, although he seems to have maintained and preferred his own colloquial terminology. The original grade repre-sented the original ground surface during the period of interest, for ex-ample, the seventeenth and eighteenth centuries at PMUM. The loca-tion of this grade was often determined by the presence of buried A horizons, humus or loam layers, or by the type and period of artifacts in a soil level. Fills or fill soils were defined largely by their artifact content and relationship to modern site features. Artifacts from these later-period fills were not generally or consistently collected. The "contact surface" was a buried living surface or grade that contained artifacts that dated to the period of interest. The depth of surfaces or layers, either below ground surface or the site's elevation datum, was recorded in Rob-bins's daily log and field notes, on artifacts bags, and also on the various section plan sheets.[45]

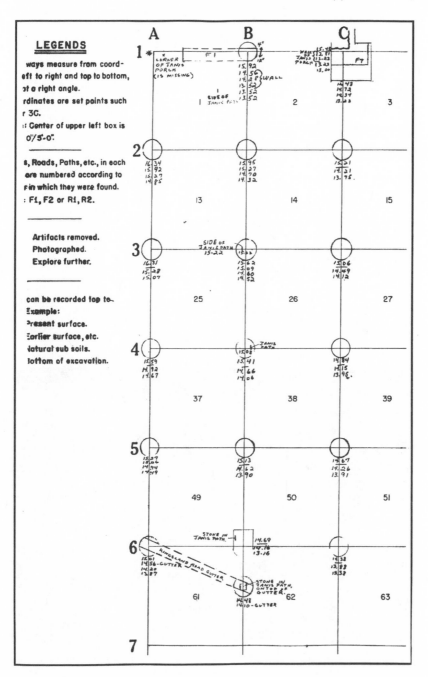

FIG. 4.3. Section plan showing 2-ft. test pits, 1958. (Courtesy of the Roland Wells Robbins Collection, the Thoreau Society, Lincoln, Mass., and the Thoreau Institute at Walden Woods.)

SECTION 56	LINE A	FRI. SEPT. 26, 1958	LEGEND	⊬ARTIFACTS REMOVED F FOUNDATION ⚫ PHOTOGRAPHED R ROAD ⚫⟋ '' IN DETAIL P PATH ↓ EXPLORE FURTHER		
	PRESENT	EARLIER SURFACES	NATURAL	BOTTOM OF EXCAVATION	ARTIFACTS	
1+0'/5'	15.90		15.06 Sand	12.10	Nearly void	
2	15.86		14.37 sand	12.15	Nearly void, some fine pea stone 9" below grade.	
+ 2+0'/5'	15.94	15.38 hard packed loam. Possible road- way or path.	14.71 sand	12.38	Nearly void.	
+ 3	16.00	15.42 hard packed loam. Possible road- way or path.	14.90 sand.	13.68	Nearly void, small piece of coal noted at lower level.	
3+0'/5'	16.05		14.98 sand	13.96	Nearly void, small pieces pea stone noted at bottom.	
3+0'/9'3" to 4+0'/1'7" is possible side of sloping roadway.	16.10	15.44 road surface 15.06 road bottom Large curshed stone, size	15.02 sand,gravel of 2 walnuts.	13.96	Loamy soils below pat void. Rubble fill begins at westerly side of path.	
4+0'/5'	16.20		15.15 coarse sand	14.32	From stone roadway to this point a 6" bed of rubble brick & plaster exists, rest- ing on natural sand.	

To the left of the table: "SAME TRENCH" and "R" bracketing the 3+0'/5', 3+0'/9'3" to 4+0'/1'7", and 4+0'/5' rows.

FIG. 4.4. Field data from 2-ft. test pits in section 56, September 26, 1958. (Courtesy of the Roland Wells Robbins Collection, the Thoreau Society, Lincoln, Mass., and the Thoreau Institute at Walden Woods.)

FIG. 4.5. Excavation of wooden dam cribbing at Philipsburg Manor Upper Mills, 1960. (Courtesy of the Roland Wells Robbins Collection, the Thoreau Society, Lincoln, Mass., and the Thoreau Institute at Walden Woods.)

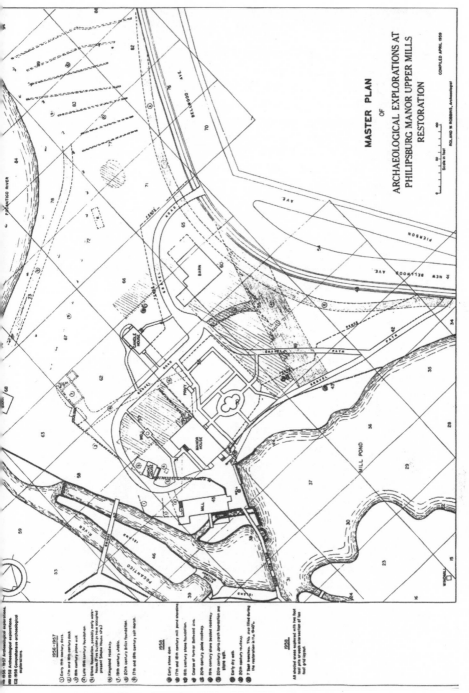

FIG. 4.6. Master plan of archaeological explorations at Philipsburg Manor Upper Mills restoration, April 1959. (Courtesy of the Roland Wells Robbins Collection, the Thoreau Society, Lincoln, Mass., and the Thoreau Institute at Walden Woods.)

FIG. 4.7. Test excavation at Philipsburg Manor Upper Mills showing the stratigraphic profile with elevations. (Courtesy of the Roland Wells Robbins Collection, the Thoreau Society, Lincoln, Mass., and the Thoreau Institute at Walden Woods.)

The excavation records from the PMUM project indicate that Robbins clearly recognized and recorded soil changes and could read and interpret stratigraphic evidence, accurately describing fill sequences and identifying features such as foundations, roadways, wells, and postholes. Robbins's plan drawings and field notes provide basic information on the excavation of each test trench, test unit, and excavation area, including soil descriptions with depths, artifact classes, and the location of historic features and modern disturbances. His daily log entries document regular record keeping at the site; these records were subsequently transferred onto formal section plans.[46] Robbins made sketches of the excavations in his field notebook and daily log and, with the help of project surveyor Hank Fridy, completed precise plan maps of many excavated sections, including feature locations such as building foundations and postholes (figure 4.8). With the help of project photographer Bill Hennessey, Robbins also meticulously photo-documented the PMUM project.[47]

While the recording of profile and plan information is critical for interpreting a site, relating these data to the artifacts recovered is even more essential. Although Robbins explained that "as we go through the

FIG. 4.8. Excavation of seventeenth/eighteenth-century mill foundation area at Philipsburg Manor Upper Mills, ca. 1961. (Courtesy of the Roland Wells Robbins Collection, the Thoreau Society, Lincoln, Mass., and the Thoreau Institute at Walden Woods.)

layers, the artifacts from each layer are carefully bagged—the soils from the various strata also have to be very carefully recorded," a review of the excavated materials suggests that this procedure was not systematically followed and that many artifacts were marked only with horizontal provenience.[48] Soil removed from excavation units was generally hand sorted for artifacts and stockpiled for later screening by staff and volunteers.[49] Artifacts recovered from the excavation were initially stored in field bags that contained basic horizontal and vertical provenience information.[50]

While the artifacts from PMUM were initially stored with basic provenience data, they were later marked with only horizontal information. It appears that as Robbins's staff cataloged the finds after the excavation and prepared artifact inventories and tables following his resignation, they did not consistently transfer all the provenience data on the artifact field bags to the artifacts and artifact catalog cards.[51]

In some cases, the materials were stored with complete locational data. For example, in 1959 Robbins recorded that his assistant helped him put "the artifacts from the various boxes and their levels in the 45-F1 area into cartons and numbering same." This statement suggests that the artifacts from the section 45, foundation 1 area were excavated and stored within their horizontal-grid boxes and by level.[52] This is further corroborated by notations from a meeting on the artifact cataloging work. Robbins wrote that "as for the transitions that took place in the 19th-century mill, they will be referred to as levels and given Roman numerals for the different periods. The 19th-century wheel pit will have a different level than the 19th-century turbine pit, etc."[53] Although Robbins seemed to confuse the terminology of level and feature, the artifacts were marked and stored with horizontal and vertical references that could be related to the depositional sequences of the site.[54] Although his vertical provenience and control over the artifacts was inconsistent, the few remaining field bags confirm that he clearly stored some artifacts with precise level and/or feature data.[55]

During the excavations, Robbins used artifacts to date the various levels and features, particularly to distinguish between more modern fills and the seventeenth- and eighteenth-century "contact surfaces" that were of primary interest for SHR staff and restoration architects. Throughout the fieldwork, he enlisted the help of consultants, including antiques experts Ben and Cora Ginsburg (general/ceramics), Helen McKearin (glass), Lura Watkins (ceramics/general), and Smithsonian curator C. Malcolm Watkins (general), for preliminary identification of diagnostic artifacts.[56]

As at Saugus, Robbins also arranged for special studies related to the overall site interpretation, including faunal analysis (Dr. Leon Hausman), geoarchaeological work on the peat beds that underlay the millpond and their relationship to sea-level rise (Dr. Elso Barghoorn), and tree-ring dating.[57] As noted for Saugus, Robbins's use of a faunal analyst to study the animal bones from several areas is of particular interest because this type of study was just not done in historical archaeology at the time. Dr. Hausman also assisted in examination and identification of seed remains, or macrofossils, removed from several "stratified soils" within the nineteenth-century mill foundation.[58]

Robbins completed several yearly interim summaries of his excavations for the directors, the most detailed being his 1959 report. This short document summarizes the dismantling of the reconstructed mill building and excavations beneath it and consists largely of a "photographic account of excavations," providing a chronological overview and initial results of the work.[59] Robbins and Wheeler later drafted an interim report that is largely descriptive and clearly intended as a brief summary of the work.[60]

The techniques and methodologies employed by Robbins at PMUM in many ways resemble those in general practice in the emerging historical archaeological community during this period. Robbins, lacking any formal training, developed his approach based on his field experiences at the Saugus, John Winthrop Jr., and Shadwell sites, a commonsense Yankee ingenuity, discussions with archaeological and museum colleagues, and his reading in the disciplinary literature. He used grid systems for horizontal control, probe and shovel testing for site survey, and general artifact provenience controls. At a time when academic practitioners in historical archaeology sought technical precision and methodological refinement and standardization, however, Robbins was using heavy equipment for "deep excavations" and taking his own approach to "get the job done," one that clearly resulted in damage to the site and a loss of critical data in some instances. While his techniques for mechanical excavation were much more controlled than has been appreciated, he was regularly chastised for his "crude" and destructive methods.[61]

As the project progressed, Robbins's work was increasingly influenced and manipulated both by museum staff, including Wheeler, Cater, and later Dr. Jack Collins, and by the architects at Perry, Shaw, Hepburn, Kehoe and Dean. Ironically, Robbins was once again working with many of the same architects that he worked with at Saugus.[62] As at Saugus, the relations between Robbins and Wheeler and the architects had deteriorated to the point of open hostility by the end of the project. Robbins was worn down by the work at PMUM—another large, complicated project—and he was clearly tired of and frustrated with his colleagues. His daily log for September 1, 1961, the day on which he packed his office to leave, reflects his concerns:

we have done an excellent job with our work at PMUM. I hope the plans for the restoration will be as good, and the restoration itself will not suffer by too many concessions brought about by pressures from within, or from lack of ability to comprehend the material facts which we unearthed. I will be happier when my report is written and I can leave and turn to other work!!![63]

The final weeks and months of Robbins's tenure at PMUM were tense and confusing for all parties. As the project wound down, Robbins began meeting with project architect Andrew Hepburn Jr. and Wheeler to discuss additional archaeological work that Hepburn considered crucial for completing the restoration.[64] On one occasion, Robbins, Hepburn, and

Wheeler met with Dr. Cater to discuss Hepburn's recommendations. Although he was generally pleased with the outcome of the meeting, Robbins recorded that Cater had shown

his typical lack of knowledge of what has been done and what is going on . . . "I didn't know that a 17–18 century dock was found below the 19 century docks"; and; "I never knew that a mill was built where the restoration built their mill about 1839"; and "I don't understand why they brought in all the broken artifacts you are finding."[65]

Cater seems to have been confused and misinformed about important interpretive issues, as Robbins reported, but he finally approved the work.

By early 1961, excavation and restoration were under way concurrently in several areas, and relations with the project managers grew increasingly tense.[66] After meeting with new museum director Jack B. Collins, Robbins noted that

I will concentrate on the sluiceway timbered area, going all the way to the southerly end of what we have been referring to as the dry dock. I will take it apart and determine what it was like originally, as well as try and find out how changes were made.[67]

Robbins seemed pleased that Collins appreciated all of his work and the difficulties associated with the project, although he was saddened to have to tell his laborers and staff that their work was coming to an end.[68] While preparing to close down the excavations, Robbins met regularly with Collins and Wheeler to prepare tentative interpretive layouts of the site, particularly during the Philipse tenure.[69] As August ended, he recorded that they

finish[ed] all the excavations: (At least all that they will permit being done.) Hank and I worked in the field plotting the ship basin, carpenter shop, etc. Bill Hennessy in this a.m. and spent part of the morning and part of this afternoon taking the final pictures of the archeological work.[70]

The plan was for Wheeler and Robbins to produce an interim report and then complete a more extensive final report. The draft of the interim "Research-Archaeological Report" was completed in September, and Robbins and Wheeler prepared a series of plan maps depicting the main periods of occupation and several reconstruction drawings.[71] In October, Robbins asked for leave to "take care of other commitments," promising Collins that he would be available if "there was anything they needed me for."[72] Collins and Wheeler had Robbins sign a letter that "contained 5 clauses stating the conditions under which I could get away until January 8th next. Whew! It makes me feel like I am on parole, not on a long overdue vacation!!"[73] Robbins never returned to finish the final report, however, due to both the growing distrust between himself and the SHR management and a dispute over his vacation pay that exemplifies the dynamics of his employment situation at PMUM.

When Robbins received a check from SHR that did not include vacation pay that he had anticipated, he called Bob Wheeler, who reported that "Jack Collins said that consultants don't get vacation time."[74] Robbins reminded Wheeler of their initial arrangement of one month vacation per year, and Wheeler agreed that he should get his vacation but that "from this would be taken all [the] time that I took off for lectures." Robbins told Wheeler that "most of the lectures were on the PMUM and Sunnyside work and that they were public relations talks." He also reminded Wheeler that "I worked nights, weekends, and that I never put in for car or traveling expenses." Robbins's entry in his daily log following the telephone conversation registers his disgust: "I have never felt so humiliated before in my life!!!!! I still can't believe it!!!!"[75] Not only had Robbins believed that he was not receiving an "ample tangible reward from the client's pocketbook," he was equally discouraged that he had been denied at least the "psychic reward of the clients's unqualified gratitude."[76]

Robbins was convinced that SHR intended to "do [him] out of [his] vacation time if they could."[77] A series of meetings between Wheeler, Collins, and Robbins failed to resolve the situation.[78] In the process of settling the dispute, Collins wrote to Robbins that he would not be allowed to lecture on his work at PMUM without written permission from SHR.[79] This only added fuel to the fire: "By cutting off my talks," Robbins noted, "he would be hurting my income considerably."[80] Although Robbins returned to the restoration briefly in 1962 to review slides of the work with Bob Wheeler, he was not asked to return to complete his report on the archaeological work.[81]

Even after his stormy departure, Robbins remarkably did not give up on completing the PMUM report, periodically corresponding with the restoration staff about finishing the work. As late as 1965, he wrote that the situation at PMUM today provides the opportunity to prepare a creditable summation of the five years of major excavations which I had the privilege to supervise. If you deem this report would be beneficial to the Restoration's final record, I would be pleased to prepare it. My compensation for this work would be on the same basis for which I was retained originally.[82]

Director Dana Creel thanked Robbins for his letter, but reported that

our staff and consultants are at work on the definitive Philipsburg Manor reports covering architecture, furnishings, and interpretation. Each of these major reports will contain all pertinent archaeological materials.[83]

As Robbins had feared and as was typical in much restoration archaeology of the period, the archaeology had been relegated to the role of footnotes in the historical and architectural reconstruction records.

During his five years at PMUM, Robbins found himself increasingly at odds with the management of SHR over the direction of the archaeological investigations. As with his work at Saugus, Robbins quickly discovered that the decision-making process regarding the archaeological work was in the hands of historians and museum professionals who had little experience in or knowledge of archaeological research. Robbins's dispute with the staff over his vacation was really just the final skirmish in a conflict that had been brewing for several years.

Although his first year of work at PMUM was marked by cooperation and mutual respect from both historian Robert Wheeler and director Harold Cater, Robbins encountered detractors early in his tenure at the site. For example, in 1956 Wheeler reported to Robbins that publicity director Jo Chamberlain was "trying to quash the archeological program" in order to move the manor house restoration and mill reconstruction on to completion.[84]

All went well for the first year or more of fieldwork. In fact, although Robbins told Cater that he had vowed after Saugus to "never take on any project which would entail more than three months [*sic*] time," he "would be quite willing to stay on [at PMUM]—there is so much to work with, and its potential is most unusual and interesting."[85] However, an incident in 1958 involving a chapter of *Hidden America* indicates that Robbins's generally positive relationship with the SHR staff had begun to deteriorate. The board of directors initially insisted that the chapter on the PMUM site be removed from the book. They eventually compromised and allowed the chapter, but only with complete editorial over-sight of the material on the PMUM excavations. Responding to their edi-torial comments, Robbins exclaimed, "they massacred it! . . . It sounds like a report—and that is what we didn't want it to sound like. . . . [It] dissolved my friendship with Wheeler."[86] The chapter was eventually in-cluded in the book after several rewrites, but the incident marked a turn-ing point for Robbins's relationship with the SHR staff. He had come to realize that he did not have the freedom over his work that he sought; he was not a coequal professional colleague but a "digging technician," as Harrington had earlier characterized the place of archaeologists in restoration work.

By the end of 1958, Robbins had become familiar with the internal staff tensions and personality problems at SHR. Robbins found to his dismay that he was increasingly drawn into the internal office politics of the organization. This was particularly disturbing because none of the parties—the board members, director Cater, or research department head Wheeler—had any real understanding of the demands of his work and its difficulties.[87]

Project planning and budgeting were constant problems for Robbins and the SHR staff due to both the depth and complexity of the features, and the lack of communication and understanding between the archae-ologist and project sponsors.[88] The completion or termination date for the archaeological work was also a regular source of confusion between Robbins, Wheeler, and the administration. SHR administrators estab-lished several unrealistic completion dates without consultation with Robbins, and he was understandably annoyed.[89] The extremely compli-cated archaeological work, combined with pressures from weather de-lays and management, again took their toll on Robbins's health.[90]

As the project progressed, another concern of Robbins's was the lack of contact that he had with the restoration architects. In 1960, Robbins took Wheeler, Cater, and architect Andrew Hepburn on a short tour of the excavations. When they returned to the site the next day, however, Robbins was not invited to join them. Although Wheeler told him that they were not "going over details," Robbins was very upset because he perceived that he had been bypassed. He told Wheeler that "he [Wheeler] was in no position to explain the details of my work and findings to Hepburn, or to anyone else for that matter."[91]

During the final year of the project, Robbins's anxiety level increased as pressure mounted to finish the archaeological investigations and begin the restoration work.[92] Robbins's relationship with Bob Wheeler continued to disintegrate as the tension increased. For instance, he noted that he was "brought up to date on Bob Wheeler's customary double-talking methods."[93] To Robbins's way of thinking, Wheeler was attempting to wrest control of the archaeological information from him. Wheeler, on the other hand, had been largely responsible for Robbins's position at the restoration and had, in a sense, sponsored him within the organization and community. The relationship between Robbins and Wheeler began with Robbins in the position of expert consulting archaeologist but was later transformed into one in which Robbins was an employee "under Wheeler's department." As their desire to complete the project and finish the restoration grew, the newly reorganized SHR management team exerted more and more control over Robbins's expanding excavations. Wheeler was increasingly placed in a position of making decisions that directly affected Robbins's work and impacted his autonomy. This was particularly troublesome to Robbins because he knew that Wheeler had little knowledge of archaeology.

Robbins's vacation battle illustrates a clear pattern in his long-term projects: he fell into conflicts with employers that eventually led to his termination or resignation. These conflicts grew out of both his self-definition as an independent consultant for museums and historical societies and his stubborn, powerful personality. Robbins sought intellectual, personal, and economic freedom; he did not want to be treated as an employee, subject to the power of others. At some level, however, he also coveted the advantages that accrued from having a permanent position in an organization such as SHR: an office, staff assistants, institutional authority, and benefits like vacation pay. Yet, Robbins was not willing to make the trade-offs that were necessary to be an employee within an organization.

Robbins had been self-employed for most of his working life and wanted to maintain that autonomy. He treated the archaeological record that he pieced together from fieldwork and other research as his intellectual property and felt strongly that he should be allowed to manipulate it or present it to the public as he saw fit. Robbins demonstrated again and again that he would share the results of his work with his colleagues and the public, but he would not share the credit for his work. His attempts to control the information he recovered became especially difficult when working within teams of researchers at major restorations such as those at Saugus and PMUM. His often tenuous position in the field, heightened at PMUM by both the tremendously complicated archaeological site and public exposure of the project, raised the stakes and intensified Robbins's anxiety. Like many of his academic counterparts, he was temperamentally ill suited to the teamwork required in these projects. *Hidden America* coauthor Evan Jones noted that "he was interested in himself—not in the vain sense of having to have an audience—he had to do what he wanted to do as best he could and he found confidence in doing the thing successfully."[94]

Although the last year of the PMUM project might give a different impression, Robbins remained passionate about his work at the site and continued to devote his entire attention and energy to it. He was a charismatic and social person, and became close friends with a very diverse group of people interested in the history of New York and the Hudson River Valley and intrigued by both Robbins and his work. In Tarrytown, Robbins gained access to a new, more refined social circle, one that included board members, company presidents, and the local elite. However, he never lost his interest in and devotion to his friends in Lincoln, and would move from a weeknight party in tony Westchester County to a small friendly gathering in Lincoln with apparent ease. Evan Jones remembered that he "never broke away from the group of friends that he had as a window washer . . . [and] in some ways he remained rather rough socially; he didn't have fancy academic terms for things archaeological."[95]

The project's spectacular press coverage and the regional attention that Robbins received after the publication of *Hidden America* gave him a new confidence in himself and verified, at least in his own mind, his position as an expert in the field. Robbins's natural sense of humor and his charismatic charm endeared him to coworkers, visitors, associates, and friends, many of whom remained close acquaintances for life. Robbins always had an "outrageous sense of humor," Mrs. Robbins recollected. "He could tell a story on himself and get the entire room laughing." "People were attracted to him," she continued.[96] Joe Butler, a former curator at SHR, remembered that Robbins "had the power to hypnotize people with archaeology—like a fundamentalist preacher."[97] In Butler's eyes, Robbins was a manipulating and controlling individual with a powerful presence and charismatic personality. Robbins was, Butler recalled, the type of person "that people either really liked or really disliked—there was no middle ground."[98]

While working at PMUM, Robbins rented a small apartment in Tarrytown during the week. It was through his friendship with Wheeler that he connected with many of the Sleepy Hollow Restorations board members and the higher echelons of Westchester society. It is ironic that Robbins and Wheeler's relationship later deteriorated and eventually became as antagonistic as it had been supportive. Even as pressure to complete the work increased, Robbins continued to enjoy the company of his friends and colleagues at the site. However, Bob Wheeler was no longer one of the bunch.[99] Overall, despite the problems, Robbins recalled that he enjoyed his time in Tarrytown. He loved the friends that he made, the dinner parties with directors and board members where he shared the latest slides of the excavations, the tennis and badminton games, and the work that he was doing at the site. Even in the face of adversity, Robbins remained thankful for his good fortune and retained an optimistic outlook about his work at PMUM.

As the project unfolded, however, the restoration goals and staff conflicts impacted Robbins's archaeological program, a situation that ultimately contributed to his early departure. Despite Rockefeller's interest and the early "concern for authenticity and substantial attention to public relations," historian Michael Kammen wrote, "Sleepy Hollow Restorations did not achieve the immediate success that Williamsburg had enjoyed."[100] A new director, hired in 1955 to "professionalize and run the cluster of Tarrytown sites," introduced programs to "attract more visitors, and . . . reach Dutch as well as Dutch-American tourists."[101] The archaeology of PMUM and conflicts with Roland Robbins were only two of the many concerns of the new staff. They regularly confronted a range of issues and faced the expectations of both their board of directors and benefactor John D. Rockefeller Jr. Archaeological assistant Susan Colby mused on the staff's special preparations for one of Rockefeller's visits to the site, remarking that

our patron saint, John D., was here on Friday and half of the people here are still cleaning dirt off their foreheads from bending so low— but he seemed to like the place very much and was particularly impressed with the "dig-it-yourself" pile [figure 4.9].[102]

The combination of special programs and the successful and well-publicized public archaeology strategy still failed to improve attendance "as much as the Sleepy Hollow Restorations administrators had hoped," even with a 39.5 percent increase in 1957.[103] In hopes of reaching higher numbers of visitors, the Sleepy Hollow Restorations staff commissioned a

FIG. 4.9. Dig-it-yourself screening area at Philipsburg Manor Upper Mills. (Courtesy of the Roland Wells Robbins Collection, the Thoreau Society, Lincoln, Mass., and the Thoreau Institute at Walden Woods.)

visitor survey designed by a Madison Avenue public relations firm.[104] The staff's desires to keep the site open to visitors and finish the archaeology as soon as possible indirectly grew out of this study.[105]

Although the motivations and needs of the restoration staff hindered his fieldwork and limited the scope of his archaeology, Robbins identified the changing layout of the mill complex and manor house over several hundred years, successfully dealt with difficult excavation conditions, experimented with new field techniques and studies, and participated and contributed, at least indirectly, to the final restored museum complex.[106] Finally, he launched a program that brought the story and excitement of the archaeological work at PMUM to the public.

The PMUM site remained open to the public during much of Robbins's excavations. Although this impacted the excavation schedule, it also provided an opportunity to experiment with presenting archaeology to visitors. Robbins and his staff developed an archaeological exhibit, guided and self-guided tours of the excavations, and the popular dig-it-yourself soil-screening program.[107] The restoration staff arranged for regular newspaper and radio stories on the work, and Robbins lectured on the excavations to business, civic, and educational organizations.

The "Dig-It-Yourself" program seems to have been initiated some-time during the spring of 1957 and, although unfortunately named, was extremely popular and received a lot of media attention.[108] A feature article in the *New York Times* resort section reported that

interest in this work has been mounting to such an extent that half of the 350 persons who visited the site on a recent day took a hand in the sifting and digging. . . . Some visitors have become so interested that they have stayed for the weekend.[109]

Robbins explained the program in a response to a complaint about his use of untrained visitors to dig on the site:

But may I point out something which I'm afraid the newspapers have not made quite clear—the articles which have been printed often give the impression that visitors are allowed to dig directly on the site. We do not have sufficient time or labor to sift through all of the loose soils that are brought up from the various levels and sections; thus we have asked for help of the general public. All of the soils that are brought up by the mechanical shovels are taken to an area close to the actual site. There they are dumped, by level and location, for interested persons, like yourself, to "paw" through. The material that you will be finding will mainly substantiate the materials that we ourselves have found.[110]

Unusual and exciting finds were displayed in the museum with a label identifying each object and the name of its "finder." The program became more popular than Robbins had dreamed, and the growing number of daily participants took up more and more of his assistants' time.[111] However, he felt that for all its work it was an important program. "It's a wonderful way to make history come alive to youngsters," he told a reporter. "They've been a big help to us, these diggers. . . . I think maybe we've got a lot of children started in an interest both in archaeology and history."[112]

A major portion of Robbins's contact with the public came from the lectures to community organizations, ranging from historical societies to schools, that he had developed and cultivated since his Walden work. During the PMUM project, Robbins gave more than 140 lectures on the excavations to groups across the region. These organizations found Robbins an interesting and entertaining speaker, one who delivered the results of his captivating archaeological explorations in the guise of a quaint Yankee workingman. As one museum director reported, Robbins's "work is characterized by scholarly accuracy and a Yankee common-sense approach. He relates the incidents with the enthusiasm of an explorer."[113]

Public exposure to Robbins's archaeological work received its largest boost from the publication of *Hidden America* in 1959; ironically, the publication also provoked the first major challenge of his work from professional archaeologists.[114] The idea for such a book was drawn from a series of newspaper and magazine articles on Robbins's work, particularly Evan Jones's "Pick and Shovel Historian." Robbins's excavations at Shadwell and PMUM, as well as his earlier work at Saugus, formed the nucleus of the book.[115] Henry Robbins (no relation), an editor at Alfred A. Knopf, had proposed the book project to Robbins in 1957. However, Robbins was reluctant to take it on due to his heavy workload at PMUM. He eventually agreed to do a "Do it Yourself" book on archaeology after writer and friend Evan Jones signed on as his coauthor.[116] The finished manuscript contained thirteen chapters, including presentations of Robbins's major digs at Walden Pond, Saugus Iron Works, Shadwell, and PMUM. Jones captured Robbins's conversational style and wove it into the narrative with his own clear, concise prose. The book also contained summaries of Native American and Viking archaeology, sections written solely by Jones and required by Knopf to give the book wider appeal.

The book was released in October 1959 (figure 4.10) and, according to Robbins, received a "very generous testimonial from C. W. Ceram [author of the popular *Gods, Graves, and Scholars*] . . . !"[117] On the day of its release, Robbins wrote, "Here's wishing it good luck—with many sales!"[118] The book proved to be a modest publishing success; however, its real significance was as the first popular work to be published on the subject of historical archaeology, setting the style and tone of many books that followed.[119] Significantly, both Ivor Noël Hume's books, including *Here Lies Virginia* (first published in 1963, also by Knopf), and James Deetz's books draw on literary devices first used by Robbins's in *Discovery at Walden* and *Hidden America* and are stylistically similar to Robbin's works. General reviewers found *Hidden America* to be well written and illustrated, a "lively and entertaining book."[120] According to one reviewer,

there could not well be a better introduction to those hidden things in our past which are within reach of everyone . . . the contribution . . . [that Robbins and

FIG. 4.10. Robbins (left) and coauthor Evan Jones sign copies of *Hidden America* at the Concord Bookshop, October 1959. (Courtesy of the Roland Wells Robbins Collection, the Thoreau Society, Lincoln, Mass., and the Thoreau Institute at Walden Woods.)

Jones] have made to public understanding and appreciation of archaeology is great.[121]

Likewise, Michael Cohn of the New York Archaeological Group wrote privately to Robbins, "I want to congratulate you on your book . . . which, in my mind, fills an important void about the romance of archaeology in places within the reach and knowledge of the interested American."[122]

Reviews by professional archaeologists were less positive and focused on the controversial final chapters: "Dig It Yourself," "Pipe Hunting, Potsherds, Arrowheads, and Artifacts," and "A Future for the Past." For instance, historical archaeologist John L. Cotter wrote that the book's

failure is that while cautioning the layman not to dig recklessly, it also informs him that he, too, can become "an archaeologist" simply by following Mr. Robbins' example and instruction. Never mind the four years' undergraduate plus three years' graduate work and three or four seasons of field experience required of the academic professional.[123]

Cotter used the analogy of a "corporation erecting a skyscraper . . . approached by an enthusiastic fellow with a set of plans under his arm who vowed he just loved engineering and drafting but had no professional training; he would," Cotter wrote, "no doubt be sent packing." Cotter summarized Robbins's work as characterized by "inquisitiveness, common sense and enterprise combined with hard work," but added, "we wish Mr. Robbins had simply said: Don't try to do any digging by yourself unless you are a trained archaeologist, or are working under the direction of one."[124]

Like Cotter, historian Lawrence Leder wrote that *Hidden America* had a significant failing:

it leaves the reader with the erroneous impression that archaeology is a simple thing, and that all the layman needs is a probe rod, a few other basic tools, and a mound or declivity into which he can dig in order to duplicate Mr. Robbins's achievements. . . . Mr. Robbins does a disservice by overemphasizing the idea that he is self-educated without explaining the extent to which he has educated himself.[125]

Leder also thought that Robbins and Jones could have written in much more detail about Robbins's own digs, rather than filling "the second half of the volume with a popular account of what has been done by others."[126] However, he added that "despite its faults, this book remains an invaluable commentary on a most important series of projects."[127]

Although the original idea of including a section instructing readers how to "dig it yourself" came from Knopf editor Henry Robbins, it appears that Robbins quickly latched onto the idea and began advocating the do-it-yourself approach to the public. "I tell them [schoolchildren]," he wrote, "there's no reason they can't have a dig in their own backyards."[128] Although Robbins initially found the dig-it-yourself program at PMUM a nuisance, and its overwhelming public appeal a bit puzzling, he was quick to appreciate its importance in terms of public support for and acknowledgment of his work. While it wasn't quite the angle that he might have hoped would be exploited by the media, the front-page coverage of this program in the *New York Times* had demonstrated the overwhelming appeal and value of involving the public in his work. Ironically, it was the success and wide coverage of both his dig-it-yourself program at Philipsburg Manor and his book that brought Robbins's work to the attention and scrutiny of the small but growing academic world of historical archaeology.

The practice of historical archaeology had witnessed major growth in the fourteen years between the end of World War II and the publication of Robbins's *Hidden America,* and yet a narrow restoration focus—linked to the historic preservation movement—remained universally visible in the historical archaeology conducted in the United States. By the early 1960s, however, university-trained professionals such as John Cotter, Edward Jelks, Charles Cleland, Charles Fairbanks, Bernard Fontana, and James Deetz were engaged in the work of separating historical archaeology from its restoration-oriented beginnings and carving out a disciplined profession. Academicians were propelling historical archaeology into the university system, the principal institutional setting of American prehistoric archaeology since World War I. These men became "leaders in the continual codification and improvement of standards of ethics for practicing professionals" in archaeology.[129] This process consisted largely of the transition to formal college-level training, as explained by Cotter in his review of *Hidden America.*[130] As such, it marked an inward focus on the part of the discipline that ignored and even devalued public participation. Historian Burton Bledstein observes that, within the culture of professionalism, "the more technical and restricted the individual areas of investigation, the more justifiable it became to deny the public's right to know or understand the professional's mission."[131] The primary orientation of the academic professional, writes historian Donald M. Scott, was not "the public-at-large; indeed it [the academy] institutionalized a sense of an unbridgeable cognitive gap between professionals and nonprofessionals."[132] In order to professionalize and upgrade the discipline of historical archaeology, practitioners had to focus on standardizing within and eliminating any outward appearances of amateur or unprofessional behavior. In this regard, it was Robbins's position as "a vociferous defender of the dig-it-yourself movement," his lack of formal training, his entrepreneurial approach, his use of mechanical equipment, and his own powerful distrust and envy of university professionals that destroyed his relationship with academic archaeologists.[133]

The techniques and methods employed by Robbins at Saugus, and particularly at Shadwell and PMUM, in many ways resemble those in general practice in the contemporary historical archaeological community, and this work set the standard for industrial archaeology at the time. Robbins developed his approach through his field experience and commonsense Yankee ingenuity, discussions with colleagues, and his reading in the literature. He used grid systems for horizontal control, probe and shovel testing for site survey, and increasingly refined artifact provenience controls. At a time when academic practitioners working from the tradition of prehistory were stressing technical precision and methodological refinement and standardization, however, Robbins was also using heavy equipment for "deep excavations" at industrial sites as a commonsense way to "get the job done." He was therefore criticized for his "crude" and destructive methods, although his techniques for mechanical excavation were more controlled than was understood at the time. Ironically, many of these methods were "introduced" into the profession with the advent of cultural resource management in the 1970s and 1980s; the professional community slowly came to realize that, when used under the proper conditions, machines such as the backhoe and Gradall could be effective and essential tools for excavation.

Robbins's extremely detailed documentation of his work at Shadwell and PMUM drew on his interest in observing and recording the world around him and exceeds the work of many of his professional academic colleagues. Perhaps most surprising is his early use of special analytical studies, such as tree-ring dating; soil, faunal, botanical, and materials analysis; and artifact conservation—techniques that became common practice in the "new" scientific archaeology of the late 1960s and 1970s. These studies, while giving Robbins confidence when working with his more educated colleagues and validating his work in the face of increased pressure and skepticism from the academic community, placed him at the forefront of modern historical and industrial archaeology, if only for a moment.

Yet, Roland Robbins was not an anthropological or scientific archaeologist, at least in the current sense of the word. For Robbins, the practice of archaeology and restoration was more art than science. In fact, he preferred to think of himself, not unlike archaeologist Ivor Noël Hume, as a historian who digs. "The Pick and Shovel Historian," he wrote, "has always been my favorite identification. After all, I am a historian who digs when the success of the subject necessitates my doing so."[134] As discussed earlier, Robbins's statement articulates the ongoing debate about the proper disciplinary home for historical archaeology. The field itself was struggling with its identity at this moment, and was in search of an intellectual home. A vigorous debate ensued between those who connected it with the scientific approach of anthropological archaeology and those who saw it as a humanistic technique that could be integrated into the study of American history.

As Robbins worked to identify, uncover, and reconstruct the buried ruins of early New England, he noted that, like Noël Hume, his "intent was to make history come alive by digging it up, getting others involved . . . making something live again in people's imaginations."[135] In *Hidden America*, Robbins wrote that "I found that simple tools and the rudiments of a scientific approach, cautiously exercised, could ferret out history that had evaded others."[136] He had already begun, however, to move toward the fringes of the developing discipline of historical archaeology. Increasingly faced with challenges from the academy, he grew more determined to practice his own brand of archaeology and restoration, embracing Thoreau's model of the practical intellectual and engaging in a philosophy that suited his Yankee blend of intense individualism and common sense.

CHAPTER 5

Historical Archaeology Comes of Age

While finishing the work at the Philipsburg Manor Upper Mills, Robbins directed a small excavation at the John Alden House in Duxbury, Massachusetts, that both exemplified his best work and brought him into an ongoing struggle with the developing academic discipline of historical archaeology. By the early 1960s, when he began the Alden site excavation, the archaeology of the Plymouth Colony and the Pilgrims was becoming the focus of university-trained archaeologist James Deetz. Robbins and Deetz initially maintained a cordial and cooperative relationship, exchanging information on their respective sites. The relationship eventually broke down in Robbins's mind when Deetz effectively excluded him from excavations on other Plymouth-period sites. Their interactions grew more combative through time as can be seen in several later encounters, particularly Robbins's excavations at the Hancock-Clarke House in Lexington, Massachusetts. Ironically, Deetz drew on Robbins's Alden work in his classic text, *In Small Things Forgotten*, and in his final book, *Flowerdew Hundred*, he used Robbins's Saugus excavations to illustrate the evocative nature and power of artifacts.[1]

By the mid-1960s, the discipline was changing, with the particularlistic, restoration-oriented phase of historical archaeology slowly giving way to scientifically minded archaeologists who argued that the discipline must sever its ties with the restoration preservationist movement if it were to advance.[2] Although a wide range of restoration-related work continued, many new research-oriented projects were begun both in university contexts and at organizations such as Colonial Williamsburg. Ivor Noël Hume applied his knowledge of stratigraphic excavation and documentary research to sites in and around Williamsburg, and a handful of student and academic archaeologists began long-term research-oriented projects on historic sites. The graduate students who completed these projects were among the first group of researchers to focus their doctoral work on historical archaeology topics. As historical archaeology emerged, academic professionals began to slowly standardize their data recovery and analytical techniques, borrowing heavily from the "New" archaeology of their prehistorian brethren.[3]

By the time that Robbins's publication on the John Alden site was released in 1969, the discipline had begun to be organized under the umbrella of anthropology as a formal scholarly pursuit. The heightened professional rhetoric of the discipline, formalized in the founding of the Society for Historical Archaeology in 1967, becomes clear in a review of Robbins's John Alden site report published in the society's new journal, *Historical Archaeology*. Although reviewer Charles F. Hayes III found the report to be an important reference and starting point "for anybody conducting future work in southern New England," he noted "now that historical archaeology has reached a degree of maturity, it is to be hoped that such future reports will contain the results of the more sophisticated analysis methods that are currently being used."[4]

Robbins's work at the John Alden site demonstrates careful research and excavation techniques, although on a much smaller scale than either the Philipsburg Manor or Saugus projects. The Alden site was, like Shadwell, a "shallow" domestic site and required, Robbins argued, a much different approach.[5] The shallow, plowed "topsoils" at Alden, he reasoned, required careful hand excavation in order to extract the greatest amount of information. Precise horizontal and vertical excavation controls were demanded to recover the scant artifacts that made up these very shallow sites, as well as to determine the spatial patterns of these early materials.

In many ways, the Alden project marked a major watershed in Robbins's career; it represented his closest approach to contemporary academic practice in terms of methodology and analytical techniques. The work was equal to and exceeded typical restoration-oriented historical archaeology projects across the region and country when conducted in the early 1960s. However, by the time of its publication in 1969, historical archaeology was undergoing refinements in excavation and analytical techniques and incorporating a broader, social science–based research orientation. Although the Alden project was conducted for a family association in the restoration tradition, resulting in a "memorial" site, Robbins devoted equal attention to research issues. As time passed, however, Robbins's methods and approach did not keep up with changing standards in archaeology. Even more damaging was his success as an independent practitioner, pitting him against academics who, from the security of their university positions, viewed Robbins's business orientation as blatant, crude hucksterism.

Robbins responded to the academy's attack on the very foundations of his career by returning to his mentor Thoreau, whose philosophy bolstered Robbins's identity as a self-reliant and independent New England Yankee. Several periods of slack consulting work combined with the exclusion and rejection he perceived from the academy served only to push Robbins further away from the mainstream archaeological community. He survived the slow periods in his archaeological business by concentrating on his successful lecturing engagements and developing projects such as his Walden Cabin Kit and marketing the publishing rights to his collection of Herbert Gleason's photographs. Yet, these projects only exacerbated his relationship with the academic crowd; to their horror he was popularizing archaeology for financial gain and trading on the literary cachet of Thoreau.

Robbins's projects during the second half of the decade, such as the Hancock-Clarke House, Strawbery Banke's Puddle Dock, and Oliver Mill Park, were small, short-term excavations conducted for local and regional governments, museums, and historical societies. As Helen Bullock told Robbins, most of these were "enthusiastic but untrained preservation organizations," which still needed convincing of the worth of doing archaeology at their sites.[6] Modest projects for small historical and preservation societies became the norm during the final decades of Robbins's career, and reflect both his extensive experience in the field and the overall sophistication of the business aspects of his consulting work. Unlike Saugus and Philipsburg Manor, these projects allowed Robbins to maintain control of the work and retain his freedom to practice as an independent professional consultant. Most importantly, these projects represent his candid, populist approach to archaeology; almost all had some type of public component, either through community involvement in a "dig-it-yourself" program, school visits, or site tours and volunteer opportunities.

As the decade began, Robbins initiated a project that demonstrates all these elements.[7] The Alden House excavation, performed for the Alden Kindred of America, Inc. was Robbins's first direct experience with a family or genealogical group (figure 5.1). Although ancestor worship had

FIG. 5.1. Members of the Alden Kindred of America at annual meeting in Duxbury, Mass., 1960. (Courtesy of the Roland Wells Robbins Collection, the Thoreau Society, Lincoln, Mass., and the Thoreau Institute at Walden Woods.)

become less fashionable before World War II, family associations maintained their viability during the postwar period through an increasing investment in the ideology of patriotism.[8] The leadership of these groups remained the province of primarily older, socially connected individuals, people who clung to historical myths and traditions in the face of a rapidly changing postwar world. Across New England, these groups sought to reestablish and solidify their ancestors' positions as regional founders and leaders through documentary research and by reconstructing or memorializing the homes and businesses of these patriots. However, the family association was also heralded as a democratizing force: "it has brought genealogy and pedigrees and an escutcheon within the reach of the common man."[9] In the postwar period, family and genealogical associations became another vehicle for the aspiring middle class. By the 1970s, interest in local and family history, particularly for groups who left few official records, was being revived and integrated into school curriculums.

Robbins was contacted by the Alden Kindred group about excavating the 1627 John Alden site in Duxbury, Massachusetts, in 1960.[10] The John Alden House site was the first home of original Mayflower settler John Alden and his wife Priscilla Mullins. The couple received their land in

Duxbury along the Blue Fish River and "near Eagletree Pond" as part of the Second Land Division to original Plymouth settlers in 1627. Although there is no record of when the Aldens built their first house, they were living in Duxbury by 1632. According to Governor William Bradford, the expansion of settlement to Duxbury was the direct result of Plymouth's growing population. The Aldens were joined by Captain Myles Standish, Elder William Brewster, George Soule, and numerous other Plymouth residents. With good agricultural soils and easy access to water transportation to Plymouth and elsewhere, the Aldens and their Duxbury neighbors successfully farmed their large properties; fresh and salt meadows provided abundant hay for cattle. The standing house on the Alden site has traditionally been dated as being built in 1653, possibly with a portion of the earlier 1627 house, but this interpretation and the 1653 date are questionable. Although changes were clearly made, the later Alden house survived largely intact, and, in 1907, the house and a three-acre parcel containing the earlier house site was purchased by the Alden Kindred of America.[11]

Robbins began his work at the Alden house site with preliminary test-hole excavations around an existing stone monument said to mark the original Alden house, including a small trench with "considerable evidence of old bricks."[12] This initial investigation indicated to Robbins that the 1627 house was not located where "the stone marker stands today."[13] His visit so impressed Alden Kindred member Russell Edwards that he wrote: "after seeing the way you work, I am more convinced than ever that we should have you supervise the search for the old site."[14]

Robbins returned to the Alden site for additional testing and recorded that "after making a few rod penetrations . . . I hit stone."[15] The stone turned out to be a wall running east-west; further probing identified a parallel wall to the north. Artifacts from the area, including bricks, nails, glass and cames from leaded windows, earthenware, clay tobacco pipe fragments, a gunflint, and a "1652 New England silver coin" were clearly of the Alden period.[16] Robbins wrote to Edwards that "in thinking over the 2 walls that I located, . . . they may be the foundations for an ell."[17] He next identified a cellar that extended to a depth of "more than 7 ft. below grade."[18] In a letter to the Alden Kindred president, Mrs. Ernest Bailey, Robbins detailed his proposed research program:

the foundation for a 17th century building . . . is situated some 60 ft. southeasterly of the stone marker. Its northerly wall is 38 ft. in length. . . . I located evidence of its cellar situated at the northwest corner. . . . the building was quite narrow, probably not over 13 to 14 ft. in width. . . . The artifacts . . . are quite numerous, and all . . . are of the 17th century period.

I hope that it will be possible for the organizations and the individuals interested in this project to carry out a complete historical and archaeological undertaking. This would mean a careful historical research study and a complete archaeological exploration. An interesting and comprehensive report which would include the history of the site and photographs of the progress of the archaeological work as well as an artist's conception of the site as it may have appeared during the 17th century should be compiled.[19]

Upon receiving the news that limited funds were available, Robbins, Edwards, and a group of volunteers staked out a grid over the site and began to remove the plowzone soil from the 10-foot grid sections.[20] Robbins excavated the cellar feature in July 1960, and although he and his assistant battled hurricane rains, they "succeeded in getting most of the fill removed from the cellar hole."[21] The cellar was excavated in three levels with volunteers screening the soil; Robbins wrote to Edwards that "it is imperative that we recover every artifact which these levels contain."[22]

Robbins reported that in checking several of the artifacts removed from the 6.5-foot-square cellar, he found that

one of them is a bronze pestle and another one is ½ of a cocks head hinge. In checking the 17th century artifacts uncovered at Jamestown, I find a hinge and a pestle identical to ours. We also removed a pair of scissors, a small hammer head, a horseshoe and several other metal pieces and nails . . . [and] considerable earthenware. All of these artifacts appear to be of the 17th century period.[23]

He went on to stress the site's importance and the need for a complete investigation:

"The more I see of the site, the more I realize its historical significance. I hope that your organization will find it financially possible to accept the recommendations which I made. . . . There should be no "short-cuts" taken with a project of such unusual significance.[24]

Russell responded that "we are all very much pleased with your work so far," and Mrs. Bailey quickly approved the additional work.[25]

In September 1960, Robbins excavated the interior of the house foundation (figure 5.2).[26] This work, he wrote, "showed that the place was probably dismantled, even to the chimney base, which was located near

FIG. 5.2. Excavation of the Alden House foundation with Geraldine Robbins excavating in fore-ground, 1960. (Courtesy of the Roland Wells Robbins Collection, the Thoreau Society, Lincoln, Mass., and the Thoreau Institute at Walden Woods.)

the center and to the southerly side of the interior."[27] The foundation and cellar evidence was cleaned and mapped and "the interior [in and around] . . . the foundation [was excavated] down to natural sands."[28] Robbins wrote that "we now have the long job of cleaning and recording the artifacts and preparing a report, etc."[29] He suggested to Mrs. Bailey that "thought be given to the rebuilding of the foundation and the cellar. To restore the house site (not the house itself) would create a very impressive monument which could be done at little expense."[30]

Robbins worked with artist Charles Overly in early 1961 to develop a plan for the restoration of the foundation, while assistant Joan McAlear completed the identification and cataloging of the artifacts.[31] He also traveled to Williamsburg, Virginia, to discuss the Alden artifacts with Ivor and Audrey Noël Hume of the Colonial Williamsburg Foundation and Jamestown curator J. Paul Hudson.[32] Both, he wrote, "agreed that the finds were . . . all of the 17th-century period."[33]

Robbins engaged his friend and colleague Evan Jones to research and write a brief historical background on the house, while he studied the

layout and form of the original foundation. He was troubled by its relatively narrow width, and he explored this dilemma by measuring similar archaeological examples such as the Joseph and John Howland sites
excavated by Sidney Strickland and later James Deetz, carefully examining the adjacent 1653 Alden House, and reviewing James Hall's plan (ca.
1853) of the Miles Standish site.[34] Robbins speculated that sections of the
extant 1653 Alden House might have been part of the original house,
noting that "the long narrow section [38 ft.] was added to the northerly
[section] probably later—however, it could have been part of the original structure."[35] Robbins also wrote that

a quick measurement of the upper foundation, which was probably the first,
showed that it was about 53 ft. long and 16 ft. wide, it being a long narrow building. Actually its length was about $3\frac{1}{3}$ times its width. This is quite interesting!
The early Alden house was 38 ft. long and 10.5 ft. wide, its length being slightly
less than $3\frac{2}{3}$ times its width. Were these early houses in the Duxbury, Marshfield
area long, narrow buildings, and if so why? The main basic plan of the 1653
Alden house is about 38 ft. by 18–18.5 ft. This is a ratio of 2 to 1.[36]

The report, containing a full summary of the project, photographic
documentation of the dig and artifacts, and detailed plan and profile
drawings of the site, was completed in 1964.[37] Robbins hoped that the
Alden family group would publish it immediately, but it was not wasn't
until 1969 that he heard that the Pilgrim Society would sponsor the publication.[38] To the original typescript, Robbins added an author's fore-
word, and Larry Geller of the Pilgrim Society prepared a brief introduction to the discipline of historical archaeology, highlighting Robbins's
contributions to the field. The book, *Pilgrim John Alden's Progress*, was
published in October 1969.[39]

Robbins's work at the John Alden site demonstrates some of his most
precise field excavation techniques.[40] He approached the problem of locating the original house site in a meticulous way, excavating by natural
strata and utilizing systematic vertical and horizontal provenience controls. The results of the initial survey provided him with stratigraphic information that guided the rest of the excavation. He observed and utilized stratigraphic evidence, reading this data with precision, accurately
describing the soil sequence, and identifying features.

Horizontal and vertical provenience controls at the Alden site were
among Robbins's most accurate. By 1960, he had advanced in his self-
education through field excavation experience, visits to other sites in-

cluding Williamsburg, and continuing dialogues with practitioners such as Ivor Noël Hume, C. Malcolm Watkins, J. C. Harrington, Henry Hornblower II, and J. O. Brew. As discussed earlier, Robbins had come to define domestic sites like Alden and Shadwell as "shallow" sites that required a much different approach than Philipsburg and Saugus.[41]

Robbins excavated within a 100-by-80-foot gridded area, removing soil layers in 10-foot-grid sections.[42] After removing the topsoils or plowzone, he excavated underlying features, such as the cellar (figure 5.3). A preliminary test suggested that the filling of "the cellar must have taken place at one time, there being no stratum to indicate the filling accumulated over a period of time."[43] Therefore, the cellar was excavated in three arbitrary levels, with Robbins plotting "all artifacts found among the rubble."[44] As with the cellar, excavations of the rubble fill beneath the topsoil and above the natural subsoils within and around the foundation were carefully controlled; the initial 10-foot blocks were divided into 2.5-foot units.[45]

The plan drawings and field notes from the excavation provide detailed information on soils, artifacts, and the location of features or disturbances (figure 5.4). The strict use of a grid provided the most precise horizontal and vertical provenience data of any of Robbins's projects.[46] Artifacts from the excavation were stored in the field bags with specific provenience information and were analyzed much more systematically than at any of Robbins's previous projects, and more thoroughly than at many restoration projects of the period.[47] Robbins provided a complete discussion of the materials as well as an inventory and artifact table in his report, relying on artifacts for feature interpretation, dating, and site interpretation.[48] As mentioned previously, he also enlisted the help of several experts for artifact identification, visits that provided Robbins and McAlear with help in clearing up general identification problems and focusing on specific diagnostic artifacts.[49]

Perhaps most significant is Robbins's comparison of the Alden site artifacts with those from several contemporary sites: the Miles Standish home in Duxbury, Massachusetts, the John and Joseph Howland sites in Kingston, Massachusetts, and the seventeenth-century Jamestown settlement in Virginia.[50] Of particular interest is a detailed analysis of the tobacco pipe stems from these early sites using J. C. Harrington's dating method, and a study of pipe bowl shapes and marks drawing on the work of Noël Hume's mentor Adrian Oswald.[51] Robbins also combined data from the temporally related archaeological sites with research on several extant buildings and used the results in his interpretation of the

FIG. 5.3. The Alden house foundation after completed excavation. (Courtesy of the Roland Wells Robbins Collection, the Thoreau Society, Lincoln, Mass., and the Thoreau Institute at Walden Woods.)

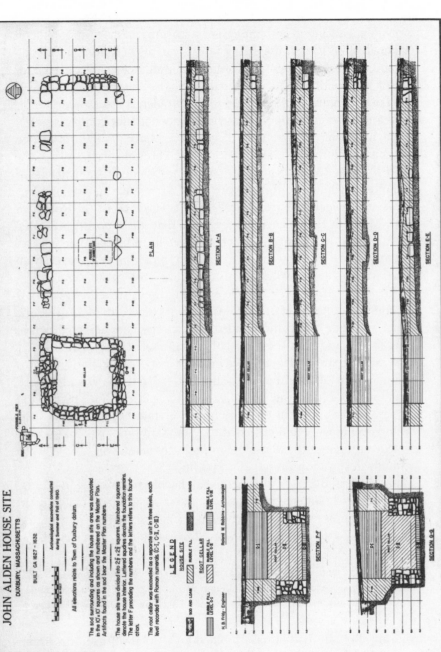

FIG. 5.4. Detailed plan and profiles of the Alden excavations. (Courtesy of the Roland Wells Robbins Collection, the Thoreau Society, Lincoln, Mass., and the Thoreau Institute at Walden Woods.)

John Alden site. He investigated the nearby 1653 Alden House because of its obvious association with the earlier structure and the tradition that it contained all or part of the earlier house, carefully examining the interior and exterior for clues to its origin and producing a measured floor plan of the building.[52] As discussed above, he considered the narrow width of the excavated Alden foundation problematic and used the 1653 house and other contemporary archaeological sites for comparison.[53]

Like his earlier Walden book, *Pilgrim John Alden's Progress* is written in a conversational style and is organized chronologically, taking the reader through Robbins's approach to the problems and "controversies" encountered while investigating the site.[54] Reviewing the book in *Historical Archaeology*, archaeologist Charles F. Hayes III of the Rochester (N.Y.) Museum and Science Center wrote that "the report is presented in a forthright descriptive manner with details of both artifactual and structural finds." Hayes went on to call it "a somewhat personal account by one who has been involved in historical archaeology at several sites in eastern North America."[55] (While engaging the reader, the "personal" and conversational style of Robbins's reports placed them outside the format and tone of technical and scientific reports as accepted within the academy, and thus they were often considered useless by his academic counterparts.[56]) Hayes noted his hope that "future reports will contain the results of the more sophisticated [artifact] analysis methods," even though Robbins's interpretative analysis, specifically his reliance on comparative examples of temporally and architecturally similar sites, was in keeping with, and exceeded, the standard types of analysis performed throughout the discipline in the early 1960s, particularly work within the restoration-preservation tradition.[57]

Nevertheless, the research-oriented archaeological excavations at the Alden site clearly suffered from some of the same problems that affected many restoration projects of the period, including the limited time and money available to complete the work. Hayes wrote in his review that

the excavations were conducted under admittedly rushed conditions and with limited financial resources. With greater community support both this and other existing sites would benefit from an approach based on less overall pressure.[58]

Ironically, Robbins had initially lobbied for a full investigation with no "short-cuts," but he proceeded with the initial investigation without a firm commitment from the sponsors to provide the time and money that he thought the work required.[59] Although Hayes believed that the

Alden site report would be an important reference and starting point "for anybody conducting future work in southern New England," it was, by its publication in 1969, already becoming dated.[60]

The 1960s witnessed the initial recognition and partial validation of historical archaeology within the larger fields of anthropology and archaeology. By the end of the decade, the discipline was beginning to change as its restoration orientation was challenged by scientifically minded archaeologists, who argued that it was "only by breaking free of the 'restoration preservationist movement' that historical archaeology can reach full maturity as an anthropological endeavor."[61] Although increasing numbers of new projects and publications launched during the 1960s document the rise of historical archaeology within American archaeology, the defining event of the period was the formation of the Society for Historical Archaeology in 1967. As was true for many emerging disciplines, the professional society played a key role in establishing communication among practitioners, promoting national visibility through its new journal, enhancing the status of practitioners, and validating the discipline's pursuit of legitimacy.[62]

Schuyler has noted that historical archaeology in the eastern United States during this period was marked by a continuation of restoration-preservation projects at both a local level and within the region's many national monuments and parks. J. C. Harrington's *Archaeology and the Historical Society* (1965) is an excellent example of efforts to bring archaeology into more standard usage in history and to provide guidance to small museum organizations interested in pursuing archaeological research.[63] This book served as a call to action for the many small museums across New England and resulted in heightened demand for Robbins's services.[64] While the book advised local historical societies on what historical archaeology had to offer, a central problem was the lack of qualified archaeologists. Harrington humorously commented that "it is not easy to dig up an archaeologist."[65] He continued that the "one thing that nearly always comes as a surprise is to find that there are no freelance archaeologists. Unlike engineers and architects, it is harder to find an available archaeologist than a Chaucerian scholar."[66] The few academic archaeologists interested in historic-sites research and available for consulting in the mid-1960s were housed almost exclusively within departments of anthropology and primarily devoted to teaching and to their own projects. Thus "freelance archaeologists" such as Robbins were in great demand.[67]

Throughout the decade, excavations at larger private historic sites such as Williamsburg or New England's Sturbridge Village expanded greatly in scope. In the early 1960s, Ivor Noël Hume reported on several sites that he investigated in the Williamsburg area. In 1960 and 1961 he excavated a group of colonial foundations and refuse pits at the Tutter's Neck site, a parcel of land located adjacent to Williamsburg.[68] Several years later, he joined forces with Smithsonian curator C. Malcolm Watkins, one of Robbins's early associates, to investigate stoneware and earthenware pottery that had been turning up on Virginia sites, particularly in Williamsburg and Yorktown.[69] Although this project did not entail any traditional excavations, Noël Hume and Watkins dug into the early documents and sifted through local ceramic collections. Their work resulted in a joint publication, *The "Poor Potter" of Yorktown*, that utilized historical and artifactual research for developing a site context, and "clearly demonstrated that a major local industry . . . operated in Virginia from ca. 1720 to 1745."[70] Noël Hume and Watkins's thesis was confirmed in 1967 with the accidental discovery of a waster dump that was part of the William Rogers pottery factory.[71]

During the 1960s, Noël Hume published several books on historical archaeology that have become classics in the discipline. *Here Lies Virginia* (1963) is a popular presentation of his work at Williamsburg as well as that of other researchers at sites such as Roanoke, Jamestown, and Green Springs.[72] As in much of Robbins's work, the writing style is popular and conversational, presenting Virginia's colonial past with a mixture of history, archaeology, and intrigue.[73] *Historical Archaeology* (1968) is a field manual that "contains a wide range of useful suggestions, [but] is essentially aimed at amateur archaeologists."[74] Noël Hume's *Guide to Artifacts of Colonial America* (1969) provided a much-needed summary description of the material culture of the colonial period and remains a standard text today.[75]

Although work in the Northeast generally continued in the restoration tradition, new trends were in evidence between 1960 and 1970.[76] Academic archaeologists continued to work under contract at historic sites, but "they also initiated similar projects as a major focus of their own research."[77] For instance, archaeologists James Deetz and Edwin Dethlefsen began what would become a classic study of gravestones in 1963. This investigation, the first historical archaeology project funded by the National Science Foundation, utilized the tightly controlled body of data provided by gravestones to look at the stylistic evolution of the stones and test the assumptions of archaeological seriation using precisely dated historical materials.[78] Deetz also continued analytical work on several previously excavated sites in the vicinity of Plimoth Plantation.[79] Ironically, Robbins bitterly recorded a visit to one of these sites while working on the Alden project, noting that "the Joseph Howland site was a mess, everything turned over in a confused mess. I believe that the Plimoth Plantation diggers worked there this year."[80]

Apparently unaware of Robbins's previous work at the Saugus Iron Works, Dover Union Iron Company, Winthrop Blast Furnace, or PMUM, or perhaps unwilling to credit it as legitimate, archaeologist Robert Schuyler reports in his 1975 dissertation, "Anthropological Perspectives in Historical Archaeology," that industrial sites also "drew attention, for the first time, between 1960 and 1970."[81] University of Pennsylvania archaeologist Vincent P. Foley's work at Bethlehem, Pennsylvania, Schuyler argues, presents an excellent example of the increasingly anthropological focus of industrial projects during this period. Beginning in 1964, Foley excavated the tannery and waterworks of the eighteenth-century Moravian settlement for Historic Bethlehem, a local preservation group.[82] Although this excavation was primarily a restoration project within the older tradition, Schuyler notes that Foley focused "not only on the processes of industrialization but also many social and cultural problems."[83]

Daniel Ingersoll's 1968 investigation of Puddle Dock at Strawbery Banke, Inc., in Portsmouth, New Hampshire, was largely free of the restoration influence. Ingersoll carried out an excavation of one small section of the dock area, across from an area tested by Robbins in 1966.[84] Schuyler notes that some early-nineteenth-century structural remains were found, but most "of the strata that contained artifacts were late 19th to early 20th century in date."[85] Ingersoll's excavation techniques were very precise, with excellent stratigraphic control. During the first season he produced a detailed cross section of the waterway and its fill, and in the second season tested a bulkhead or wharf found at the end of the preceding year's work. Horizontal control was maintained using a 5-foot grid system, and excavation proceeded vertically, with layers divided by using visible natural soil strata and designated cultural features. "To determine stratigraphy," Ingersoll noted, "squares were excavated just peripheral to the master sequence squares."[86] In his Ph.D. dissertation Ingersoll provided excellent descriptions of stratigraphy, dating, and features, and focused a great deal of attention on the artifact analysis. According to Schuyler, the dissertation provided a "basic source on 19th-century material culture and its transformation under industrialization."[87]

Several years earlier, Robbins had heard of an upcoming restoration project at Strawbery Banke during his 1963 survey work at the Governor John Wentworth Farm in Wolfeboro, New Hampshire, and immediately sought to get involved.[88] A series of letters were exchanged between Robbins and Strawbery Banke's executive vice president, Carl A. Johnson, and in 1965 Johnson contacted Robbins about working "on some archaeological research in Strawbery Banke next year."[89] The museum, he explained, had been invited to participate in a joint research program, and "one aspect . . . will be archaeological investigations of the compound, with emphasis on old Puddle Dock."[90] Robbins was delighted to get the news and wrote to Johnson that he had recalled a "tingling of excitement when you took me on a tour of Strawbery Banke."[91]

The land around Puddle Dock, a tidal creek of the Piscataqua River, was rapidly settled in the 1690s. By the 1720s, the area was a densely populated mixture of wharves, warehouses, dwellings, and commercial structures including a pottery and tannery and was the center of the growing city of Portsmouth. In the late eighteenth and early nineteenth centuries, the Market Square became the city's new commercial center and Puddle Dock became largely a residential neighborhood. During the nineteenth century, the area increasingly became one of rented houses and industrial operations. By the turn of the twentieth century, Puddle Dock was filled and built over. In the 1950s, the area was slated for urban renewal but was eventually saved through the preservation leadership of resident Dorothy Vaughan. The area became the property of Strawbery Banke Museum in the early 1960s. Although Robbins wouldn't actually work with them again at Strawbery Banke, the museum's first master plan was created with the help of the architectural firm of Perry, Shaw, Hepburn, Kehoe and Dean of Boston.[92]

Robbins and Johnson met with Professor William R. Jones of the University of New Hampshire's (UNH) Department of History in early 1966 to discuss the Puddle Dock project.[93] The Puddle Dock work was to be a summer field experience for UNH undergraduate and graduate students with interests in colonial history, to give them "first hand knowledge of colonial site archaeology."[94] However, it was revealed at the meeting that only two thousand dollars was available for the work; Robbins reluctantly agreed to excavate small sections of the dock making "maximum use . . . of volunteer workers."[95] Robbins was to "plan and guide the performance of the excavation and the recording of significant data, supervise the progression of the work, and give lectures (on site) on the methods and yield of excavation."[96] After starting the work, he

FIG. 5.5 Robbins studying and recording wooden wharf features at Puddle Dock, Strawbery Banke, Portsmouth, N.H. (Courtesy of the Roland Wells Robbins Collection, the Thoreau Society, Lincoln, Mass., and the Thoreau Institute at Walden Woods.)

"remained concerned about expectations for his participation," commenting that "the good professor still talked as though I was expected to be there during the [entire] summer to direct students."[97]

Robbins began his excavations to locate the dock by trenching with a backhoe and quickly identified heavy log cribbing.[98] He also opened a trench to follow evidence of a pier, noting that it tied into a wharf "of a different construction, indicating that one must have been an extension of the other" (figure 5.5).[99] Excavating in front of the pier to determine the bottom of the vertical planking, he sought "to see if it could be determined what kind of fill the wharf [pier] had been built upon, if any."[100]

When the UNH students arrived at the dig, Robbins set up a grid system, mapped his test trenches, and continued excavation in the wharf area.[101] This wharf, he now believed, was "the pier that shows in the 1813 map."[102] A typical day with Professor Jones and his history students was later described by graduate student Ann Marie Nielsen:

[students] arrive at Strawbery Banke [and] Mr. Robbins conducts them on a tour of the site, explaining the techniques he uses to expose history hidden in the earth. He describes what has been unearthed to date, and then puts the students to work scraping the timbers of the wharves, and sifting the rubble for artifacts.[103]

With funds for the work quicky exhausted, Robbins completed the master plan and section plan drawings in December 1967, ending his involvement with the project.[104]

When Robbins contacted Johnson in February 1968, hoping to arrange to continue his previous work at Puddle Dock, he was informed that the archaeological work at Strawbery Banke would be continued by Daniel W. Ingersoll Jr., a graduate student from Harvard University.[105] The "Harvard graduate and three students," Robbins reported, will "dig about 100' west of my dock excavations."[106] In 1972, Robbins once again wrote to Strawbery Banke, hoping to interest them in more excavations at Puddle Dock. His letter was answered by curator James L. Garvin, who had worked with Robbins during his previous excavations at Strawbery Banke.[107] Garvin judiciously wrote that Robbins's work, as well as that by others, had "convinced us that there is a vast body of material awaiting discovery at Puddle Dock, and that this material should not be disturbed until we can afford to excavate very carefully."[108] Unfortunately, he told Robbins, the money was not available, and, therefore, "we have decided to discontinue all work on the site until we're prepared for a proper program."[109]

The Strawbery Banke project was from the start a very particularistic project in terms of the archaeology. The archaeological goals of the project were simple and straightforward: locating and excavating small portions of the original Puddle Dock. The educational nature of the project was the impetus for the work and was, at least in concept, more exceptional. This was especially true at a time when restoration needs were still responsible for most historical archaeology projects. The project also marked the first time that Robbins was formally invited to participate in an academic project and teach college students. Although his comments regarding the UNH professors suggest his wariness of and resentment toward academics, Robbins actually got along reasonably well with the UNH staff. Yet, he was perplexed over their demands on his time given his very small fee; working from the security of a tenured position in the university, the faculty members had little idea about the realities of surviving as a consultant.

Robbins's work at Strawbery Banke demonstrates the typical approach that he had developed for a preliminary survey of a "deep" site. His goal for these preliminary projects was straightforward: to identify the archaeological remains—foundations and artifacts—and assess the potential for further exploration and study. His decisions about where to excavate at Puddle Dock were guided by these goals and the specific desires of the Strawbery Banke staff. Prior to excavation, Robbins reviewed documentary information on the area, particularly early maps of Portsmouth showing Puddle Dock.[110] Colonel George L. Prindle, chair of Strawbery Banke's Archaeology Study Committee, described Robbins's excavation work in a 1967 report, writing that

the operation consisted of uncovering a long section of . . . a bulkhead of heavy timbers and planks, evidently constructed in two different periods, portions of one or two docks, and many glass bottles, fragments of Chinaware and part of a ship's timber. Tons of earth were moved and piled to one side. It was difficult to determine just what artifacts come from the earth fill, or from the original surface.[111]

Archaeologist Daniel W. Ingersoll Jr. later reported that

the extensive excavation by Robbins produced thousands of artifacts, but, unfortunately, only square provenience was given to the artifacts; vertical provenience either artificial or stratigraphic, was apparently not assigned. It has been Mr. Robbins's practice in the past to use power equipment to get down to older deposits after the stratigraphic sequence is discovered by test trenching and this may have been the case here since a backhoe was used. Therefore, much of the material removed by machine may not have been given vertical provenience because it was not regarded as old enough.[112]

Ingersoll was correct in his assessment of Robbins's use of power equipment to remove "modern," nineteenth- and twentieth-century fill. His speculation about vertical provenience of artifacts is also likely correct; Robbins typically did not record any artifacts from these types of upper fill deposits. Artifacts provenienced with horizontal information would typically be from the contact layer or early surface that Robbins sought.[113] In the case of the wharf and pier structures at Puddle Dock, these artifacts likely came out of the "peat layer" below the modern fill and above the "blue clay" that Robbins identified as natural subsoil.[114] It is also likely that Robbins was not as systematic about saving artifacts as he was at other projects because he viewed the Puddle Dock excavations as a very preliminary look at the wharf structure and anticipated more extensive excavations in the future. In this sense, the artifacts from this initial excavation work were a "bonus" to Robbins, a phrase that he used on many occasions, and a legacy from the early years of the restoration-preservation tradition.[115] Similarly, the 1960 excavation of the oldest house site in St. Augustine by a group of anthropologists, including John Griffin, concentrated on the architectural remains; the authors said that their project "would not attempt to give a full report of the artifacts recovered. It will only concern itself with the ceramics, which are of distinct aid in dating, and a few other items which indicate something of construction."[116]

The restorative and educational nature of the Puddle Dock project propelled the archaeological research, particularly in terms of the limited time and money available to Robbins. His work was initially commended by both the staff of Strawbery Banke and the UNH Department of History. Carl Johnson wrote that

your accomplishments in the excavation of Strawbery Banke's Puddle Dock have far exceeded our expectations. All associated with the Joint Archaeological Research Program fully appreciate your forceful and tenacious application, with a minimum of assistance, toward the early success of the program. We are happy that you were able to take the leadership of the program and we look forward to the continuation of the work into the next phase.[117]

However, it is apparent from the 1967 report by Prindle and subsequent comments by Garvin that the quality of Robbins's work was soon thought to be less than acceptable by the Strawbery Banke staff. This is particularly evident in comments by Ingersoll and in Garvin's carefully worded reply to Robbins's 1972 inquiry about additional excavations.[118]

The period from 1960 to the early 1970s was one of change and reorientation within historical archaeology. The number of practitioners grew from an unorganized handful of individuals in 1960 to a fledgling subdiscipline boasting more than four hundred members by 1970. During this period, more and more individuals were working within departments of anthropology.[119] "The reason for this growth is clear," Schuyler explains: "as interest in historic sites grew and recognition of the contribution archaeology could make also grew, government and private agencies had to turn to anthropologists as they constituted almost the only source for new historic-sites archaeologists."[120] The movement to link historical archaeology with anthropology on both theoretical and technical levels was under way, but according to Schuyler, "most archaeologists working on historic sites could be anthropologists and yet not truly historical archaeologists."[121] Contracting for short-term historic-sites projects committed to restoration and preservation goals "allowed anthropologists to be very non-anthropological about digging historic sites; they acted like and indeed were technicians serving other, especially restoration, interest[s]."[122] Although an anthropological orientation had been established by the early 1970s, the long association between the field and the restoration-preservation movement was still very evident and in some areas, particularly the Northeast, continued to dominate the scene.

The academic community's establishment of formal professional standards beginning in the mid-1960s slowly resulted in restricted access to the discipline. Robbins found himself increasingly excluded by academicians; he did not fulfill the norms of their world. These professionals were repulsed by his excavation methods, populist approach to the discipline, and crass business techniques. Robbins's standing and self-promotion as the "Pick and Shovel Historian," a commonsense Yankee workingman, lowered his status in the eyes of his more polished academic rivals. He was too quick to jump into the excavation with the "workmen" and wield a shovel; as Floyd Johnson remembered, "he just went in there and worked as hard as any of the people that we hired to do the digging."[123] Robbins reacted to his exclusion in a number of ways, particularly by intensifying his identification with Henry D. Thoreau. Robbins's career, after all, was also a personal pursuit devoted to maintaining both a livelihood and a respectable place in the community. In this way, he saw his quest for a legitimate place in society as like that of Thoreau, who struggled to find a suitable means of living within his world. Thoreau's brand of individualism and self-reliance was attractive to Robbins, and he both benefited and suffered by it.[124]

In a general sense, the postwar era was an age of anxiety, Kammen notes, one that caused people to "think wistfully about individualism, self-reliance, and other verities associated with the colonial period and the early republic."[125] The postwar period also witnessed a heightened desire on the part of Americans for membership in the growing middle class.[126] However, "the fear of falling," wrote Bledstein, "knawed away at every climber, and this fear—ubiquitous in the middle class—was often the source of a general anxiety within individuals which no amount of monetary security, public honors, or personal confidence seemed to eliminate."[127] Robbins's personal anxieties over and struggles for middle-class status and economic independence, which took root in the Great Depression, and his snubbing by the academic establishment compelled him to reject the professional "community of the competent" and embrace a philosophy of individualism, one that grew stronger throughout his life. "The middle-class person," argued Bledstein, "was not merely self-reliant, he was absorbed in his own egotism."[128] Interestingly, *Hidden America* coauthor Evan Jones characterized Robbins as a "terrible individualist—terrible in the other sense. Robbie just didn't care about what other people were doing. I don't mean that he was insensitive or rude. He just wanted to do his thing and follow his interests."[129] His individualistic approach and lack of formal education helped him to focus extraordinary energy on investigating historic sites. He was unhindered by the conventions and constraints of formal education and also by what people thought. "It may have made him better," commented archaeologist Paul Heberling, "because he was not hung up on all the extraneous problems that we [professionals] often are [dealing with]."[130]

Robbins's approaches to archaeological research and excavation did not improve with respect to the increasingly rigorous standards of the professional community; if anything, they deteriorated with his increasing alienation by the academic community, and his growing desire to separate himself and his work from that of the academy. This spiral of alienation by academic archaeologists heightened Robbins's self-doubts and insecurities. The late 1960s were a very confusing time for him, a period filled with mixed messages. He was well aware of negative comments about his work and his qualifications from within the academic archaeological community, yet he still received positive feedback from some quarters of the archaeological profession, from many, if not all, of his clients, and from the public.[131] For instance, Robbins was invited to be the guest speaker at the Second Annual Symposium on Historic Site Archaeology in the Northeast Region, held at Bear Mountain, New York, in 1966. The organizers wrote that "it is the unanimous opinion of all . . . that if you could . . . [lecture] our second meeting would be a tremendous success. We tentatively plan to have as the theme of this symposium: *Historic Site Archaeology Today: Its Importance and Problems,* a subject I feel you are eminently qualified to discuss." Following his lecture, the organizers wrote that "your talk was a tremendous success. We could not have had a better finish to what I believe was a good meeting."[132]

It is clear from Robbins's writing that he was concerned and increasingly anxious about his standing in the discipline because of his lack of formal education. He often, like Thoreau, reflected on the value of being self-educated and having a native New England commonsense understanding of the world. In fact, he saved and highlighted an editorial published in the *Concord Journal* in 1965 that underscored his anxiety about succeeding without an education:

schooling, particularly at the college level and the graduate school plane, has become an American obsession which may one day return to haunt us. Secondly, the word drop-out has taken on the connotations of a dirty word, used chiefly to describe quickly and easily the problem adolescent.[133]

Author Ed McCaffrey went on to quote remarks by the Right Reverend George W. Casey of Lexington, who meditated on the definition of higher education as the only basis of learning and essential to success:

This impression [that there is no place other than college to learn anything] is wrong, and proven so by the long tradition of success in America on the part of self-taught men. . . . Undoubtedly most of the successful men of our history who did not do so, would have gone to college if they had the time and the opportunity . . . [however], they wouldn't have gone to just any old college and just to go through it. They would have been too smart to waste the time. . . . In most professions and in some big businesses degrees are *sine qua non* . . . and there is no other way than going to school and getting one. . . . But with the libraries, correspondence courses, newspapers even, seminars, etc., now available a man can get all the information he needs and sharpen his wits as well as the next without ever putting his foot in college. And in many instances he would be just as well off if he didn't.[134]

As he endeavored to come to terms with his lack of education and its relationship to his place within the specialty of historical archaeology, Robbins faced a growing distance between himself and professional academic archaeologists. As this gulf widened, he began to refer to himself using alternative titles, such as restorer, explorer, and historic-site consultant, to increase his identification with his mentor Thoreau and to locate his projects within the framework of what he called "American Heritage Studies, covering ecology, environmental awareness, and history."[135]

Robbins found many things about Thoreau appealing. Quick to pick up on Thoreau's curiosity about the past, he quoted him in an early promotional flyer: "nothing so restores and humanizes antiquity and makes it blithe as the discovery of some natural sympathy between it and the present."[136] Robbins and Thoreau had interests in common. For example, in "The Bean Fields," Thoreau recorded his own discovery of the buried artifacts of past cultures:

I disturbed the ashes of unchronicled nations who in primeval years lived under these heavens, and their small implements of war and hunting . . . and also bits of pottery and glass brought hither by the recent cultivators of the soil.[137]

In "Former Inhabitants," Thoreau was intrigued with the settlers of Walden woods and the remains of their dwellings, and in a sense foretold the condition of his own cabin some one hundred years later:

Now only a dent in the earth marks the site of these dwellings, with buried cellar stones . . . some pitch pine or gnarled oak occupies what was the chimney nook, and a sweet-scented black-birch, perhaps waves where the door-stone was.[138]

Thoreau also had a decidedly negative view of higher education that, as discussed above, resonated with Robbins. After spending the day listening to Thoreau's negative comments about education and educational institutions, a visitor recalled that

Emerson pleaded always for the college. . . . This aroused the wrath of Thoreau, who would not allow any good to the college course. . . . When the curriculum at Cambridge was alluded to, and Emerson casually remarked that most of the branches of learning were taught there, . . . Thoreau . . . replied "Yes indeed, all the branches and none of the roots."[139]

Like his mentor Thoreau, who designed innovative pencil-making machinery and became an accomplished land surveyor, Robbins had a knack for engineering and was extremely mechanically inclined.[140] He had an innate curiosity in how things worked, and his wife remembers that he had an inventive mind and was always "thinking up things—

mostly electric or mechanical."[141] He also became a very proficient surveyor and draftsman, practicing this craft during his field projects.

Within the context of his identification with Thoreau and his increasing alienation from the academy, archaeology became more narrowly focused for Robbins.[142] "As a historic-site consultant," he wrote, "archaeology is only one of my tools. Interpretation and faithful presentation, restoration, or reconstruction are vitally involved." Increasingly at odds with the evolving techniques of excavation and standardization of the professional archaeological community, he put his energies into what he saw to be the larger project of crafting, literally sculpting, "American Heritage" sites or parks from the ruins and remains that had been recovered through his investigations. Robbins's emphasis on heritage studies connected with a general trend, a "heritage syndrome," notes Kammen, that began in the 1950s and has lasted in one form or another until the present. In a world of change and discontinuity, "a sense of permanence and timelessness carried enormous appeal."[143] The past, writes historian David Lowenthal, is crucial for our sense of identity; "to know what we were confirms that we are."[144] This perception of self-continuity "depends wholly on memory," and "history extends and elaborates memory by interpreting relics" and written records.[145] Relics, such as the ruins and artifacts unearthed by Robbins in New England and the northeastern United States, "trigger recollection, which history affirms and extends backward in time."[146] Sociologist Dean MacCannell suggests that "restored remnants . . . are [also] reminders of our break with the past and with tradition."[147]

The delivery of a national heritage or collective memory became "vastly easier and more comfortable" with the success of mass-market print media such as *American Heritage* magazine, the enormous impact of television, and increased mobility brought about by the automobile.[148] "Tradition," Kammen notes, "had been made readily available to the mobile middle class."[149] The tangible reminders of the past represented by the Oliver Mill ruins, Robbins told a crowd at the site's dedication ceremony, would remain after the spirit of the celebration had "dwindled with the reality of the present" and after people had settled "back to the normal level of their everyday way-of-life."[150] Robbins understood the appeal of physical manifestations of the past and eagerly sought to deliver them to the public; the discipline of historical archaeology, he thought, was simply headed in the wrong direction. His split from and bitterness toward the academy is apparent in a 1971 letter to E. Gilbert Barker, an architect and planner who worked with Robbins at the Crown Point site in New York:

It would seem to me, Gil, from many years of close association with it, the term Historic Sites, has earned a standing of much misunderstanding and misuse. It has been placed on a pedestal above the reach of the man in the street, . . . whom it is all about![151]

The academic community was directing its energies at developing standardized educational requirements and a foundation of method and theory, closing off access and effectively eliminating and devaluing both practitioners like Robbins and the input of the public at large.

Robbins's increasing emphasis on the relationship between site restoration and the landscape and environmental aspects of historic sites can be seen in his multiyear project at the Oliver Mill Park restoration in Middleborough, Massachusetts. In his report on these excavations, Robbins played off of Thoreau's statement that "in wilderness is the preservation of the world."[152] The wilderness, Robbins argued, preserves, reclaims, and recycles abandoned communities.[153] "The site," he continued, "is obliterated and reclaimed by nature's octopus-like spread of snarled vegetation and brush and reforestation."[154] The ruins of Peter Oliver's colonial mills, Robbins thought, provided an "excellent example of the natural elements reclaiming that which man had [originally] borrowed from nature."[155]

The Oliver Mill project, Robbins reasoned, provided an opportunity to put history within the reach of the common man, "whom it is all about."[156] At the dedication of Oliver Mill Park during the town's tercentenary celebration, he noted that the occasion was a "tribute to the citizens of Middleborough for their vision and the desire to reestablish the physical features of the colonial times, so that they would serve as a constant reminder of their heritage."[157] It was relatively easy to get people to talk about the history of the community, he thought, but this project represented a more "lasting physical accomplishment."[158]

The Oliver Mills site was first developed in 1734, when a group of Middleborough, Massachusetts, residents petitioned for permission to build a dam, forge, rolling and slitting mill, and gristmill along the Nemasket River. The works were built shortly thereafter, and by 1741 the Reverend Peter Thatcher owned the property and operated a bloomery forge at the site. Peter Oliver, a provincial official and judge moved to Middleborough from Boston and with Jeremiah Gridley purchased the ironworks from Thatcher in 1744. The new owners made improvements and the works became an important source of iron goods for the British military. By 1758, Oliver purchased Gridley's interest in the ironwork and became sole owner. By the time that Oliver fled to England in 1776, the mill had eight waterwheels and was "producing 70 to 100 tons of wrought bar iron per year."[159] The works were acquired by John Ritchie in 1780 and then passed through several owners until purchased in the late 1790s by General Abriel Washburn and Judge Thomas Weston. Washburn and Weston converted the operation into a shovel manufacturing shop. The owners altered or removed many of the Oliver period structures and built several new shovel shop buildings on the north shore of the river. The shovel operation continued into the 1850s. It was an interest in creating a public park at the site as part of the town of Middleborough's upcoming Tercentenary celebration in 1969 that brought Robbins to the site.[160]

The Oliver Mill project is significant because it exposes Robbins's shaky foundation in historical archaeology by the late 1960s. On the one hand, he applied his commonsense approach and experience to the excavations and reconstructions of the site and dismissed the need for academic credentials. On that same basis and to his great disgust, the park managers later hired a stonemason to complete a portion of the archaeological work. On the other hand, when the stonemason proved inadequate, as Robbins had predicted, the park hired university-based archaeologists, who lacked Robbins's practical experience in excavating and reconstructing industrial sites. Poised between the ordinary tradesman and the impractical academic, Robbins was drawn into regular skirmishes to defend and justify his position.

After an initial survey that identified several stone foundations and included preliminary excavation on the eighteenth-century ironworks complex, Robbins presented his findings to park commissioners and members of the Oliver Mill Park Coordinating Committee. According to Robbins, the members "expressed pleasure in the progress that had been accomplished during the previous three months."[161] However, during a review of the project's budget he learned that

there was an outstanding bill for $3,000 for work done before my field work was undertaken. . . . [and] it was voted that my project would terminate the next day.[162]

Although caught off guard, Robbins made preparations to comply with the request and terminate work by the end of the following day. However, the next day he recorded that

upon returning from lunch I was startled to find the equipment, the workmen, and the tools were out of the excavations and were preparing to leave the project. . . . I was informed that [park superintendent] Joseph Masi had . . . told the men . . . to terminate the field work at noon.[163]

Robbins left the site in a state of confusion, he wrote, but was later assured by committee members that "money from other sources would soon be made available."[164]

Robbins made a presentation to the Coordinating Committee, reviewing previous work and discussing the future development of the site; he also reviewed his recommendations and estimates for additional excavation and restoration during 1968.[165] Although the approved budget contained some funds to complete the excavations, it did not include money for artifact cataloging, mapping, or report preparation.[166] The committee agreed to proceed immediately with masonry work to stabilize the ruins, and to have Robbins complete the outstanding archaeological investigations. Because his workload would not allow him to start soon enough to satisfy the Oliver Mill representatives and avoid delaying the stonemason, the committee voted to "have the stonemason . . . excavate the present raceways not excavated so that he can complete the work contracted by him this year."[167]

Robbins was furious and wrote a long letter to Masi detailing the sources of the project's problems and delays.[168] Of the decision to have the stonemason excavate the raceways, he fumed,

in my twenty years as a consultant for historical restorations I have never encountered such a travesty of irresponsible restoration. Permitting the stonemason to archaeologically excavate the original Peter Oliver mill raceways is as ludicrous as engaging a nurse to perform an intricate surgical operation.[169]

This encounter and Robbins's response are particularly interesting in that this was the same argument that academic professionals were using against Robbins. For example, John Cotter's analogy compared Robbins to a "fellow with a set of plans under his arms" who "just loved engineering and drafting but had no professional training, applying to a corporation to erect a skyscraper. He would," Cotter mused, "no doubt be sent packing."[170]

Just prior to sending his voluminous letter to Masi, Robbins learned that the committee had engaged Richard Humphrey and other archaeologists from Plimoth Plantation, Inc., and Brown University to complete the excavation. Aware of the problems that would result from introducing new players, Robbins wrote to Masi that "I can appreciate the unfortunate position in which you have placed another archaeologist by subjecting him to the confused mess."[171] Robbins simultaneously wrote to Humphrey to offer his assistance. "A refinery-forge was a complex operation" he concluded; "however there are shortcuts that can be followed when excavating such a site. This comes only with experience. Good luck with your work. Do let me know if I can be of any assistance."[172]

No surprise to Robbins, the arrangement with the professional archaeologists did not seem to work out; perhaps Masi was upset that the academically trained Humphrey and his colleagues worked even more slowly and methodically than Robbins. In his daily log for April 6, 1969, Robbins wrote that

Bob Candee said that Joe Masi had a falling out with the archaeologist . . . from Plimoth Plantation and Brown University . . . and he fired him. Ain't that something!! Apparently the guy wasn't sure of himself and this work (this I can believe).[173]

Robbins could certainly believe this outcome. He had warned Masi of the likelihood that problems would ensue with a new archaeologist and had indirectly warned Humphrey in his letter about the complexity of this type of site and the need for experience.

Comments on the project by archaeologist Marley Brown, then a student of James Deetz's at Brown University, further clarify and expand the story. Brown relates how he and Deetz would regularly drive by the Oliver Mill site on the way to Plymouth. He remembers that as they passed the site, Deetz would comment that they needed to stop Robbins from digging. Although the reason for Robbins's departure appeared to Robbins to be funding shortages, Brown speculated that Deetz might have called the town officials and urged them to end Robbins's involvement. In any event, Brown notes, Deetz's students were then engaged to excavate the site. However, it quickly became apparent that "they had no idea what they were doing" in terms of excavating a complicated industrial site.[174] Shortly thereafter, they either left or, as Robbins reports, were fired. Brown suspects that the falling-out was not so much over the archaeology itself but over the restoration work. Robbins, Brown notes, commanded many skills, including the ability to oversee the reconstruction of dry-laid stonework, but this was outside Deetz's ability and interest.[175] Robbins had been correct about the site's complexity and the special knowledge needed to excavate and, particularly, to restore such an industrial site.

Robbins's persistent and tenacious crusade to properly, as he saw it, finish the project finally paid off. In 1969, town manager Anders Martenson asked him to consider returning to Oliver Mill Park. Robbins completed the excavation of the refinery-forge and old dam; the repair and preservation of stonework at the southern end of the dam, the raceways, the foundation of the refinery-forge, and the stone foundation on the southern embankment; the repair and preservation of the raceway boards and timbers; the excavation and restoration of the south side of the millpond; and the removal of soils washed into the site area. He also made plan drawings of the site and ruins, recorded the artifacts, and prepared a report.[176] Marley Brown recollects driving by the site again with Deetz after Robbins had returned to complete the work, and Deetz complaining to him that they should never have gotten involved with the site in the first place.[177]

The restoration nature of the Oliver Mill Park project influenced the archaeological research. Limitations of time and money, combined with Robbins's own focus on the creation of physical monuments to the past, resulted in an approach that was seen as being at odds with the prevailing methods of historical archaeology. Yet, the academic researchers that briefly took over from Robbins found that they could do little better in terms of excavating a complicated industrial site. In the end, Robbins excavated and restored the eighteenth- and nineteenth-century mill complex, both gathering and destroying archaeological data in the process (figure 5.6). He ignored the potential usefulness of the overburden or "modern fill layers" in terms of their temporal relationships, removing them with little or no controls. While Robbins focused on the intact site features described above, and carefully documented this work, he recorded only the horizontal provenience of artifacts and features, not the critical vertical and temporal relationships.[178] His methods of data collection and excavation at Oliver Mill Park, informed largely by the commonsense approach developed at other industrial sites, have tradition-

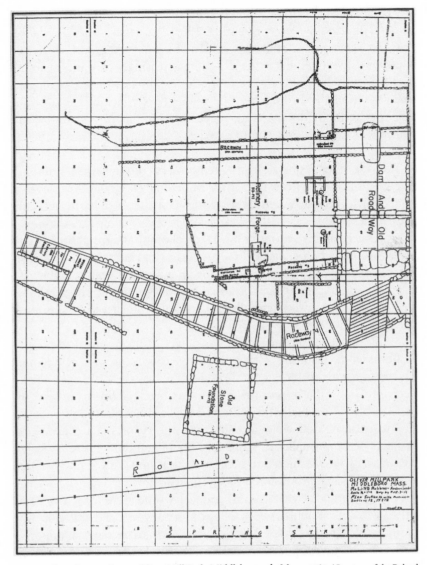

FIG. 5.6. Plan of excavations at Oliver Mill Park, Middleborough, Mass., 1969. (Courtesy of the Roland Wells Robbins Collection, the Thoreau Society, Lincoln, Mass., and the Thoreau Institute at Walden Woods.)

ally been viewed as crude and extremely destructive to the site. A recent project, directed by Ben Ford and Matthew A. Kierstead of PAL and related to stabilization and reconstruction work at the park, reviewed Robbins's investigations at the site. Not surprisingly, the authors found that his work did not conform to modern standards for archaeological excavation and recording. Yet, the researchers concluded that "while Robbins undoubtedly altered the appearance of the site and destroyed a number of features, he seems to have left a significant portion of the site for future study."[179]

As with other restoration-oriented projects of the period, Robbins's application of data from the Oliver Mill site to larger anthropological and historical issues was entirely lacking. The essence of his projects was creating a tangible past—uncovering and reconstructing foundations—an approach directed toward physical display and interpretation. In this sense, Robbins was engaged in a process of crafting usable and marketable history, a craft that brought together his own interest in the past, his yearning for stability and personal foundations in the rapidly changing world of the mid–twentieth century, and his belief in the power of the past to educate.

While short-term projects such as Oliver Mill continued to provide Robbins with consulting work, he was increasingly forced to supplement his income with entrepreneurial projects such as the Walden Cabin Kit venture. These enterprises only further distanced him from the academy as examples of his blatant commercial bent. Although Robbins continued to excavate archaeological sites into the 1980s, his archaeological projects became smaller in scope and the demand for his services less frequent. By 1964, he noted to a colleague that "the last 3 years have been very poor in my professional business of historical research. If I had known 3 years ago what I know today, I would have turned to some other work."[180] Robbins's lack of success, however, did not stop him from continuing to pursue new projects. With archaeological opportunities sparse, he supported himself primarily by lecturing (figure 5.7) and increasing his attention to Thoreau, becoming president of the Thoreau Society in 1964. Thoreau, too, had been only moderately successful with his published writings, and had entered the lecture circuit in the late 1840s to promote his work and pay the bills.[181]

Along with radio and television interviews, Robbins's public presentations bolstered his self-esteem and established his reputation as a

FIG. 5.7. Robbins lecturing in the early 1950s. (Courtesy of the Roland Wells Robbins Collection, the Thoreau Society, Lincoln, Mass., and the Thoreau Institute at Walden Woods.)

historic-sites archaeologist. He was an accomplished lecturer, speaking to women's clubs, college audiences, schoolchildren, and corporate presidents. Between 1945 and 1980, he presented approximately seven hundred lectures to an estimated seventy-five thousand people, who, it appears, found him an engaging and interesting speaker.[182]

Robbins's success with his Walden presentation prompted him to prepare lectures on the Minute Man statue and his rural Vermont poetry and verse. He added a Saugus Iron Works lecture in 1948 and, in the promotional literature for this talk, began to identify himself as an archaeologist of the colonial period for the first time. Proclaiming himself a "Poet, Author, Photographer, and Lecturer of the New England Scene," Robbins advertised his lectures in *Yankee* magazine, locating his identity in the guise of the quintessential New England Yankee. Donald Smith, director of the New York Museum Association, summarized Robbins's lecture to the Association as "an excellent story of the fascinating and painstaking job he has done in archaeology. His work is characterized by scholarly accuracy and a Yankee common-sense approach."[183] Robbins had realized that lecturing could provide a significant income, and his well-publicized work at Saugus brought new demands for his lecturing skills. As the years passed, his lecture brochures became increasingly sophisticated, with new lecture offerings and testimonials from his sponsors and audiences (figure 5.8).[184]

Lecturing benefited Robbins in several ways: it supplemented his income on a regular basis, was an excellent publicity vehicle, and allowed him to network with groups and organizations in search of a historic-sites archaeologist. As J. C. Harrington said in 1965, it was "harder to find an available [historical] archaeologist than a Chaucerian scholar."[185] Yet, the benefits of Robbins's lectures were far from his alone. Thousands of men, women, and children laughed and learned with Robbins, often getting their first introduction to historical archaeology.[186] Robbins, "a polished public speaker" according to Evan Jones, addressed a wide range of organizations, from local clubs and schools to regional historical and archaeological conferences.[187]

Despite his lecturing successes in both the public and professional spheres, Robbins was uncertain about his relationship with professional archaeologists from the very beginning. This uncertainty was often masked in his Thoreauvian attitude of individualism, stubbornness, and irascibility. Robbins wrote that

I have probably come as close as any of my contemporaries to meeting and visiting with Henry David Thoreau in person. Maybe I did it the hard way. But then I did it my way. And by doing it my way I found a contentment suitable for my way of life.[188]

His initial success was due, in large part, both to the youthful nature and the preservation orientation of historical archaeology and to his enduring passion and excitement for historical and archaeological research. He had been, as he said, in the right place at the right time. But more than that, he was good at what he did, in terms of both his research and the public presentation of this work.

Beginning in 1964, a particularly slow period in his archaeological work, Robbins maintained a heavy lecture schedule and dabbled in several new entrepreneurial ventures, including the Thoreau–Walden Cabin Kit, a build-it-yourself replica which only further alienated him from the

ROLAND ROBBINS

Saugus Ironworks Restoration

Excavator

PILGRIM JOHN ALDEN'S HOME
Circa 1627
DUXBURY, MASSACHUSETTS

SAUGUS IRONWORKS 1646
*America's First
Successful Ironworks*
SAUGUS, MASS.

SLEEPY HOLLOW RESTORATIONS
*Dutch trading post
on the Hudson 1683*
TARRYTOWN, N. Y.

COLONIAL CROWN POINT
1731-1783
LAKE CHAMPLAIN, N. Y.

SHADWELL 1737-1770
*Birthplace of
Thomas Jefferson*
CHARLOTTESVILLE, VA.

STERLING FURNACE
*Producer of iron for the
chain spanning the Hudson
at West Point 1778-1783*
TUXEDO, N.Y.

DUPONT'S EARLY POWDER
ROLLING MILLS 1822-1824
WILMINGTON, DEL.

THOREAU'S WALDEN POND
CABIN SITE
1845-1847

Thoreau at Walden

The

"Pick and Shovel"

Historian

PRESENTS

HIS COLORFUL

AND ENTERTAINING

ILLUSTRATED LECTURES

Hidden America

Highlights of Robbins' most important digs and discoveries and restorations. You will be fascinated and excited as you review the unbelievable adventures that unearthed the ruins of America's early way of life.

The Road to Ruins and Restorations

More than 3 centuries of American Living. This is a special treat where the club sponsoring a Robbins' Lecture can choose the subjects which appeal to them most. The Road to Ruins and Restorations includes any three of the following subjects: Pilgrim John Alden's Home in Duxbury *circa* 1627; Thomas Jefferson's Birthplace; Thoreau's Cabin At Walden Pond; The 1646 Saugus Ironworks; The 1644 John Winthrop, Jr., Ironworks: Philipsburg Manor Upper Mills, a 17-18 century Dutch Settlement at Tarrytown, New York; Colonial Crown Point, Lake Champlain, New York; Sterling Furnace and DuPont's Early Mills.

Yankee Country

A rare treat of New England yarns and humor. Superb color scenes, including many illustrations of rural life through the four seasons of the year, also dramatic upside down reflections. And featuring the Strange Tale Of Human Hibernation In Vermont.

Co-Author of HIDDEN AMERICA, Roland Robbins is subject of countless articles in national magazines and newspapers. Has made many appearances on TV and Radio, before college audiences, at all types of clubs, historical societies, luncheons, dinners and conventions.

Robbins has been called back for lectures by the same organizations as many as four and five times — so great is his audience appeal.

Lecturer - Author - Photographer - Historian - Archaeologist

FIG. 5.8 Robbins's promotional brochure, ca. 1962. (Courtesy of the Roland Wells Robbins Collection, the Thoreau Society, Lincoln, Mass., and the Thoreau Institute at Walden Woods.)

academy.[189] Borrowing once more from Thoreau, Robbins noted in the brochure that,

if it is your wish to "live deliberately"—to make a place in your life to house your dreams, your privacy, or your own personal life style . . . then the Thoreau–Walden Cabin is your happy answer.[190]

"The Thoreau–Walden Cabin," he wrote to prospective buyers, "has its origins in the cabin built in the woods at Walden Pond by Henry David Thoreau in 1845. Rediscovered in 1945 and reconstructed by Roland Wells Robbins, the Cabin is now available to the discriminating buyer."[191] The kit included all the wooden elements for the frame, plans, and instructions for assembly. The framing members were numbered and pre-jointed "for setting up the Cabin with maximum efficiency."[192]

The idea for the kit grew out of suggestions from the many visitors to the replica of Thoreau's house that Robbins had built in his backyard (figure 5.9).[193] During the late 1960s and 1970s, visitors were drawn to Robbins's replica to worship at the house of Thoreau and spend the night in a reproduction of his forest home. Over time, Robbins realized that many of the pilgrims wanted a Thoreau house of their own.[194]

The press and public responded enthusiastically to the initial kit in 1964, but several academic members of the Thoreau Society thought it an "insipid, blatant, commercialized venture" and quipped that Robbins might also make "polyethylene Walden ponds for pseudo-rustics . . . and . . . sell small dashboard statues of Thoreau himself."[195] Another detractor wrote to Robbins in 1981, "now why don't you just tell the truth! At $2,495 (plus), you're capitalizing on that great man's name for the entirely selfish purpose of getting rich."[196] Although some academic purists derided the house replica venture, most welcomed Robbins's first Thoreau house reproduction. Walter Harding remembered that "Roland offered it to visiting scholars and enthusiasts to sleep over . . . and I brought my National Endowment for the Humanities seminar students to the cabin replica each year."[197] It is ironic that as Robbins attempted to respond to his increasing exclusion from archaeology by identifying with Thoreau, he once again came into conflict with academics, this time those pushing to professionalize the Thoreau Society. Thomas Blanding identified with the irony, remarking:

It almost seemed that you were describing through the example of Roland what many of us now feel is happening in the field of Thoreau studies, and maybe in

FIG. 5.9. Roland Robbins standing in the doorway of the Thoreau–Walden Cabin replica located at his home, ca. 1964. (*Courtesy of the Roland Wells Robbins Collection, the Thoreau Society, Lincoln, Mass., and the Thoreau Institute at Walden Woods.*)

some ways in the world in general, this polarity of intellectualism that looks down its nose at popularization, and vice versa, the distrust of intellectualism by some.[198]

Blanding believed that Robbins's replicas allowed people to "experience this house that actually symbolized Thoreau—not just stepping into the house, but stepping into the symbol, stepping into Thoreau's life."[199] "For me," he reflected, "this came to overshadow any sense of commercialism in the venture."[200]

The period between Robbins's Philipsburg Manor and John Alden excavations and the completion of his work at Oliver Mill Park witnessed tremendous change within the discipline of historical archaeology. As he began the PMUM project in 1956, Robbins was still a figure of some prominence within historical archaeology in New England and the Northeast, particularly in the public's eye, and one of only a handful of pioneers practicing the craft of historical and industrial archaeology. His work at PMUM was made highly visible through coverage in the press and broadcast news and was even reported on positively in the "Notes and News" section of *American Antiquity,* professional archaeology's main academic journal of the period.[201] Likewise, the 1959 publication of *Hidden America* marked the first widely disseminated volume on American historical archaeology and brought Robbins additional notice. The extremely visual nature of the Philipsburg Manor excavations, both structurally and artifactually, combined with Robbins's charismatic personality and his unqualified enthusiasm for his subject, created the perfect situation for engaging the public and promoting the importance of historical archaeology. It was a period that valued the presentation and enhancement of physical structures and other evidence as reminders of the past, particularly as suburban development increasingly impinged on the cultural landscape, and as the Cold War caused Americans to think about their democratic social system and seek to defend its values by turning to the country's colonial beginnings.

By 1970, however, Robbins had been eclipsed by the academic profession. Having reached an age when most academics and professionals would have retired and turned their work over to the next generation, he continued to vigorously pursue his chosen career with an overpowering degree of independence that only further alienated him from the profession. In a very revealing statement, Evan Jones commented that by the late 1960s Robbins

had done his thing and he didn't know it. He helped to stimulate the discipline but once the thing got rolling the academic attitude was bound to prevail, and more and more people were made to feel that it was a legitimate pursuit, so they went to it as students—whereas they wouldn't have when Roland was beginning.[202]

For the college-educated Jones, the academy was unquestionably bound to prevail; the pursuit of historical archaeology would not be legitimate until it became taught within a university. Paul Heberling recalls that "academic archaeologists were particularly brutal toward him, taking a superior attitude and disparaging him—not only what he did, but what he wrote."[203] Although he desperately sought approval and praise for his life's work, Robbins was continuously placed in the position of defending his participation in historical archaeology in light of what was viewed as his outdated field and analytical techniques, his crass business tactics, and his encouragement of direct public involvement in archaeology.

CHAPTER 6

A "Thoreau Yankee" Meets the Academy

By the early to mid-1970s, historical and industrial archaeology were becoming established within the sanctuary of the university system and slowly boasting a more anthropological orientation. However, the long association between these fields and the restoration-preservation movement was still very evident, particularly in New England. With the passage of the National Historic Preservation Act of 1966 (NHPA), archaeological excavations of historic sites expanded exponentially, as did the literature of the field. Throughout the decade, the discipline continued to struggle to define itself as a viable profession, generating and enforcing new standards for practice and developing new educational requirements for admittance.

Although Robbins completed several excavation projects that were mandated under the NHPA and was able to capitalize on the interest in historic sites generated by the nation's bicentennial, he found himself increasingly marginalized by professional academic archaeologists who considered his lack of education and excavation standards unacceptable, and his populist views downright alarming. At the beginning of the decade, his work at the Hancock-Clarke House was bluntly criticized by university-based archaeologists James Deetz and Charles Tremer. Several years later, he was declared unqualified to conduct archaeological investigations based on the standards and guidelines of the National Park Service. At the 1977 Dublin Seminar on historical archaeology, he was humiliated by professionals who dismissed his excavations and publications and poked fun at his folksy, unsophisticated demeanor. The experience was the final blow for Robbins in terms of his relationship with the world of academics. Thoreau scholar Brad Dean remembers meeting Robbins for the first time in the mid-1970s and receiving a stern lecture about the world of professional archaeology; he recalled being struck by Robbins's extreme loathing for academics.[1]

In the early 1980s, major health problems forced Robbins to admit to himself that his career was coming to its end, and he sought recognition for his contributions to the discipline. He believed strongly that he had not been given proper credit by academic professionals for his many pioneering efforts in industrial and historical archaeology and restoration throughout the Northeast, not to mention his important contributions to contract and public archaeology. Colleague Evan Jones observed, "I really don't think that he was able to appreciate the fact that he had done a hell of a lot just by being what he was, and to hell with . . . the academic judgment."[2]

University-based historical archaeologists struggled to create their professional caste or "community of the competent" throughout the 1970s and 1980s. As late as 1976, the founding members of the Society for Historical Archaeology were still urging the membership to "professionalize our organization!"[3] Historical archaeology went through a series of stages and processes typical of emerging professions. In the early stages of a developing discipline, the membership of the group is very diverse; members are not "homogeneous with respect to the amount of knowledge and community orientation they possess."[4] This was certainly true as historical archaeology sought to define itself in the 1950s and 1960s, the first few decades of its existence, and can be seen in the active participation of such figures as Ivor Noël Hume and Robbins. Leaders, generally the older and more elite members of a group, typically work to strengthen community orientation by "constructing and publishing codes of ethics."[5] As seen in historical archaeology, these individuals, almost exclusively academics, worked to establish or strengthen the professional organization to provide "self-control, socialization, and education of members, communications with the public, and the defense of professional interest[s]."[6]

Emerging professions have long sought to "locate the center of their authority within university schools," particularly if they already have a marginal connection there.[7] "By defining its functions comprehensively and constantly expanding its clientele," Bledstein asserts, "the American university . . . serve[d] to enhance the public's image of a unified professional authority in the society."[8] The university also became the principal force to lobby for membership standards, uniform procedures, and consistent terminologies.[9] Beginning with John Cotter's courses in the mid-1950s, historical archaeology has attempted to establish itself in the university within departments of anthropology. However, anthropology's initial rejection of historical archaeology as "tin-can archaeology" resulted in a lingering period of indecision, when practitioners questioned the proper disciplinary orientation, resulting in the inclusion of historical archaeology in both history and American civilization/studies departments.[10] Perhaps not surprisingly, the only university alliance that Robbins, "the historian who digs," had during his career was with the History Department at the University of New Hampshire.[11] Like Robbins, Ivor Noël Hume also forged his disciplinary allegiance with American historians rather than anthropological archaeologists. Both Robbins and Noël Hume found that they were granted a degree of legitimacy by historians that they never received from anthropologists. Although many historical archaeologists were settling into anthropology departments around the country during the 1970s and the Society for Historical Archaeology was growing, the debate of over the proper disciplinary allegiance for historical archaeology was still alive. The discipline had yet to gain the full respect of American archaeology at large and persisted in its heavy focus on restoration and preservation projects.

Perhaps the state of historical archaeology's emerging "community of the competent" can best be summarized by an account of the 1971 annual meeting of the Society for Historical Archaeology in Tallahassee, Florida, as told by archaeologist Kathleen Deagan. The meeting hotel for the conference was being shared with the entourage of presidential candidate George Wallace, Deagan relates, and

confused reporters interviewed Wallace supporters and archaeologists alike, and Stan South was so compelling that they aired his interview on Tallahassee TV. Jim Deetz . . . went skinny dipping in the hotel pool—which fortunately was not aired on TV, and a long series of other even more colorful events took place throughout the meeting. As a graduate student at the time, I was thrilled by the whole thing and said "sign me up for historical archaeology!"[12]

By the end of the decade, historical archaeology in the United States had slowly altered both its methods and its theoretical approaches. The particularistic research of the restoration and preservation tradition was slowly giving way to an orientation that favored anthropological theory and scientific certainty.[13] Articles published in the journal *Historical Archaeology* reflect a growing concern with producing specific research designs, standardizing field techniques, and improving the quality of professional reporting. In addition, theoretical questions of cultural process and pattern were increasingly asked of the excavated materials in what were designed to be "controlled experiments;" the search was on for broad rules and laws of human behavior and culture.

The movement to more anthropologically oriented research in historical archaeology was slow at first. This was particularly true for New England, where, with the exception of the pioneering work of scholars such as Deetz and Dethlefson, archaeologists allowed "their sites to be selected for them by organizations committed to the preservation and restoration of historic buildings and sites."[14] In addition to the 1970s excavations at Plimoth Plantation to reproduce the Pilgrim Village, Deetz and other Plimoth Plantation archaeologists worked at various sites in the region, including the Quaker Meeting House in Newport, Rhode Island, the Wellfleet Whaling Station on Cape Cod, a seventeenth-century domestic site in Portsmouth, Rhode Island, and the Old Jail site in Barnstable, Massachusetts.[15] Three other New England museums, Strawbery Banke in New Hampshire, Historic Deerfield in Massachusetts, and the Pemaquid Restoration in Maine, also began long-term historical archaeology projects during this period.[16]

During the 1970s, historical archaeology was still under way at many smaller historic sites across New England, including the Fairbanks Homestead in Dedham, Massachusetts, the Peake House in Medfield, Massachusetts, and the Golden Ball Tavern in Weston, Massachusetts.[17] The U.S. bicentennial celebration provided a "favorable climate and practical opportunities for certain kinds of archaeological research," particularly in New England.[18] Town bicentennial commissions worked with local historical societies and local governments, sponsoring excavations at sites across the region; Robbins would successfully tap this source of work at sites in the greater Boston area.[19] Local historical societies also supported archaeological investigations at many New England sites, including the Greene-Bowen House in Warwick, Rhode Island, the Anthony House in Edgartown, Rhode Island, and Forts Shirley and Pelham in western Massachusetts.[20]

In addition to the archaeological projects conducted through local and regional historical societies, commissions, and house museums, the federal government funded archaeology in New England through the National Park Service (NPS). These projects included excavations of domestic sites within the Minuteman National Historic Site in Lexington,

Massachusetts, the excavation of the Wellfleet Tavern on Cape Cod National Seashore, and investigations at the Salem Maritime National Historic Site in 1973.[21] At Saugus Iron Works National Historic Site, the NPS
also conducted an evaluation of Robbins's archaeological work in the
late 1940s and early 1950s, and performed new test excavations at the
site.[22] This work was carried out by archaeology graduate students in
the anthropology department at Brown University who conducted "an
evaluation of [Robbins's] project . . . from the standpoint of professional historical archaeology and its current standards."[23] In an attempt
to avoid a direct critique of Robbins's work, the authors explain that they
emphasize the assessment of the potential of the site for further archaeological work, "rather than . . . judging the quality of archaeology done
by Robbins."[24] While they provide a thoughtful and balanced analysis
and largely avoid judging Robbins's work, the very presence of the dis-
claimer in the introduction suggests their overall view of his work.[25] In
fact, the report makes little attempt to reassess Robbins's work in any interpretive way, other than to determine where he worked and to eliminate these areas as having potential for future excavations.

Although the discipline was changing, Schuyler notes, it was not until
the mid-1980s that historical archaeology began to shed "its famous
place and famous person styles of research and its historical particular-
ism," and practitioners began to address the "broader humanistic and
scientific goals" of anthropology.[26] University-based archaeologists perceived that this trend would bring progress and advancement to the
practice of historical archaeology; by the mid-1980s, they exulted in
the "apparent maturation in the discipline's intellectual, physical, and
emotional well-being."[27] Although members of the profession began to
establish a smooth, seamless veneer for the discipline, historical archaeology was far from unified in either its theory or its methods. Archaeologist William Adams boasted that earlier "shouting matches and temper
tantrums" had disappeared and been replaced with new theoretical developments, alliances with history, and increased "confidence and certain knowledge" in research directions.[28] Yet, Adams candidly admitted
that, even in 1993, historical archaeology was "basically at the sophomore
level; we think we know far more than we do, and we try to appear far
wiser than we really are."[29] For an emerging and marginal discipline, appearance was everything.

The mid-1980s witnessed the realization by many historical archaeologists of what Roland Robbins had long known: neither the exclusive

use of the humanistic or the scientific approaches "adequately addressed their research needs." Archaeological data, they found, could not be entirely understood within a scientific framework of laws and rules, because of the fundamental human agency of free will.[30] However, archaeological data could be collected and studied, and reports written, in a scientific manner, to allow comparison of the materials in and between sites.[31] Researchers attempting to address social and cultural behaviors needed systematically collected and reported scientific evidence in order to draw inferences from groups of excavated sites. During the 1980s, historical archaeologists began to study their excavated sites and materials within dynamic cultural systems, such as households and neighborhoods. Sites were no longer exclusively chosen by historical societies and museum staff interested in restoration; researchers began to prepare reports and essays that addressed larger cultural issues such as consumerism, community interaction, social control, racial dynamics, economic participation, and political manipulation. For a brief moment, when universities were prospering and government contracts were ample, historical archaeology sought the luxury of purely theoretically driven research. However, it could not long remain innocent of the demands of commerce and fund-raising.

In its anguished struggle to standardize and professionalize, the discipline rejected many of the earlier practitioners and their "amateurish" ways.[32] Professionals make claims to certain levels of technical performance and certain standards, and may be forced, as historical archaeologists did with Robbins, to label those outsiders who fall short of these levels and standards as "charlatans."[33] Less "professional members of the emerging profession resist these innovations, sometimes violently."[34] For a man like Robbins, with his fiercely individualistic and stubborn character, these changes were not easy to integrate into his established way of doing things. The discipline of historical archaeology labored hard during the 1970s and 1980s to separate itself from what it considered the unscientific and unprofessional restoration and preservation focus of its founders and also from those whom it saw as marginal practitioners, such as Robbins, who continued to hang on against all odds.

The long struggle by historical archaeology to define itself and its membership spanned the lifetime of Robbins. From the mid-1960s onward, he felt the repeated rejection of professionals as they tightened their ranks and sought to strengthen both their internal and external control over the discipline. These practitioners were attempting to distinguish the value of their training and education from Robbins's common-sense work experience, on-the-job training, and Yankee ingenuity. As early as 1869, Harvard's president Charles W. Eliot wrote that ignoring specialized training for professionals, particularly those in leadership positions, was a "national danger":

The vulgar conceit that a Yankee can turn his hand to anything we insensibly carry into high places, where it is preposterous and criminal. We are accustomed to seeing men leap from farm or shop to court-room or pulpit, and we half believe that common men can safely use the seven-league boots of genius.[35]

The balance between experience and on-the-job training versus university education has long been a topic of debate in archaeology and continues to the present. Archaeologist Dan Mouer has noted that archaeology is "really two very different sets of skills residing under the same roof."[36] Mouer views excavation and laboratory work as "really sophisticated crafts," the type of skills that could be learned by someone like Robbins through apprenticeship and on-the-job training. Sounding a bit like Robbins, he goes on to note that "no school work, per se, can teach someone how to dig a site." However, he sets these experiential skills against "the knowledge of theory, applications, and context" that must be gained in graduate school.[37] So practitioners without an advanced degree, like Robbins, were and are relegated to the position of craft specialist, to the status of "digging technician" as Harrington called it, with little chance for advancement or respect within the discipline. Also sounding like Robbins, archaeologist Steve Boxley lamented the value accorded university degrees over extensive experience, writing that he got the sense that "non-degreed people are fine for shovel work in the field, as long as they leave all the "important" theory work for the Ivory Towered degreed people."[38] For academics, experience was important, even essential for the archaeologist, but a professional had to have formal university training as well to pursue the larger questions of human experience and culture within the framework of anthropology.

As the archaeological profession united within the confines and strictures of the academy, Robbins became bitter and resentful and would often disparage professional archaeologists.[39] Robbins felt strongly that his extensive experience at historic and industrial sites was being overlooked and devalued by people who had, in his mind, much less experience. By the end of the 1960s, the professionals were looking down on

Robbins and his work, and their criticism became more frequent and odious.

In 1970, Robbins's autonomy to practice his craft and his ability to earn a living were directly challenged by archaeologist James Deetz. This confrontation developed out of Robbins's participation in planning a project to investigate a Plymouth-period site in Duxbury, Massachusetts. The 350th Anniversary Committee of the town of Duxbury wanted Robbins to "do a preliminary study of . . . old mill sites" in hopes of reconstructing one as its anniversary project.[40] Robbins and Pilgrim Society director Larry Geller inspected several mill and dam sites in the Duxbury area, and focused on what Geller reported was the "1st Pilgrim Mill" at the Holmes Dam.[41] The committee was very interested, and Geller informed Robbins that "things are moving fast."[42] Robbins arranged with artist Charles Overly to prepare a sketch of the site and visited the site again himself to take color slides; these would be used at a meeting to "to sell the town on the idea of making the site available for restoration purposes."[43]

The committee requested that Geller and Robbins prepare a brief statement about the survey and its costs, and Robbins recommended a study consisting of

selected clearing . . . at the dam . . . . archaeological tests . . . to determine if the existing dam is built upon the site and remnants of an earlier dam, or dams. A study of the deeds and records tracing the . . . mill to its origin and site. . . . a report on this survey which would include a plan recording the areas tested and photographs of this work.[44]

He also recommended additional work if "the preliminary survey revealed that evidence and remnants of Stephen Dean's corn mill survives."[45]

The proposal was forwarded to the committee; although it approved the preliminary survey, there were concerns that a reconstructed mill would conflict with a commercial gristmill operation in town. Prior to the next town meeting, which was to have discussed the plans, Geller received a call from Plimoth Plantation archaeologist James Deetz, who had "found out about the plans for the preliminary survey at the site . . . [and] was all upset . . . said they never had a mill before the 1630s, and didn't think Larry's research was thorough enough."[46] Robbins recorded in his log that he [Deetz] said that they (Plimoth Plantation) will do the dig free. He also said that my *Pilgrim John Alden's Progress* didn't tell anything new (sour grapes). Larry [Geller], to say the least, was all put out by Town Politics and Plimoth Plantation.[47]

Robbins later learned from Geller that "Deetz has been on the phone telling 'the right persons' that Plimoth Plantation will excavate the mill site for free. Naturally the town will not pay to have it excavated if they can get it done for free!"[48] Robbins complained to Geller that

Deetz and his bunch have never excavated a mill site (and the one they were engaged to do some work on [Oliver Mill Park] fired them after their first work as being most incompetent in this field). I said that in view of the fact the 350th Anniversary Committee was in charge of the project (of which I conceived the idea) I thought it only fair that they invite both Deetz and I to discuss with them our individual experiences in the field of excavating mill sites, particularly along rivers and tidewater ways. . . . AND OUR TALKS SHOULD BE ILLUSTRATED WITH PICTURES OF OUR WORK!!!!!![49]

Robbins could not match Deetz's educational qualifications, but he could challenge him to a duel of sorts. They could settle the dispute in the democratic arena of the New England town meeting, Robbins thought, based on real-world experience. Robbins's total disgust with the situation is evident in his comment that "THE DISHONESTY OF MANKIND SURFACES AGAIN!!!"[50] "All this," he noted, "is too local and complicated, let alone petty, for me to get further involved until they [the town] come to some agreement (if they ever do!)."[51]

Robbins's relationship with academic archaeologists continued to deteriorate as the decade unfolded. He found himself increasingly at odds with the world of university-based archaeology and its practitioners' aspirations to professionalize their approaches and methods from the security of their institutions. His sense of detachment from the discipline became crystal clear in 1973, when he received copies of reviews of his 1965–1966 work at the Hancock-Clarke House prepared by university-affiliated professionals.

In October 1964, the Lexington Historical Society had inquired of Robbins about the "possibility of locating the Hancock-Clarke House."[52] The structure, an early New England house museum, had been moved from its original site in the 1890s, yet members of the society "had dif-

ferent ideas as to where the house had once stood."[53] The site was originally the home of the Reverend John Hancock and later the Reverend
Jonas Clarke. Reverend Hancock had come to Lexington, Massachusetts,
in 1698 and built a small parsonage on the Hancock-Clarke House site.
It appears that Hancock's son Thomas, a wealthy Boston merchant, enlarged the house in the 1730s. The Reverend Clarke succeeded Hancock
as minister in 1752 and moved into the parsonage. The house was reportedly a stop on Paul Revere's infamous April 18, 1775 ride to Concord.
Colonial leaders John Hancock (Rev. John Hancock's grandson) and
Samuel Adams were staying with the Clarkes that evening, and Revere
stopped to bring the leaders news of the advancing British troops. The
house was acquired by the Lexington Historical Society in the late nineteenth century and moved from its original location. It was a desire to
return the house to its original location that brought Robbins to the site
in the mid-1960s.

Robbins visited the site in 1964 and began limited testing to determine the viability of a full-scale dig, quickly identifying a stone foundation wall.[54] Indecision within the society delayed the start of the project
until the fall of 1965.[55] After relocating the previously identified foundation (figure 6.1), Robbins and his crew began to "clean out the rubble
and soils that filled the cellar" of the 1698 house with a backhoe and shovels.[56] "The artifacts," he recorded, "were mostly of the late 19th-century
period."[57] After completing the 1698 house cellar (6-F1 in figure 6.1), the
workers excavated the fill from the adjacent 1734 house cellar (6-F2).[58]
Robbins noted that this cellar was filled "with coal and coal ashes and
contained bones, nails, a bone handled knife, a small bottle, glass etc. All
of this stuff looked of the late 19th century."[59] Robbins and crew next located a well northeast of the cellars, and a third cellar foundation (6-F3)
west of the 1698 cellar.[60] Excavation of this cellar was begun almost immediately. While working on the final excavations north of the 1698 cellar, yet another cellar (3-F1) was located that contained artifacts that
appeared to date exclusively to the eighteenth century.[61] This new cellar,
Robbins hypothesized, "must have been associated with the 1698 house."[62]

The following year, Robbins designed a dig-it-yourself screening area
to finish sifting the cellar fill for artifacts, and extended his testing to an
area behind the barn. He also identified another stone-lined cellar, west
of the northwest corner of cellar 6-F3.[63] Robbins hand excavated the cellar the next day and noted that "it appears to have been a narrow cooling
cellar . . . about $7\frac{1}{2}'$ in depth. . . . The few artifacts found were of a late

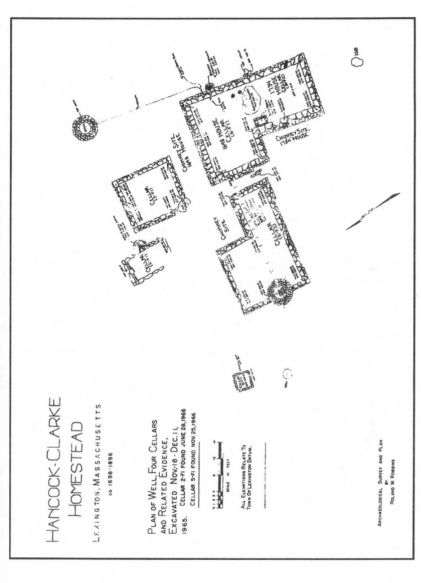

FIG. 6.1. Plan of the Hancock-Clarke Homestead excavations, Lexington, Mass., 1966. (Courtesy of the Roland Wells Robbins Collection, the Thoreau Society, Lincoln, Mass., and the Thoreau Institute at Walden Woods.)

nineteenth-century period, it would seem."[64] Following this excavation, he discovered that the Historical Society had decided not to proceed with any new work beyond removing the remaining soils, grading around several of the cellars, and testing at the tentative site of the new museum building.[65] Members of the society approached Robbins again in 1969 to investigate the well that he had identified in 1965, and he recorded that it

had been filled with stones from the foundation of the house when it was moved across the street in 1896 it would appear, based on the concrete on some of the stones and some of the brick evidence removed from the fill in the well.[66]

The removal of the fill proceeded to a depth of 10.5 feet, where water was encountered; the artifacts from the bottom were late nineteenth century.[67]

Robbins went to work on the analysis of excavation results within several weeks of completing the fieldwork, and he finished his manuscript report in 1966. "The Archaeological Excavations of the Hancock-Clarke Homestead" is a descriptive report and includes a brief review of the site history, a discussion of the master grid and datum, presentations on the excavation of the cellars and well, descriptions of the cellars, a brief presentation on the early artifacts recovered from cellars 6-F3 and 3-F1, a summary of the results, and recommendations for the site.[68] Like many of Robbins's earlier works, the report is written in a conversational style and organized chronologically, taking the reader through his approach to the problems and "controversies" encountered at the site. Typical of other restoration-oriented reports of the period, the Hancock-Clarke report is descriptive and pays little attention to artifacts or site interpretation. Unlike the earlier Alden report, the Hancock-Clarke report is almost exclusively a story of the dig, containing very little specific data.[69]

Robbins's work at the Hancock-Clarke House demonstrates an approach to excavation that certainly valued foundations over artifacts, and it illustrates some of the problems inherent in working with small historical societies (figure 6.2). Robbins's decisions about the excavations at the Hancock-Clarke House were initially influenced by the very specific goals of the Lexington Historical Society, related to locating and excavating the foundations in advance of moving the house back to its original site.

Robbins's management of this project was typical of his arrangements with local historical societies and other associations. The project was controlled by a written agreement with the society that detailed the

FIG. 6.2. Lexington Historical Society board members visit the Hancock-Clarke excavations. (Courtesy of the Roland Wells Robbins Collection, the Thoreau Society, Lincoln, Mass., and the Thoreau Institute at Walden Woods.)

expectations of both parties. Robbins was to excavate the original foundations of the house "archaeologically in a careful and professional manner so that the excavation shall preserve all pertinent evidence dating before the twentieth century."[70] Robbins was to provide the labor, materials, tools and equipment, engineering, photography, and insurance, pay for all other associated expenses, and prepare a final report; the excavated soils were to be screened by society volunteers.

The restoration and contract–oriented nature of the Hancock-Clarke project influenced the archaeological research design, particularly in terms of the time and money available to Robbins to complete the work. Both the Lexington Historical Society and Robbins went into the project with the very specific goal of locating and excavating the cellar of the house that had been moved in 1896. The society hoped to eventually relocate the house on its original site.[71] The discovery of additional cellars (6-F3 and 3-F1) was unexpected and surprised both parties. Robbins felt that he had provided extra service by excavating the newly discovered cellars (6-F3 and 3-F1), and he used much the same techniques that he had determined adequate for the cellars that held the house at the time of its move in 1896 (6-F1 and 6-F2). Although he reasoned that the new cellars had been abandoned and filled prior to the nineteenth century, Robbins did not excavate the fill in these cellars with the types of stratigraphic controls that would likely have been used by his academic colleagues.

The response of academic archaeologists to Robbins's work at the Hancock-Clarke site was damning. A 1971 review by archaeologist Charles W. Tremer begins with a section that sets Tremer up as the professional expert, defining for his audience the differences between amateurs and professionals.[72] It is "indeed unfortunate," he writes, "that a professional archaeologist was not consulted or employed to direct the excavations of so important a site."[73] Although amateur archaeologists like Robbins make meaningful contributions to the discipline, Tremer notes that "amateurs are just that—amateurs."[74] "Amateur archaeologists," he continues in a stream of professional jargon,

rarely have the formal training and theoretical conceptualization to appreciate the archaeological problem, and the methods that must be employed in order to extract the fullest possible knowledge from the artifactual and structural remains. The unfortunate result is usually that a site excavated in this manner— lacking valid methods and conceptualization of the archaeological problem as seen by the professional archaeologist—gives little knowledge toward explaining the problems at hand. And more important is that the excavation techniques that have been erroneously employed cause the destruction of parts of the site and loss of knowledge that then cannot be recovered.[75]

This scenario, Tremer reports, prevailed at the Hancock-Clarke site, where "the excavations conducted in 1965–1966 by Mr. Robbins reflect no appreciation or understanding of the archaeological problem at hand, but rather the crude clearing of the stone foundations."[76] The basic problems with Robbins's approach and excavation techniques were "the use of a back-hoe and the ignoring of any possible vertical stratigraphy present in the foundation fill [which] has prevented any possible analysis that might have answered the questions present."[77] The usefulness of the artifacts has been lost, Tremer reports, "due to the lack of sufficient records being kept as to location, provenience, and so on."[78] Robbins's report, he writes, "cannot be considered an archaeological report. It is a description of various procedures of probing and digging."[79] Furthermore, the report "does not conceptualize the archaeological problem, and synthesize the artifactual and structural remains found in any way that would help explain or clarify the historical sequence at the H-C site."[80] Although Tremer writes that he, as a professional archaeologist, "did not want to disparage the ambitious efforts of Mr. Robbins . . . , it must be recognized that the previous excavations have fallen far short of acceptance, and at times prove to be destructive to the valid reconstruction of the historical sequence of the H-C house."[81]

In a subsequent review, archaeologist James Deetz of Plimoth Plantation agreed with Tremer about the problems with Robbins's work. According to Deetz, the problems with Robbins's work were related to "inadequate excavation procedures and virtually non-existent analytical work following the completion of the field exercise."[82] However, Deetz noted, "since the site cannot be re-done in another way, the most reasonable course is to work as efficiently as possible with that which is available."[83] Deetz argued that Robbins's excavation techniques precluded any type of vertical stratigraphic control within the cellar fill. Based on the techniques of recovery and a brief review of the artifacts, he believed that it would be quite difficult to resolve the problems of temporal and functional relationships between the four cellars. He noted that "it is absolutely standard and proper procedure in excavating cellars to remove them by hand, using trowels, and controlling this excavation in some type of vertical sections."[84] Prior to the complete excavation, Deetz continued, a small test excavation is made to "determine the extent and nature of the layering . . . the results . . . are used as a guide for the subsequent removal of the cellar fill."[85] "Removal of untested fill," he cautioned, "particularly with power shovels, is in the worst tradition of 'Williamsburg' archaeology of the 1930's, to put it mildly."[86]

Deetz's likening of Robbins's work at Hancock-Clarke to the early Williamsburg excavation suggests that he did not have all of Robbins's field notes and documentation or did not use them in his assessment of the project.[87] For instance, Robbins reports that he dug small tests along the walls in several of the cellars to determine the nature and depth of the fill prior to mechanical excavation, recording this information in his daily log and photo logs.[88] Photographs of the work also indicate that, even when working exclusively with power equipment, Robbins would establish a trench cut through the cellar and then excavate using the profile as a guide. In the case of the first two cellars, historical research suggested that they had been filled in 1896 when the house was moved, and

this was confirmed by the artifacts; therefore, Robbins felt justified in removing them as a single context.[89]

Deetz noted that questions remained concerning nonexcavated or
partially excavated features such as the chimneys. He also explained that
the house may have been bigger than the cellars, sitting on footers or
piers, a point also considered by Robbins.[90] The remaining questions,
Deetz summarized, could be answered by careful study of the artifacts
and additional excavation around the house to identify features that were
not excavated or only partially excavated by Robbins.[91] Deetz felt that an
analysis of the artifact collection and reexcavation of the cellars might be
all that was necessary to answer the temporal and functional questions
necessary for moving the house back to its original site.[92]

Although Robbins did not record his reaction to these negative com-
mentaries when he received them in November 1973, they caused a heated
dispute within the ranks of the Lexington Historical Society. Charles H.
Cole II, a local architect and board member of the society, wrote an
angry letter to Roland B. Greeley, president of the society.[93] Cole noted
that the Tremer report was "extremely critical in every way of the work
of the archaeologist."[94] "I would like to know who authorized such a
study," he wrote:

I can't help but feel that it was a most unethical procedure. As a professional architect, I know it would be very unethical in my profession to do such a thing
without notifying the original professional hired.[95]

Cole noted that the Deetz report on stabilizing the ruins "digresses into
criticism of the original exploration," although the comments are relatively mild.[96] The real issue for Cole was the original contract between
the society and Robbins, and from his point of view "the Society, for
their $3,000, got far more than their money's worth."[97] "If they wanted
an Indian culture unearthed of 2000 or more years, or the Hancock-
Clarke house site excavated in that manner, they should have been prepared to pay ten times as much, —and believe me, what they did pay was
all they could afford at the time."[98] Cole ended the letter by requesting
an apology to Robbins for "extremely unethical conduct." "Furthermore," he wrote, "if anyone knows how to preserve existing excavated
historical sites your original archaeologist can do it better than most. You
have only to inspect his restoration of foundations in the Fort Ticon-
deroga area to know that!" Ironically, Robbins's work in the Fort Ticon-

deroga area at Crown Point was by this time being severely criticized by professional archaeologists as well.[99]

While Robbins certainly resented the comments of Tremer and Deetz, it appears that he did not voice his opinion at the time. However, the episode undeniably had the effect of making him more wary of academic practitioners in the developing discipline of historical archaeology, and it no doubt reinforced the view of critics within the professional community that this type of outcome was to be expected from the work of "amateurs" like Robbins. Once again Robbins had been reminded of his shortcomings by professional archaeologists. The result was to bring out his populism and his representation of himself as the "Pick and Shovel Historian," the self-educated everyman with Yankee common sense and a healthy respect for the past.[100] Scorning the professionals' attempted control, he pressed forward with his own brand of archaeological research and restoration, one that unquestionably continued to do some damage to the sites he excavated.

The dismissal of Robbins's work by Tremer and Deetz also depicts the growing intellectual differences between the "amateur" Robbins and the new university "professionals." In the spirit of his generation, Robbins searched for foundations. His essential assumption was that his own modern culture could be deduced from and inspired by a return to its origins. By contrast, the next generation of researchers embraced an anthropological conception of culture, which could envision that earlier Americans had a worldview and way of life radically different from our own. For instance, Deetz's *In Small Things Forgotten* (1977) put historical archaeology firmly in the service of cultural history and advanced the field of material culture studies.[101] Paradoxically, in developing his picture of the changing worldview of early Americans, Deetz drew on Robbins's excavation of the John Alden House.[102] While in one sense their work was worlds apart, in another sense Deetz imitated Robbins. He used the literary devices pioneered by Robbins, including writing in a popular style and surrounding the text with the romance of archaeology. Deetz exploited the drama of uncovering the past and, like Robbins, even interjected the rhetoric of controversy with a discussion of the "Valley of the Moon" and "Mystery Hill" sites.[103] Both the title and the introduction of Deetz's book are reminiscent of Robbins's *Hidden America*, implying that the historical archaeologist recovers the neglected and the obscure, showing the hidden significance in the ruins and artifacts below ground.[104]

Robbins persisted in his search for foundations throughout the 1970s. He continued his work for small historical societies, bicentennial committees, and municipalities, supplementing these projects with contracts conducted under recently enacted federal preservation legislation. Although cultural resource management (CRM) had its formal beginnings in the Antiquities Act of 1906, it was not until the passage of the National Historic Preservation Act in 1966 (amended 1980) and the National Environmental Policy Act (NEPA) in 1969 that a solid foundation was laid for the protection of these resources.[105] The passage of this legislation precipitated a dramatic upsurge in the demand for contracted archaeological services. By 1980, a survey of the membership of the Society for Historical Archaeology (SHA) indicated that over half of the members worked within a "federally-mandated historic preservation framework."[106] The fundamental legislative changes that affected archaeology and the influence of the bicentennial are reflected in the growth of membership in the SHA from approximately 300 in 1970 to over 1,400 by 1980.[107] While the bicentennial celebration was, according to archaeologist Bert Salwen, an "attractive and interesting, but transitory," phenomenon, the establishment of a strong national preservation program brought major, lasting change to the practice of archaeology.[108]

The rapid growth in contract archaeology quickly outdistanced the discipline's ability to manage issues such as personnel and quality standards. The combination of new contract projects and the demand created by the bicentennial for archaeological excavations at small historical museums and municipal properties quickly depleted the already meager contingent of archaeologists qualified for and/or interested in performing historical excavations. University-based research organizations, such as Deetz's research center at Brown University, were simply unable or unwilling to take on many of these small jobs.[109]

Robbins, already familiar with the world of consulting and contracts, successfully competed for these projects, particularly those from small museums and bicentennial committees. He was less successful with cultural resource management projects because the academic community began to tighten the standards of research as federal agencies issued more specific guidelines. At the same time, major archaeological organizations such as the Society for American Archaeology recommended certification of professionals and began to craft minimal standards and codes of ethics for archaeological research.[110]

In the early 1970s, Robbins ran headlong into the discipline's push for higher standards when officials of the National Park Service rejected his qualifications as an archaeologist. Following a lecture by Robbins to the Historic Wethersfield Foundation in Wethersfield, Connecticut, William J. Morris, director of the Connecticut Historical Commission, approached Robbins and indicated that he was interested in acquiring his services as a consultant for the commission. Because the work in question was federally funded, Morris submitted Robbins's name and résumé to the keeper of the National Register for review. Morris reported to Robbins that the keeper replied that Robbins's "qualifications did not meet their [National Register] criteria."[111] The matter was referred to the National Park Service, which concluded that Robbins did not have certain "academic credits to qualify for government work." Morris noted that "it seems that on occasion you have committed the cardinal sin of utilizing mechanical equipment which apparently cannot be tolerated under any circumstances."[112] He added that "I want you to know that my opinion of you and your work has not changed one iota."[113]

Although Robbins cavalierly wrote to Morris that "I was delighted to learn that the National Park Service refused to accept my qualifications," he was both devastated and outraged by this rejection of everything that he had worked for during his long career.[114] He immediately enlisted Senator Edward W. Brooke of Massachusetts to help in clearing his name. Explaining the problems that the Connecticut Historical Commission had encountered with the keeper of the National Register and the National Park Service, Robbins defended his previous work and use of mechanical equipment.[115] He cited his work at Saugus, where he had learned to

use the appropriate tools and equipment, mechanical or otherwise, to accomplish the job that had to be done. This included excavations that couldn't hope to be achieved with shovels and trowels alone.

THERE WOULD BE NO NATIONAL PARK TODAY AT THE SAUGUS IRON WORKS RESTORATION IF I HAD NEGLECTED TO USE MECHANICAL EQUIPMENT THERE WHEN IT WAS NEEDED AND WHERE IT WAS NEEDED! THE MASSIVE EXCAVATIONS THAT UNEARTHED THE ENTIRE BASIC PLAN AND RUINS OF THE ANCIENT SAUGUS IRON WORKS WERE COMPLETELY SUCCESSFUL ONLY BECAUSE OF THE PROPER USE OF MECHANICAL EQUIPMENT AND HAND TOOLS![116]

Robbins closed his long letter to Brooke by noting that "there is something terribly wrong with their system [National Park Service] when a person who has excelled in his profession . . . finds that he cannot assist his government with his talents because of some bureaucratic pitfall."[117]

Senator Brooke wrote to Robbins that he had asked the Park Service for a "complete report" on the situation.[118] Having received no answer from Brooke, Robbins inquired in September 1970 and again in February 1971.[119] In April 1971, Senator Brooke forwarded a reply from the Park Service but noted that "it seems to me that the Park Service has not completely answered your questions."[120]

The Park Service reply from Acting Director Raymond L. Freeman is, as Brooke hints, a classic bureaucratic evasion of the question. In fact, it is nothing more than a description of the process for designation of the state historic preservation officer (SHPO) under the National Historic Preservation Act of 1966.[121] Morris wrote to Robbins that, "having seen a copy of Mr. Freeman's reply to Senator Brooke, I most heartily agree [with the senator] that it was evasive to the point of being childish."[122] In May 1971, Robbins wrote to Senator Brooke in reply to Freeman's letter:

Mr. Freeman evaded answering specific questions that for the past year I have endeavored to find answers for. The questions pertain to why a citizen with my vast and most successful experience as a consultant on Colonial and Early American Landmarks and Their Restoration cannot be engaged on projects that are receiving Federal subsidies.[123]

He ended his letter by asserting that "my twenty-three years of outstanding achievement in the field of Historical Restoration work does not qualify me for acceptance to the National Register, according to the National Park Service. I want a specific answer to this decision."[124]

In July 1971, Senator Brooke forwarded another reply from Acting Director Freeman.[125] Freeman explained that

Mr. Robbins indicates that State and municipalities may not engage him and receive Government assistance. The National Park Service has not, nor could it, set any condition which would prohibit State and local authorities from employing Mr. Robbins.[126]

While this answer seems to have satisfied Robbins, it still avoids the primary question of professional qualifications required by the keeper of the National Register and the National Park Service for participating in federal projects under historic preservation legislation.

Even with the formal ruling by the NPS regarding his lack of qualifications, Robbins completed five projects within the framework of Section 106 of the NHPA between 1971 and 1980. He obtained these projects through his network of contacts in New England archaeology and preservation, for example, Dr. Maurice Robbins (no relation) of the Massachusetts Historical Commission and William J. Morris of the Connecticut Historical Commission.[127] With his attention focused on projects that were generated by interest in the bicentennial celebration, Robbins pursued no CRM-related work in the mid-1970s. When his bicentennial projects waned, he picked up several more Section 106 investigations.

In the years immediately preceding the nation's bicentennial, Robbins was engaged to work on six separate archaeological excavations that grew out of local communities' desires to commemorate the event. In 1974 and 1976, he excavated at the Governor Moses Gill Mansion in Princeton, Massachusetts. Working for the Princeton Bicentennial Committee, Robbins performed a small survey that involved excavations to identify and mark the location of the house site. Robbins also worked on the Moore Memorial State Park project in Paxton, Massachusetts, performing excavation and restoration work on an early mill. In 1975 and 1976, he returned to the Oliver Mill Park in Middleborough, Massachusetts, and also completed a preliminary survey to locate and mark the site of the Lexington Meeting House for the Lexington Bicentennial Committee. The final two bicentennial ventures were an excavation and restoration project at the Rogers-Sheldon East Bridgewater Iron Works and a survey of the Clinton Blast Furnace. These projects all had small budgets with very limited goals. In almost every case, they were directed primarily at locating and marking or partially restoring significant sites within the community as physical reminders of the past.

Robbins remained busy with lectures and seminars up through the bicentennial, and also participated in several university programs. In the bicentennial year he was invited to Juniata State College in Huntingdon, Pennsylvania, as lecturer-in-residence. Robbins was recommended for this endowed visiting scholar program by English Department faculty member Jack Troy, a longtime Thoreau Society member and acquaintance of Robbins. During his stay at Juniata, Robbins presented public slide lectures and met with students and faculty.[128] Troy introduced Robbins to Paul Heberling, an archaeologist in the school's Anthropology Department, and the two became fast friends. Heberling remembers that the faculty loved Robbins's lectures; however, "the students were a bit jaded."[129] Roland had an "intense interest and enthusiasm for every-thing he did," and it soon wore off on Heberling.[130] He remembers being fascinated by their trips to local sites, particularly ironworks. Robbins, he recalled, would just walk around and point out where the industrial features would be found; "he has such an astute, alert awareness of iron complexes that he immediately would recognize what he had."[131] "I don't think," Heberling continued, "that he had any peer in the details and understanding of ironworks."[132] Although Heberling could not evaluate Robbins's impact on the students, he stated emphatically that "Roland was individually responsible for a change in interest [from pre-historic to historical archaeology] on my part."[133]

Spurred by the nation's birthday celebration, the 1970s also witnessed the rise of a new public history movement, and Robbins found himself to be a natural proponent. He was a popularizer with a long-term inter-est in bringing historical archaeology to the masses and in helping them to participate in digs themselves. In *Old Glory: A Pictorial Report on the Grass Roots History Movement and the First Hometown History Primer*, editor James Robert noted that there was

a new breed of archaeologist out digging up the past, cataloguing everything they find, and then struggling to put these ancient clues together. They aren't professionals—they're just ordinary curious people—secretaries, truck drivers, students. . . . who are coming out in ever-increasing numbers to work alongside professional archaeologists.[134]

Robert described the extensive volunteer training program and oppor-tunities available through the Arkansas Archaeology Survey, and noted that "prehistoric archaeology requires a certain amount of experience and expertise. . . . Purely Historic Archaeology—such as Roland Robbins is involved in—is something you can do yourself, right now."[135] Rob-bins, Robert continued,

is not a popular man among elitist archaeologists. Not only do they consider him personally unqualified to be carrying out archaeological research, but the fact that he dares advocate that others follow his example and begin digging up American history too—well, that's dreadful. . . . He stresses his belief that his-tory under the ground belongs to every American, and anyone has a right to do first-hand research (if he obtains permission from the landowner). Of course, Robbins insists that amateur archaeologists fulfill their responsibilities to soci-ety, too—orderly, careful work; complete cataloging; excavation for the sake of knowledge and not to collect trinkets.[136]

Although Robbins embraced the democratization of archaeology, he also stressed the absolute necessity of careful fieldwork and proper recording. To some extent, Robbins imagined that a commonsense application of excavation techniques and the ability to meticulously record and document the work came as easily to everyone as it did to him. As *Hidden America* reviewers Cotter and Leder noted, in this sense he undervalued his skills and overstressed his extensive self-education. "Mr. Robbins does a disservice," Leder commented, "by overemphasizing the idea that he is self-educated without explaining the extent to which he has educated himself."[137] Robbins's focus on self-education derived from both a long-term pride in his accomplishments and an insecurity about his lack of formal education. His push for others to follow his road, to become archaeologists themselves, is not surprising. This approach was another way for him to validate his own work and fulfill his "quest for credentials of merit," and by this point it also gave him some satisfaction knowing that this position rankled academic archaeologists.[138] *Hidden America* coauthor Evan Jones observed that

if any professionals would have treated Robbie as an equal and worked with him, they would have found him cooperative and charming. He hated to be condescended to by professionals, either archaeologists or historians, and made to think that he was just a digger. . . . Robbie was very intelligent—he was much smarter than most of them gave him credit for.[139]

Robbins was determined to make his own way and bemoaned in 1971 that

the thing that has screwed up progress in the Historic Sites field is the name itself, and the limitation of the training and the lack of vision found in the "professionals" in this field. Very little will ever be accomplished in the Historic Sites sciences until it, and the people administering its present policies mature. This may be a long time in the making. And I don't plan to wait around until the field "grows up."[140]

By the end of the decade, Robbins was both ignored and mocked by the professional community while presenting his work at the Dublin Seminar for New England Folklife's conference "New England Historical Archaeology."[141] Robbins was initially baffled by a letter from program chairman Marley R. Brown III, who wrote to confirm his lecture title: "The Future of Historical Archaeology in New England." "It sounds," Brown noted, "like it will be extremely interesting and should provide the basis for an enlightening discussion."[142] Robbins replied to Brown that "an error has been made in [the title of my talk], a subject I would not venture to intrude upon." Robbins went on to inform Brown that his illustrated talk was titled "History Recycled." "It will demonstrate how old industrial sites, deserted years ago and reclaimed by nature and wildness, are found, excavated, repaired and rehabilitated for recreational and park purposes."[143]

Robbins traveled to the Dublin School prior to the seminar to set up his exhibit of color photographs. During this visit, he met with organizer Peter Benes and donated one hundred autographed copies of his book *Pilgrim John Alden's Progress* and fifty copies of *The Story of the Minute Man,* noting in his journal that "these are to be sold, with all money going into their [Dublin Seminar] fund."[144] While the others were at lunch, Robbins edited his talk, pathetically noting that "I wasn't invited to eat, [but] Peter did bring me back a cup of coffee."[145]

The lecture was for Robbins the supreme embarrassment. He lamented in his journal that "MY TALK WAS A DISMAL FAILURE!!!"

I must say that I was not in good speaking form . . . and I got *no encouragement* from the audience, and I was aware of snickering and distracting and unattentiveness. . . . To say the least a rude and brainwashed audience! Their whole movement appears to have a propaganda basis that discounts my life work. . . . Work that most of them could never achieve, even if they want to follow in my footsteps!!!

No one talked to me after the meeting. . . . Looked through me as though I wasn't present! No one mentioned my exhibit, nor offered to help dismantle it, or carry it out in the pouring rain!! *To say the least, I found myself in a most embarrassing position* I can ever recall that would be associated with my professional work!!!

Well, I had to find out . . . and I did. I shall simply travel my way alone with any future programming I undertake. I can't believe that they could look at clearly defined major projects showing the highlights of the before-during and after results and not be responsive!![146]

Program chairman Marley Brown has quite a different recollection of Robbins's presentation. He remembers really enjoying Robbins's talk:

I was very impressed with Roland's lecture, it was extremely well done, both a good presentation and excellent use of slides. His lecture was on par with most of the seminar's papers and his archaeology was better than most of the non-academic archaeologists on the program.[147]

Although Brown did not specifically remember any negative comments or "snickering," he acknowledged that it was certainly very possible.[148] The younger graduate students in the audience, Brown continued, particularly those who had worked with Jim Deetz, may have had a negative opinion of Robbins. Deetz was openly vocal about his contempt for Robbins and his work, and harbored a general disregard for contract archaeology.[149] Brown conjectured that Robbins's consulting work had created ill will among the young professionals; "we were doing this work for free as Deetz's students and Robbins was working right down the road and getting paid for it."[150] It is not just ironic, but significant, that although Deetz worked from the security of the university, many of his graduate students—those who scorned Robbins's hucksterism, that is, his self-promotion of archaeology as a business—were later employed in contract archaeology or cultural resource management.[151] They were compelled to practice contract archaeology because of underlying economic and political circumstances. As these university-trained archaeologists slowly began to embrace cultural resource management as a legitimate pursuit, they faced many of the same conditions that Robbins had encountered during his thirty-five-year career, including institutional constraints, monetary pressures, and lack of standing within the discipline.[152] In this sense, Robbins's career has much to say to the archaeologists of today who work in an environment of retrenchment in higher education and disappearing funding for the humanities.[153]

Having repeatedly suffered dismissals by professional archaeologists, Robbins became bitter. He perceived academics as hypocrites; they were actively engaging in the business of archaeology and began employing many of the methods, such as excavation with heavy equipment, for which he had earlier been criticized. He frequently noted that he accomplished a task in a much simpler fashion than many "professional colleagues" with all their scientific techniques and tools. In a 1985 interview, he anxiously noted that academic archaeologists are "the most insecure people I ever encountered. . . . they have to have a committee agree before sticking a spade in the ground. The man who works alone, Thoreau used to say, can leave today."[154] For Robbins, the archaeologists had, in Thoreau's words, "become the tools of their tools."[155] He saw them as afraid to vacate the safety of the classroom, using "improved means to an unimproved end."[156] Robbins rebelled against the control that the scientific archaeological community exerted on his ability to earn a living and share his study of the past with the public. In the face of repeated disapproval and criticism, he continued to work on smaller

FIG. 6.3. Roland W. Robbins in 1976. (Photograph by Keith Martin.)
(Courtesy of Geraldine Robbins.)

projects generated through the enthusiasm of the bicentennial celebration and based on his local reputation with historical societies and
museums.[157]

For most of his life, Robbins had loved his work with a great passion
and thus remained positive and philosophical about his career, even as
he harbored tremendous bitterness toward the academy (figure 6.3).
However, as he grew older, he began to worry that his lifetime of archaeological research had amounted to very little. Thoreau scholar Brad
Dean remembers Robbins during the 1970s and 1980s as "a bitter old
man very concerned that his contribution be recognized."[158] When his

health began to decline in the summer of 1982, Robbins felt an urge to make a pilgrimage to sites that he had excavated during his career. Mrs. Robbins recalled that they initially visited several small sites, stopping only briefly. "When we got to Sleepy Hollow [Philipsburg Manor]," she continued, "he did go around quite a bit more [but was disturbed that nobody recognized him]. He was really quite depressed after that. I think he had begun to have a feeling that he had worked so hard and this was all he got—it wasn't satisfying to him."[159] During his slow recovery from major heart surgery in the fall of 1982, Robbins began to organize his immense collection of personal papers and photographic materials. He had hoped to sell his papers and slides to a major repository both to protect them and to help provide for his family when he died. Although he wrote dozens of letters and found institutions that would accept the collection as a donation, none would buy it.[160] Kristina Joyce, a local artist who helped Robbins with the second edition of *Thru the Covered Bridge,* remembered that

he was aware of the fact that his life was drawing to a close, and I got the feeling that he wanted to communicate to a younger person who didn't know anything about his past—to show me all the things he had done—I think that he wanted to be appreciated by a person of the next generation.[161]

For all of his lack of confidence and the controversy that surrounded his career, Roland Robbins was a pioneer in both industrial and historical archaeology, made important contributions to contract archaeology, and developed an approach to presenting archaeology to the public that would eventually be adopted as standard practice in the profession.[162] It is evident that Robbins lived from project to project and contract to contract and, at an early date, had to fashion his own set of approaches to the practice of historical archaeology that echo many of the conventions of modern cultural resource management. He worked hard to earn a living in a very new and unstable environment. Robbins administered his projects professionally and had many successful years from consulting, although his yearly workload and income fluctuated greatly. He remained flexible, never completely giving up the odd-jobs work that filled in between archaeological contracts. He rarely became "despondent or down in the dumps about the lack of work in archaeology," noted his wife Geraldine.[163] He wrote in his tenacious Yankee style in 1967 that "when things get tough, and they have since the year began, both business-wise and lecture-wise, there isn't a damn thing I can do about it except complain and keep on plugging."[164]

From the beginning of his career, Robbins's earnings as a consultant were supplemented by lecturing and odd-jobs work. Geraldine Robbins recalled that "he really never gave up the [window-washing] business; he left the door open . . . [and in] several slow times went back to [it]."[165] Robbins's successes in consulting were due to his savvy approach to marketing and to the management of his contracts. In this sense, he was ahead of most cultural resource consultants, then principally academics, who lacked business and management skills. Robbins scheduled short survey jobs between his larger projects and even during his vacations from the longer projects, because he knew that these small "preliminary survey" jobs could turn into more extended projects—and, often enough, they did. Therefore, he considered it important to do several of these each year, often pro bono or at least for reduced fees. As mentioned above, Robbins used a variety of direct-marketing approaches, such as letters of introduction and brochures, lectures, and preliminary surveys, to obtain new projects. Because of his early reputation for good work, he received important referrals from his clients, whether small historical societies or local governments.

Robbins ultimately succeeded in locating and reconstructing important American monuments and in capturing the public's interest. He accomplished a great deal during his career, excavating and restoring many early domestic, commercial, and industrial sites using a methodical and thoughtful approach that particularly suited his goals. In the end, these goals of locating and restoring foundations and buildings, and some of the methods he used to accomplish them, directly resulted in the destruction of irreplaceable archaeological information and data. Yet, at the same time, he also pioneered various approaches to excavating and analysis, particularly at industrial sites, that reflect many aspects of the discipline's evolving practice. In this sense, the legacy of his work is complex and complicated.

Beyond a doubt, Robbins excavated more early ironworks sites than any other archaeologist of the period, and he was completely familiar with the entire process of iron making. Industrial archaeology, formally established in the early 1950s, had a long tradition as an avocational pursuit in England.[166] Although several studies on industrial sites had been published in the United States by the late 1960s, and the subject had gained some popular attention, it was the late 1970s before it "made itself known in the university curriculum."[167] As suggested earlier, Robbins's interest in industrial sites can be examined from within the long-standing tradition of Yankee tinkerers. His preoccupation with these sites stemmed from his roots as a manual laborer and his innate curiosity about how things worked, particularly mechanical devices and processes.

Robbins's work at industrial as well as domestic and military sites was informed by his excellent visual skills: "he was very astute visually . . . he saw so much, not just in detail, but in terms of landscape and relationships of landscape."[168] Archaeologist Paul Heberling recalled a visit that he and Robbins made to the Greenwood Furnace: "He just walked around and looked at the terrain." "He had such an astute, alert awareness of iron complexes," Heberling continued, "that he immediately recognized what he had."[169] Robbins's passionate pursuit of and research on industrial sites resulted in the accumulation of a tremendous wealth of archaeological and historical data on a variety of early enterprises that has real value to address present research questions and concerns.[170]

Throughout his extended career in archaeological and historical research, Robbins supported himself and his family and cultivated a vocation that temporarily offered him the satisfaction, success, and recognition he sought. While his work was understandably questioned and rejected by many academically trained archaeologists, it was eagerly welcomed by the general public, who visited and participated in his projects by the thousands. Reviews and comments on his publications and presentations indicate that he succeeded in making "history come alive . . . , [in] making something live again in people's imaginations."[171] Through his lectures, volunteer and dig-it-yourself programs, and teaching opportunities, Robbins skillfully conveyed to eager students the excitement and importance of historical archaeology. Thomas Blanding remembered that although Roland enjoyed the attention of the public, "he was a very giving, generous-spirited person. I think in many ways he was a born teacher."[172]

Since the early 1980s, public archaeology has developed into an organized subarea within both prehistoric and historical archaeology.[173] This has come about through the advent of post-processual archaeological theories and a reawakened awareness that public support is essential for the long-term survival and development of the discipline.[174] Robbins's school programs and hands-on projects anticipated the current integration of archaeology into the school curriculum by twenty-five to thirty years. For instance, he became involved with an outdoor education program administered by the Ridgewood Public Schools in Ridgewood, New Jersey, in 1966. The program was designed to provide outdoor educational activities in "archaeology, cartography, conservation, geology, history, and pond ecology."[175] Each summer for several days, Robbins introduced students to field archaeology. In the second year, the students discovered the pre–Revolutionary War Hewitt Iron Works furnace in Ringwood State Park. Over the next five years, Robbins worked with the students to explore and excavate the furnace site. School superintendent Malcolm Katz wrote to Robbins that

> the experience that our junior high school students had with you was the most stimulating and worthwhile educational experience we have been able to provide. Your ability to capture the interests of these young people and to work with them such that they felt the "scent of discovery" was at the heart of their learning during that week.[176]

The director of the Ridgewood outdoor education program explained to Robbins that educators across the country were beginning to see the importance of this type of hands-on learning experience, and ended by telling him that "your effect upon children and adults, as a teacher, is of such magnitude that one can not help but wish you were a member of our staff."[177]

Robbins pioneered the development of public archaeology in schools, at sites, and through his publications and lectures. Paul Heberling has argued that Robbins's major contributions were to "get people interested in archaeology and bring attention to historic-sites archaeology," in that order.[178] "He saw it almost as a mission," remembered Heberling, "getting people involved in these sites so that they could participate in their own heritage."[179] Much of Robbins's message to the public focused on the importance of the tangible remains of the past and the thrill of discovery. James Deetz has eloquently described the importance of the emotional appeal of the past and its connection to intellectual pursuits. Using Robbins's excavation at Saugus as his example, Deetz writes:

> One can look at the ironworking equipment excavated at seventeenth-century Saugus, Massachusetts, and point out that it tells us a story of early attempts at ironworking in the colonies. One can even suggest that the excavation led investigators into an area of research on seventeenth-century ironworking technology that might not have been pursued had the archaeology not been done. Yet the equipment per se tells us little new about the subject, for its history and technology are well attested to in documents, both in England and America. So to justify the excavation of this material in intellectual terms is a shaky propo-

sition. But the emotional impact of these objects is palpable, reminding us in ways that no written account could of what it must have been like in the rough New England frontier, trying to develop a technology in the face of considerable odds. That is the true value of such objects, and if by some chance they do contribute something new to our knowledge, well and good. But they need not, for it is their intrinsic worth that justifies their recovery.[180]

Ironically, more than thirty years earlier, Robbins revealed to a radio audience in New York that he had worked under the same emotional attraction. "I think the thing that interested me [at Saugus]," he recalled,

was that it was so ingenious in being able to take and harness this rough country in all its aspects, not only build docks at the head of the river, but there nature had been very generous with ore deposits and large trees that could be felled and converted to charcoal for fuel.[181]

As Robbins argued for decades, it is equally important to convey this emotional aspect of archaeology to the public. Deetz adds:

If the field is to continue to grow and prosper . . . it is imperative that the emotional content of our subject not be buried beneath layers of dull, jargon-ridden reporting. This is not to suggest that the artifacts themselves be celebrated . . . context is all important. But we must also not lose sight of the intrinsic worth of those things which we also consider in their associational context and relative numbers.[182]

In many cases, however, by continuing to "find things out in his own way," focusing on the emotional impact of archaeology and its ruins, and continuing to excavate well into his retirement years, Robbins, like other pioneers, destroyed important archaeological information at sites. The central failing of his work at many of the sites he investigated relates to insufficient and/or inconsistent attention to recording and proveniencing artifacts in terms of their vertical position in the soil. This information is essential for understanding the way in which a site developed and the relationships between artifacts and features, such as foundations or cellars, and thus for interpretation of site chronology and function. Although information was regrettably lost, particularly in his later projects, Robbins's meticulous documentation and recording of all his work at these sites mitigates this loss to some extent by providing a tremendous body of detailed information that allows current researchers to

tease out new data for interpretation.[183] The quality of his documentation is so thorough that his excavations have the potential to provide
even more usable data than that available from many "professionally"
excavated sites of the period.

To the dismay of the professional archaeological community, Robbins
also actively encouraged the general public to become "pick and shovel
historians," declaring that the past was not the exclusive property of
university-trained archaeologists. His suggestions in *Hidden America*
that individuals could dig it themselves caused John Cotter to write that
the book's "failure is that, while cautioning the layman not to dig recklessly, it also informs him that he, too, can become an archaeologist
simply by following Mr. Robbins's example and instruction."[184] However, Robbins clearly understood the importance of public involvement
in archaeological projects in both an educational and a financial sense,
and was highly successful in reaching the public with the stories of his
discoveries and of archaeology in general. Although he realized the importance of connecting with the public early in his career, it was not
until the early 1980s that "public" archaeology became the buzzword of
the profession. In this respect, Robbins's distance from members of the
discipline, who were at that time professionalizing, turning inward, and
grasping for control, enabled him to succeed in reaching the public.

Because of his public orientation, his restoration and antiquarian interests, his outdated excavation techniques, his reliance on mechanical
excavation, and his combative style and stubborn temperament, Robbins's
work has been largely forgotten or ignored by "scientific" researchers who
consider it useless or simply worthless. In this sense, Robbins's research
projects provide an important opportunity to analyze approaches to
studying the past that have existed outside of the academy. Even more
significant is the high level of skill and resourcefulness demonstrated in
his records, field notes and diaries, photographs, and maps.[185]

Although they have long been ignored and underrated, the voluminous materials on Robbins's excavations, both artifactual and documentary, have enormous importance for archaeologists in the early
twenty-first century and beyond. Jamestown pioneer J. C. Harrington
has asserted that

it must be obvious than any excavating done 80, 50, or even 25 years ago, in-
evitably had its shortcomings. Of course, we wouldn't do it the same way today,
but there is no point in crying over spilt milk. Rather than lamenting the faults

of previous projects, it would be more productive to make the best possible use of information and artifacts from those projects.[186]

More recently, Marley Brown has remarked that Robert Schuyler and Stanley South have clearly demonstrated that "archaeological material previously recovered from historic sites can serve as a valuable data base for further analysis, regardless of the reasons behind the original excavation."[187] Of equal importance is the instructive value of Robbins's life and career for archaeologists. He pioneered public involvement and contract archaeology within a setting of institutional constraints and monetary pressures—the same circumstances that face practitioners today. In Robbins's approach, business success, historical knowledge, and popular appreciation of the past went hand in hand. His rivals eschewed both business and popularity in pursuit of professionalism. The contest over professionalism concealed many similarities of practice between Robbins and his critics. Ironically, the field has ultimately come to embrace many of Robbins's positions and practices in terms of consulting, the meaning and use of ruins, and the importance of public participation and support.

Robbins's life and early work show that he had a variety of reasons for embracing historical and industrial archaeology as a career. It is clear that he was working within a system that desired to create monuments and shrines as symbols of the American past, particularly those that would celebrate New England's Yankee past. He worked within and was often directed by the many small historical societies, museums, and family associations that desired to identify and interpret the physical remains associated with their sites. The available alternatives were few, particularly during Robbins's early career. The academy was out of reach for the self-educated Robbins, and most academic practitioners saw the field as "tin-can archaeology." The only other organization involved in historical archaeology was the federal government, and its projects were staffed largely by university-trained prehistorians. Therefore, most of Robbins's projects were short-term and undertaken for historical sites and museums, organizations that brought a wide array of intentions and desires to the table that often conflicted with archaeological goals.

Like any pioneer, Robbins also desired to build a shrine to his personal success as well as to the man who represented the independence and self-determination that he so desperately sought. "Do I think [Thoreau] wanted me to find [the cabin]? You're damned right I do! I think he wanted me to stay right there until I found the damned thing!"[188] Although he was a good-natured man, Robbins had the pioneer-type personality. "He was irascible and could be caustic," friend and colleague Paul Heberling remembered.[189] "Yes, he was self-centered and thought fundamentally of himself. What he was doing—what the reaction of the world to him was." But he was also a wonderful person, Heberling recalled: "people that couldn't deal with him were probably rather insecure themselves."[190] Writer Frederick Turner remarked to him, "you know, Mr. Robbins, you're a character. 'Oh, I know I'm a character,' he shot back with a high laugh, 'and I love it!'"[191]

For Robbins, his work and his life had been a series of problems. "Yes", his friend Heberling recalled, "he loved the problems—that gave him something to explore."[192] He met his impending death the same way, "almost enthusiastically—it was a problem—he talked about it ahead of time and wondered about it."[193] He spent his final weeks as he had spent his life, working on his papers and walking through the woods of Walden Pond. Even during his final illness, remembered friend Tom Blanding, "he was never too busy or tired, to entertain a Thoreauvian or offer him the hospitality of the Walden House."[194] On February 8, 1987, Robbins died in his own bed in the house that he had cherished for over fifty years, surrounded by his entire family.

The results of his work, still visible in many state parks and historical sites, now provide a new generation with symbols of the American past, and the archaeological community with a legacy of excavations that pose as many questions as they provide answers. In building and accepting these symbols, Robbins made himself an emblem of Thoreauvian self-determination, an unlettered, self-educated man of action, with common sense and a thoroughly Yankee background, who could be called the "People's Archaeologist." Perhaps Thoreau's reflection on his experiment at Walden best characterizes Robbins's lifework: "If one advances confidently in the direction of his dreams, and endeavors to live the life which he has imagined, he will meet with a success unexpected in common hours."[195]

Appendix

Archaeological Projects of Roland Wells Robbins

Site Name	Organization	Date(s)	Location	Site Type	Project Type
Thoreau House (Walden Pond)	N/A	1945–1947	Concord, Mass.	Domestic	Excavation/Restoration
Saugus Iron Works	First Iron Works Assoc.	1948–1954	Saugus, Mass.	Industrial/Ironworks	Excavation/Restoration
Falling Creek Iron Works	Chesterfield Hist. Soc.	1951, 1961–1962	Falling Creek, Va.	Industrial/Ironworks	Prelim. Survey
Old Glebe House	Rev. Charles Harriman	1952	Woodbury, Conn.	Industrial/Ironworks	Survey/Excavation
Lincoln Beehives	N/A	1953–1963	Lincoln, Mass.	Domestic/Farm	Survey
Dover Union Iron Company	Miss Amelia Peabody	1954	Dover, Mass.	Industrial/Ironworks	Excavation/Restoration
Shadwell, The Peter Jefferson House	Thomas Jefferson Birthplace Memorial Park Commission	1954–1955	Shadwell, Va.	Domestic	Excavation/Restoration
Eleutherian Mills/ Birkenhead Mills	Hagley Foundation	1955	Wilmington, Del.	Industrial/Mill	Survey/Excavation
Monticello "Mulberry Road"	Thomas Jefferson Memorial Foundation	1956	Charlottesville, Va.	Domestic	Prelim. Survey
John Winthrop Jr. Blast Furnace	City of Quincy, Mass.	1956	West Quincy, Mass.	Industrial/Ironworks	Excavation
		1965	West Quincy, Mass.	Industrial/Ironworks	Restoration

Philipse Castle/ Philipsburg Manor Upper Mills	Sleepy Hollow Restorations/ Historic Hudson Valley	1956–1961	Sleepy Hollow, N.Y.	Industrial/Mill	Excavation/Restoration
Crown Point State Park	W. R. Slack	1956	Crown Point, N.Y.	Military/Revolutionary	Prelim. Survey
	Bulwagga Bay Assoc./ Colonial Crown Point, Inc.	1959–1960	Crown Point, N.Y.	Military/Revolutionary	Excavation/Restoration
	Barker & Henry/ Architects-Engineers for State of N.Y.	1967–1968	Crown Point, N.Y.	Military/Revolutionary	Survey/Excavation/ Restoration
Wharton Tract/ Batsto Ironworks	New Jersey Dept. of Conservation & Economic Development	1957	Burlington Co., N.J.	Industrial/Ironworks	Prelim. Survey
Brothers House, Apothecary Gardens, Moravian College Campus	Historic Bethlehem, Inc.	1958–1959	Bethlehem, Pa.	Domestic	Survey/Excavation
Temple Hill	National Temple Hill Assoc., Inc.	1959–1960	Newburgh, N.Y.	Military/Revolutionary	Prelim. Survey
Sterling Blast Furnace	The Sterling Forest Corp.	1959, 1961– 1962	Sterling Lake, N.Y.	Industrial/Ironworks	Excavation/Restoration
John Alden House	Alden Kindred of America	1960–1964	Duxbury, Mass.	Domestic	Excavation/Restoration

(*continues*)

Site Name	Organization	Date(s)	Location	Site Type	Project Type
Capt. John Sands House	Block Island Tercentenary Committee	1960	Block Island, R.I.	Domestic	Survey
Parson Barnard House/Anne Bradstreet House	N. Andover Hist. Soc.	1962	N. Andover, Mass.	Domestic	Survey
Gov. John Wentworth Farm	N.H. Dept. of Resources and Economic Development/Division of Parks	1962	Wolfeboro, N.H.	Domestic	Prelim. Survey
Manursing Island	Mrs. Ellen C. McKay	1962	Rye, N.Y.	Domestic	Prelim. Survey
Nassawango Iron Works	Worcester Co. Hist. Soc.	1962	Snow Hill, Md.	Industrial/Ironworks	Prelim. Survey
		1977, 1978, 1980, 1984	Snow Hill, Md.	Industrial/Ironworks	Excavation/Restoration
Dover Furnace/South Boston Furnace Co.	N.Y. City Mission Soc.	1963	Dover Furnace, N.Y.	Industrial/Ironworks	Prelim. Survey
Hasenclever Blast Furnace	Edward Ryerson	1963	Ringwood State Park, N.J.	Industrial/Ironworks	Prelim. Survey
Peter Folger Homestead/Tristam Coffin Homestead	Miss Dorothy Whitman	1964	Nantucket, Mass.	Domestic	Prelim. Survey

Site	Organization	Location	Year	Type	Work
Hancock-Clarke House	Lexington Hist. Commission	Lexington, Mass.	1965	Domestic	Excavation/Restoration
Katahdin Iron Works	Maine Bureau of Public Improvements	Brownville Junction, Maine	1966	Industrial/Ironworks	Excavation/Restoration
Puddle Dock	Strawbery Banke, Inc.	Portsmouth, N.H.	1966	Commercial/Wharf	Survey/Excavation
Hewitt Iron Works	New Jersey Dept. Of Conservation & Development	Ringwood State Park, N.J.	1967	Industrial/Ironworks	Excavation/Restoration
Oliver Mill Park Restoration	Oliver Mill Park/Town of Middleborough	Middleborough, Mass.	1967, 1969, 1971–1973, 1975–1976, 1980	Industrial/Mill	Excavation/Restoration
Von Steuben Mansion	Bergen Co. Hist. Soc.	River Edge, N.J.	1967–1968	Domestic	Prelim. Survey
First Parish Church Cellar Site/Wheeler Property Pottery	Weston Hist. Soc.	Weston, Conn.	1967–1968	Domestic/Industrial	Survey/Excavation
Hammondville Furnace/Ironville Forge	Penfield Foundation	Crown Point, N.Y.	1968	Industrial/Ironworks	Prelim. Survey
Gilmanton Iron Works	Gilmanton Hist. Soc.	Gilmanton, N.H.	1968	Industrial/Ironworks	Prelim. Survey
Rockport Lime Kilns	Town of Rockport	Rockport, Mass.	1969	Industrial/Lime Kilns	Prelim. Survey
Kent Furnace	Connecticut Hist. Commission	Kent, Conn.	1970	Industrial/Ironworks	Prelim. Survey
Rev. Samuel Parris Parsonage	Danvers Hist. Soc.	Danvers, Mass.	1970	Domestic	Excavation/Restoration
Tufts Street Meter Bldg.	U.S. Coast Guard	Boston, Mass.	1971	Commercial	Survey

(continues)

(*Continued*)

Site Name	Organization	Date(s)	Location	Site Type	Project Type
Old Mill Park	Town of Bolton	1972	Bolton, Mass.	Industrial/Mill	Prelim. Survey
Revolutionary War Encampment, Avon Mountain	Connecticut Dept. of Transportation	1972–1973	W. Hartford, Conn.	Military/Revolutionary	Prelim. Survey/ Excavation
Fort Ticonderoga	Fort Ticonderoga	1972–1973	Ticonderoga, N.Y.	Military/Revolutionary	Prelim. Survey
Fort Stamford	City of Stamford	1973	Stamford, Conn.	Military/Revolutionary	Prelim. Survey
Richard Smith Forge/ Colebrook Mills	Colebrook Hist. Soc.	1973	Norfolk, Conn.	Industrial/Ironworks	Prelim. Survey
Gov. Moses Gill Mansion	Princeton Bicentennial Committee	1974	Princeton, Mass.	Domestic	Survey
Moore Memorial State Park	Massachusetts Dept. of Natural Resources	1976	Princeton, Mass.	Domestic	Excavation
		1974, 1979	Paxton, Mass.	Industrial/Mill	Excavation/Restoration
	The Friends of the Mill Village, Inc.	1976	Paxton, Mass.	Industrial/Mill	Excavation/Restoration
Beaver Dam Village	School of Cultural Arts, Inc.	1974	Westhampton, L.I., N.Y.	Domestic	Prelim. Survey

Site	Organization	Year	Location	Category	Type
Lexington Meeting House	Lexington Bicentennial Committee	1975	Lexington, Mass.	Religious	Survey
Rogers-Sheldon East Bridgewater Iron Works	East Bridgewater Bicentennial Commission	1975–1976	East Bridgewater, Mass.	Industrial/Ironworks	Excavation/Restoration
Clinton Blast Furnace	Newark Watershed Conservation & Development Corp.	1976	Newfoundland, N.J.	Industrial/Ironworks	Prelim. Survey
Cape Ann Industrial Park	Tibbetts Engineering Corp.	1977	Gloucester, Mass.	N/A	Survey
Lakeville Industrial Park	Town of Lakeville	1978–1979	Lakeville, Mass.	N/A	Survey
Rev. Daniel Shute Site	Hingham Hist. Commission	1980	Hingham, Mass.	Domestic	Prelim. Survey
Clove Furnace Historic Site	Orange Co. Hist. Soc.	1982	Arden, N.Y.	Industrial/Ironworks	Prelim. Survey
		1983–1984	Arden, N.Y.	Industrial/Ironworks	Excavation/Restoration
Munroe Tavern	Lexington Hist. Soc.	1982, 1983, 1984	Lexington, Mass.	Commercial	Excavation
Sabbathday Lake	The United Society of Shakers	1985	Poland Springs, Maine	Domestic/Commercial	Prelim. Survey

Notes

Introduction, pp. 1–8

1. James Dodson, "The Man Who Found Thoreau," *Yankee* 49 (1985): 62; Evan Jones, "Pick and Shovel Historian," *Collier's*, Aug. 5, 1955, 28–31.
2. Dodson, "The Man Who Found Thoreau," 62; John Cotter, personal communication, 1996.
3. Marley R. Brown III, "A Survey of Historical Archaeology in New England," in *New England Historical Archaeology*, ed. Peter Benes, *The Dublin Seminar for New England Folklife, Annual Proceedings, 1977*, (Boston: Boston University, 1978), 6.
4. Dodson, "The Man Who Found Thoreau," 116.
5. Lynn A. Bonfield and Mary C. Morrison, *Roxanna's Children: The Biography of a Nineteenth-Century Vermont Family* (Amherst: University of Massachusetts Press, 1995), 122.
6. Joseph A. Conforti, *Imagining New England: Explorations of Regional Identity From the Pilgrims to the Mid-Twentieth Century* (Chapel Hill: University of North Carolina Press, 2001).
7. Roland W. Robbins and Evan Jones, *Hidden America* (New York: Alfred Knopf, 1959), 11.
8. C. Malcolm Watkins to Roland Wells Robbins, Mar. 21, 1952, the Roland Wells Robbins Collection, the Thoreau Society, Lincoln, Mass.
9. J. C. Harrington to Roland Wells Robbins, Aug. 11, 1952, the Roland Wells Robbins Collection, the Thoreau Society, Lincoln, Mass.
10. John L. Cotter, "Review of *Hidden America*," *Archaeology* 14 (1961): 221.
11. Michael Kammen, *Mystic Chords of Memory: The Transformation of Tradition in American Culture* (New York: Alfred A. Knopf, 1991), 538.
12. Dodson, "The Man Who Found Thoreau," 116.

13. James Deetz, "Other Peoples Garbage," *Odyssey* series, 1988, distributed by PBS Video.

14. Donald M. Scott, "The Profession That Vanished: Public Lecturing in Mid-Nineteenth-Century America," in *Professions and Professional Ideologies in America,* ed. Gerald L. Geison (Chapel Hill: University of North Carolina Press, 1983), 27–28.

15. Carl Becker, "Everyman His Own Historian," *American Historical Review* 37, no. 2 (1932): 221–236.

16. The discipline was reacting to years of damage to sites by looters and pothunters and even well-meaning amateurs. The cardinal rule was that excavations must be carefully executed and well documented because the very process of archaeology destroys the site.

17. Frederick Turner, *Spirit of Place: The Making of an American Literary Landscape* (Washington, D.C.: Island Press, 1992), 48.

Chapter I. The Road to Ruins and Restoration: Historic Preservation and Historical Archaeology on the Road to Walden Pond, pp. 9–26

1. James M. Lindgren, *Preserving Historic New England: Preservation, Progressivism, and the Remaking of Memory* (New York: Oxford University Press, 1995), 6, 52.

2. Conforti, *Imagining New England.*

3. Lindgren, *Preserving Historic New England,* 10.

4. Charles Eliot Norton, 1889, quoted in James M. Lindgren, "'A Constant Incentive to Patriotic Citizenship': Historic Preservation in Progressive-Era Massachusetts," *New England Quarterly* 64, no. 4 (1991): 601.

5. James M. Lindgren, *Preserving the Old Dominion: Historic Preservation and Virginia Traditionalism* (Charlottesville: University of Virginia Press, 1993), 3–4; David Lowenthal, *The Past Is a Foreign Country* (Cambridge: Cambridge University Press, 1985), 121–122.

6. Curtis Guild Jr., 1907, quoted in Lindgren, "'A Constant Incentive to Patriotic Citizenship,'" 594–608.

7. William J. Murtagh, *Keeping Time: The History and Theory of Preservation in America* (Pittstown, N.J.: Main Street Press, 1988), 30.

8. Lindgren, *Preserving Historic New England,* 29.

9. James M. Lindgren, "The Gospel of Preservation" in Virginia and New England: Historic Preservation and the Regeneration of Traditionalism" (Ph.D. diss., College of William and Mary, 1984).

10. Lindgren, "The Gospel of Preservation," 9.

11. Lindgren, *Preserving Historic New England,* 27.

12. T. J. Jackson Lears, *No Place of Grace: Antimodernism and the Transformation of American Culture, 1880–1920* (New York: Pantheon Books, 1981), 301.

13. Lindgren, *Preserving Historic New England*, 27.

14. Michael Wallace, "Reflections on the History of Historic Preservation," in *Presenting the Past: Essays on History and the Public*, ed. Susan Porter Benson, Stephen Brier, and Roy Rosenzweig (Philadelphia: Temple University Press, 1986), 167.

15. Nathaniel Hawthorne, 1852, quoted in Lowenthal, *The Past Is a Foreign Country*, 111.

16. Charles B. Hosmer Jr., *Presence of the Past: A History of the Preservation Movement in the United States before Williamsburg* (New York: G. P. Putnam's Son's, 1965), 29–40.

17. Hosmer, *Presence of the Past*, 62.

18. Murtagh, *Keeping Time*, 30.

19. Wallace, "Reflections on the History of Historic Preservation," 168–169.

20. Michael Wallace, "Visiting the Past: History Museums in the United States," in *Presenting the Past: Essays on History and the Public*, ed. Susan Porter Benson, Stephen Brier, and Roy Rosenzweig (Philadelphia: Temple University Press, 1986), 139.

21. Lowenthal, *The Past Is a Foreign Country*, 122.

22. Hosmer, *Presence of the Past*, 131. The DAR, with its national organization headquartered in Washington, D.C., was founded to encourage "historical research and preservation of relics and sites connected with the Revolution."

23. In the South, preservationists "attempted to make museums out of buildings associated with famous men," and reestablish the gentility of the Old South. Hosmer, *Presence of the Past*, 63; Wallace, "Reflections on the History of Historic Preservation," 169–170. Addressing an Association for the Preservation of Virginia Antiquities gathering at Jamestown, Professor John Leslie Hall proclaimed that "this island is to us what those sacred spots were to the older nations. It is at once our Acropolis, our Palatine Hill, and our isle of Thanet. Let us ever love it and preserve it." Lindgren, *Preserving the Old Dominion*, 1–2.

24. Hosmer, *Presence of the Past*, 102–103.

25. Hosmer, *Presence of the Past*, 110–111.

26. Lindgren, *Preserving Historic New England*, 101–102; Hosmer, *Presence of the Past*, 115–118. Robbins excavated the 1627 John Alden House for the Alden Kindred in 1960.

27. Lindgren, *Preserving the Old Dominion*, 9–10; Edwin Bacon, *Historic Pilgrimages in New England; Among Landmarks of Pilgrim and Puritan Days and of the Provincial and Revolutionary Periods* (New York and Boston: Silver, Burdett & Co., 1898); Clara Walker Whiteside, *Touring New England on the Trail of the Yankee* (Philadelphia: Penn Publishing Co., 1926).

28. Lindgren, "'A Constant Incentive to Patriotic Citizenship,'" 603; George F. Dow, n.d., quoted in Lindgren, "'A Constant Incentive to Patriotic Citizenship,'" 603.

29. Lindgren, *Preserving Historic New England*, 38.

30. Lindgren, *Preserving Historic New England*, 121.

31. Lindgren, *Preserving Historic New England*, 38.

32. William Sumner Appleton, 1916, quoted in Lindgren, *Preserving Historic New England*, 92.

33. Hosmer, *Presence of the Past*, 271.

34. Lindgren, "'A Constant Incentive to Patriotic Citizenship,'" 603.

35. Lindgren, "'A Constant Incentive to Patriotic Citizenship,'" 597.

36. Lindgren, "'A Constant Incentive to Patriotic Citizenship,'" 598.

37. Lindgren, *Preserving Historic New England*, 22.

38. Hosmer, *Presence of the Past*, 237–239.

39. Lindgren, "'A Constant Incentive to Patriotic Citizenship,'" 605.

40. Lindgren, "'A Constant Incentive to Patriotic Citizenship,'" 605; Lindgren, *Preserving Historic New England*, 134–152.

41. Lindgren, *Preserving Historic New England*, 11.

42. Lindgren, *Preserving Historic New England*, 101.

43. Lindgren, *Preserving Historic New England*, 105.

44. Carl Russell Fish, 1910, quoted in Robert L. Schuyler, "Anthropological Perspectives in Historical Archaeology" (Ph.D. diss., University of California at Santa Barbara, 1975), 37–38.

45. Jacob W. Gruber, "Artifacts Are History: Calver and Bolton in New York," in *The Scope of Historical Archaeology: Essays in Honor of John L. Cotter*, ed. David G. Orr and Daniel G. Crozier (Philadelphia: Laboratory of Anthropology, Temple University, 1984), 18.

46. Gruber, "Artifacts Are History," 17.

47. Gruber, "Artifacts Are History," 19. The Field Exploration Committee, formed by Bolton and Calver and members of the New-York Historical Society, was among the first organizations engaged in historical archaeology research.

48. Bolton, 1918, quoted in Gruber, "Artifacts Are History," 21–22.

49. Robbins's possession of their book demonstrates that he was aware of the work of these pioneers and likely built on their methodological approach. However, the publication of this book in 1950 clearly postdates the Walden excavations. William L. Calver and Reginald P. Bolton, *History Written with Pick and Shovel; military buttons, belt plates, badges and other relics excavated from Colonial, Revolutionary, and War of 1812 camp sites by the Field Exploration Committee of the New-York Historical Society* (New York: New-York Historical Society, 1950).

50. Schuyler, "Anthropological Perspectives," 42.

51. Samuel H. Yonge published his findings in the *Virginia Magazine of His-*

tory and Biography in 1904 and followed this with his monograph, *The Site of Old "James Towne,"* later the same year (1904; reprint, Richmond, Va.: The Association for the Preservation of Virginia Antiquities, 1930).

52. Yonge, *The Site of Old "James Towne."*

53. J. C. Harrington, "Jamestown Archaeology in Retrospect," in *The Scope of Historical Archaeology: Essays in Honor of John L. Cotter,* ed. David G. Orr and Daniel G. Crozier (Philadelphia: Laboratory of Anthropology, Temple University, 1984), 31–32.

54. Charles B. Hosmer Jr., *Preservation Comes of Age: From Williamsburg to the National Trust, 1926–1949* (Charlottesville: University of Virginia Press, 1981), 31.

55. Prentice Duell, an archaeological draftsman at the University of Pennsylvania, was hired for the position in 1929. Hosmer, *Preservation Comes of Age,* 32–34, 37.

56. Moorehead (n.d.) quoted in Linda Derry and Marley R. Brown III, "Excavation at Colonial Williamsburg Thirty Years Ago: An Archaeological Analysis of Cross-Trenching Behind the Peyton Randolph Site," 1987, Office of Archaeological Research, Colonial Williamsburg Foundation, Williamsburg, Va., 8. Moorehead, the supervisor of archaeological excavations at Colonial Williamsburg at various times, had worked with archaeologist A. V. Kidder during his survey of the Pecos River Valley.

57. Hosmer, *Preservation Comes of Age,* 58, 60.

58. Hosmer, *Preservation Comes of Age,* 60.

59. Derry and Brown, "Excavation at Colonial Williamsburg Thirty Years Ago," 7.

60. Ivor Noël Hume, *Historical Archaeology* (New York: Alfred A. Knopf, 1968), 73–74.

61. Derry and Brown, "Excavation at Colonial Williamsburg Thirty Years Ago," 8–9.

62. Schuyler, "Anthropological Perspectives," 42. American archaeology, particularly prehistoric archaeology, began to be established as a recognized subfield of anthropology in the early 1920s and increasingly organized within the university. The founding of the Society for American Archaeology in 1934 brought together academic and museum archaeologists. Thomas C. Patterson, "The Last Sixty Years: Toward a Social History of Americanist Archaeology in the United States," *American Anthropologist* 88 (1986): 7–26.

63. Schuyler, "Anthropological Perspectives," 44; Kammen, *Mystic Chords of Memory,* 470–471.

64. Schuyler, "Anthropological Perspectives," 45.

65. Thomas F. King, *Cultural Resource Laws and Practice: An Introductory Guide* (Walnut Creek, Calif.: AltaMira Press, 1998), 13–23.

66. Schuyler, "Anthropological Perspectives," 46.

67. Patterson, "The Last Sixty Years," 14.

68. Robbins would encounter similar situations on many projects, particularly Saugus and Philipsburg Manor.

69. Ivor Noël Hume, *The Virginia Adventure, Roanoke to James Towne: An Archaeological and Historical Odyssey* (New York: Alfred A. Knopf, 1994), 414–415.

70. Noël Hume, *The Virginia Adventure*, 415.

71. Harrington, "Jamestown Archaeology in Retrospect," 35.

72. Noël Hume, *The Virginia Adventure*, 416.

73. W. J. Winter, 1935, quoted in Noël Hume, *The Virginia Adventure*, 416.

74. Harrington, "Jamestown Archaeology in Retrospect," 36.

75. Schuyler, "Anthropological Perspectives," 48.

76. J. C. Harrington, "From Architraves to Artifacts: A Metamorphosis," in *Pioneers in Historical Archaeology: Breaking New Ground*, ed. Stanley South (New York: Plenum Press, 1994), 7.

77. Karin Goldstein, "Harry Hornblower (1917–1985)," Plimoth-on-Web, www .plimoth.org/archaeology/hh2_arch.htm (Plimoth Plantation: The Living History Museum of 17th-century Plymouth, 2001).

78. Schuyler, "Anthropological Perspectives," 50–51. The preparation and presentation of site reports is considered the ethical responsibility of all excavators, as the process of excavation itself results in the destruction of the archaeological record and resource.

79. Schuyler, "Anthropological Perspectives," 72.

80. Schuyler, "Anthropological Perspectives," 73.

81. Stanley South, ed., *Pioneers in Historical Archaeology: Breaking New Ground* (New York: Plenum Press, 1994), vi–vii.

82. Wallace, "Visiting the Past," 142.

83. Wallace, "Visiting the Past," 142.

84. William Sumner Appleton, n.d., quoted in Hosmer, *Presence of the Past*, 268.

85. Hosmer, *Preservation Comes of Age*, 65.

86. In the mid-1940s, the Williamsburg staff assisted with several Rockefeller-funded projects near his home in Tarrytown, New York, including Philipse Castle and Sunnyside. They apparently did not like spending Rockefeller money on what they saw as the "amateur approach" to restoration being taken by the Tarrytown Historical Society and were not happy with the quality of either the archaeology or the architectural research. The Philipse Castle site was later investigated by Robbins under contract with Sleepy Hollow Restorations as part of a thorough reanalysis and reevaluation of the original 1940 restoration (see chapter 4). Hosmer, *Preservation Comes of Age*, 67, 70–71.

87. Wallace, "Reflections on the History of Historic Preservation," 171.

88. Lindgren, *Preserving Historic New England*, 5.

89. Kammen, *Mystic Chords of Memory*, 295.

90. Kammen, *Mystic Chords of Memory,* 295.

91. Kammen, *Mystic Chords of Memory,* 505.

92. Kammen, *Mystic Chords of Memory,* 505.

93. Lowenthal, *The Past Is a Foreign Country,* 265.

94. Everett B. Mero, *Celebrating a 300th Anniversary: A Report of the Massachusetts Bay Tercentenary of 1930* (Boston: Tercentenary Conference of City and Town Committees, 1931), 102–103.

95. Lowenthal, *The Past Is a Foreign Country,* 269–270.

96. Kammen, *Mystic Chords of Memory,* 342.

97. Lindgren, *Preserving Historic New England,* 5.

98. Kammen, *Mystic Chords of Memory,* 342.

99. Kammen, *Mystic Chords of Memory,* 343.

100. Harrington, "Jamestown Archaeology in Retrospect," 29.

101. Harrington, "Jamestown Archaeology in Retrospect," 36.

102. Harrington, "Jamestown Archaeology in Retrospect," 39.

103. Harrington, "Jamestown Archaeology in Retrospect," 40.

104. Harrington, "Jamestown Archaeology in Retrospect," 39.

105. Schuyler, "Anthropological Perspectives," 73.

106. Brown, "A Survey of Historical Archaeology in New England," 4.

107. A complete history of historic preservation and historical archaeology is beyond the scope of this work and already the subject of several excellent works: Hosmer, *Presence of the Past* and *Preservation Comes of Age;* Lindgren, "The Gospel of Preservation," *Preserving the Old Dominion,* and *Preserving Historic New England;* Schuyler, "Anthropological Perspectives"; Gordon R. Willey and Jeremy A. Sabloff, *A History of American Archaeology* (San Francisco: W. H. Freeman and Company, 1974).

Chapter 2. House Hunting for Henry David Thoreau, pp. 25–57

1. Lawrence Buell, "The Thoreauvian Pilgrimage: The Structure of an American Cult," *American Literature* 61, no. 2 (1989): 175–199.

2. Early cairns were used to mark human burials and protect the body from scavengers.

3. Bronson Alcott quoted in James Dawson, "A History of the Cairn," *Thoreau Society Bulletin,* no. 232 (Summer 2000): 1–3.

4. Jeanne M. Zimmer, "A History of Thoreau's Hut and Hut Site," *ESQ* 18 (1972): 136.

5. Theodore F. Wolfe, *Literary Shrines: The Haunts of Some Famous American Authors* (Philadelphia: Lippincott, 1895), 73.

6. Walter Harding and Michael Meyer, *The New Thoreau Handbook* (New York: New York University Press, 1980), 207.

7. Harding and Meyer, *The New Thoreau Handbook*, 208.

8. Eric Cheyfitz, "Matthiessen's *American Renaissance:* Circumscribing the Revolution," *American Quarterly* 41 (1989): 347.

9. Walter Harding quoted in Roland W. Robbins, *Discovery at Walden* (Stoneham, Mass.: George R. Barnstead & Son, 1947), xiii.

10. Kammen, *Mystic Chords of Memory*, 339.

11. Robbins was born in Worcester, Massachusetts, on March 21, 1908.

12. Roland W. Robbins, "Roland Wells Robbins and the Saugus Iron Works Restoration," n.d., the Roland Wells Robbins Collection, the Thoreau Society, Lincoln, Mass., iv.

13. Fred Robbins was born in Albany, Vermont, and Lucy May Davis was born in Acton, Massachusetts.

14. Robbins, "Roland Wells Robbins and the Saugus Iron Works Restoration," v.

15. Robbins, "Roland Wells Robbins and the Saugus Iron Works Restoration," v.

16. Geraldine Robbins, interviews with author, July 31 and Aug. 1 and 3, 1992, Lincoln, Mass.

17. Robbins, "Roland Wells Robbins and the Saugus Iron Works Restoration," ix.

18. Robbins, "Roland Wells Robbins and the Saugus Iron Works Restoration," viii.

19. Robbins, "Roland Wells Robbins and the Saugus Iron Works Restoration," ix.

20. Robbins's school experience may have been colored by a learning disability affecting both his reading and his writing capacities. He regularly commented in his daily journals and project notes on the physical drain he experienced from reading and writing. Roland W. Robbins, "Tennis Notebook [1961–1968, 1970]," the Roland Wells Robbins Collection, the Thoreau Society, Lincoln, Mass.). While his reading and writing problems were a constant irritation, he devised successful strategies for coping with them and, in retrospect, kept extraordinarily detailed daily journals and produced vast correspondence. Geraldine Robbins recalled her husband's struggles with reading and writing throughout his life, and suggested the possibility of dyslexia. Geraldine Robbins, interview with author, July 2, 1990.

21. Robbins, "Roland Wells Robbins and the Saugus Iron Works Restoration," ix.

22. Town of Acton, "Annual Report, 1929," Town of Acton, Mass.

23. Irwin Robbins, personal communication, 1994. Irwin remembered that his Uncle Fred was devastated by his wife's death. After the death of his parents, Robbins had little contact with his older married brothers, who by then had families and concerns of their own, but he remained close to Leonard.

24. Roland W. Robbins, *Thru the Covered Bridge* (1938; reprint, Rutland, Vt.: Academy Books, 1986); Robbins, "Roland Wells Robbins and the Saugus Iron Works Restoration," ix.

25. Robbins, "Roland Wells Robbins and the Saugus Iron Works Restoration," x.

26. Robbins, *Thru the Covered Bridge*, n.p.

27. For example, his poems appeared in the *Rutland Daily Herald, Burlington Free Press*, and *Brattleboro Reformer*, and in several anthologies of New England verse.

28. Howard L. Hindley, ca. 1932, quoted in Robbins, *Thru the Covered Bridge*, n.p. Walter Hard was Vermont's unofficial poet laureate. Walter Hard Jr. and J. Kevin Graffagnino, *Walter Hard's Vermont People* (Middlebury: Vermont Books, 1981), ix.

29. Robbins, *Thru the Covered Bridge*, n.p.

30. Geraldine Robbins, interviews with author, July 31 and Aug. 1 and 3, 1992.

31. Geraldine Robbins, interviews with author, July 31 and Aug. 1 and 3, 1992.

32. Robbins, *Thru the Covered Bridge*, n.p.

33. Geraldine Robbins, letter to author, Oct. 26, 1995.

34. Robbins, *Thru the Covered Bridge*, n.p.

35. Mrs. Robbins remembered that the bank thought that they were a good risk because of Roland's reputation as a hard worker. She also noted that they repaid Roland's uncle within several years of building the house. Geraldine Robbins, personal communication, 1996.

36. Geraldine Robbins, letter to author, Oct. 26, 1995.

37. Geraldine Robbins, letter to author, Oct. 26, 1995.

38. Geraldine Robbins, letter to author, Oct. 26, 1995.

39. Geraldine Robbins, letter to author, Oct. 26, 1995.

40. Roland W. Robbins, *Thru the Covered Bridge* (Stoneham, Mass.: George R. Barnstead & Son, 1938). Two of Robbins's poems were also collected in Louise Hall Littlefield's compilation *The Triad Anthology of New England Verse* (Portland, Maine: Falmouth Book House, 1938).

41. Robbins, "Roland Wells Robbins and the Saugus Iron Works Restoration," x.

42. Robbins's poems were reviewed in the *Boston Herald, Burlington Free Press, New York Herald Tribune, Boston Globe*, and *Concord Herald*.

43. *Burlington Free Press*, "More Vermont Verse," n.d., editorial page, the Roland Wells Robbins Collection, the Thoreau Society, Lincoln, Mass.

44. Conforti, *Imagining New England*, 268.

45. Conforti, *Imagining New England*, 273.

46. Conforti, *Imagining New England*, 271, 284.

47. Conforti, *Imagining New England*, 288.

48. Conforti, *Imagining New England*, 288.

49. Kristina Joyce (interview with author, Aug. 8, 1993), a friend and local artist who later illustrated the second edition of Robbins's book of poems, remembered that Roland "told me over and over again how much these poems had meant to him when his mother died during the Depression years."

50. Geraldine Robbins, letter to author, Oct. 26, 1995.

51. Robbins, "Roland Wells Robbins and the Saugus Iron Works Restoration," xi.

52. Roland W. Robbins to Rowland Allen Wells, Jan. 23, 1962, the Roland Wells Robbins Collection, the Thoreau Society, Lincoln, Mass.

53. Robbins, "Roland Wells Robbins and the Saugus Iron Works Restoration," xi.

54. Roland W. Robbins, *The Story of the Minute Man* (New London, N.H.: Country Press, 1945).

55. The Minute Man image also appeared in propaganda campaigns to garner support for the war effort.

56. Dodson, "The Man Who Found Thoreau," 117.

57. Robbins and Jones, *Hidden America*, 14.

58. Philip Van Doren Stern, ed., *The Annotated Walden: Walden; or, Life in the Woods* (1970; reprint, New York: Marboro Books Corp., 1992), 245.

59. Dawson, "A History of the Cairn," 2–3.

60. Robbins, *Discovery at Walden*, 5. Robbins had met French while working on his Minute Man statue research project.

61. Robbins, *Discovery at Walden*, 6.

62. Robbins, *Discovery at Walden*, 9.

63. Robbins, *Discovery at Walden*, 9. Geraldine Robbins would continue to help her husband on projects throughout his career. "When he would get behind," she recalled, "I would help him out." (Robbins, interview with author, Feb. 2, 1996.

64. Roland W. Robbins, "#1 Thoreau Hut Notes," the Roland Wells Robbins Collection, the Thoreau Society, Lincoln, Mass., 2.

65. Robbins, "#1 Thoreau Hut Notes," 5–6. The early markers were installed by Raymond Adams of the University of North Carolina and Raymond Emerson of Concord in 1931. Raymond Emerson to Raymond Adams, Aug. 19, 1931, and Feb. 16, 1932. The Raymond Adams Collection, the Thoreau Institute, Lincoln, Mass.; Dawson, "A History of the Cairn," 2.

66. Robbins, *Discovery at Walden*, 9–18.

67. This "prodding rod" was a piece of quarter-inch steel rod stock that was sharpened on one end and had a handle welded to the other. Mrs. Robbins indicated that her husband had it made at a local welding shop. It is interesting that Robbins uses the same term, "prodding rod," that was used by the team of Calver and Bolton in first part of the twentieth century. Bolton, 1918, quoted in Gruber, "Artifacts Are History," 21–22.

68. Robbins, "#1 Thoreau Hut Notes," 22.

69. Robbins, *Discovery at Walden,* 17–18. Aaron Bagg was a writer and naturalist who Robbins met at the Walden centennial.

70. Robbins, *Discovery at Walden,* 18.

71. Robbins, "#1 Thoreau Hut Notes," 25.

72. Prior to his trip to the brickyard, Robbins had visited the library to read all that he could find on bricks and brick making. This is the first instance of Robbins's seeking expert assistance for specific research problems.

73. Robbins, "#1 Thoreau Hut Notes," 28.

74. Robbins, "#1 Thoreau Hut Notes," 29–30.

75. Robbins, "#1 Thoreau Hut Notes," 32–34.

76. Robbins, "#1 Thoreau Hut Notes," 35. The artifacts, including 165 pounds of plaster, 111 pounds of bricks including three whole bricks, thirty-four nails; and one round metal ring, were recovered from the top 12 inches of soil.

77. Robbins, "#1 Thoreau Hut Notes," 42.

78. Robbins, "#1 Thoreau Hut Notes," 45–46.

79. This information helped to prove that the site was not that of New Yorker Edward Stuart Hotham, who, desiring to experience Thoreau's stay at the pond, built a cabin near Thoreau's in November 1869 and lived in it until May 1870. William Ellery Channing noted that Hotham's cabin was "by the pond on the bank, in front of Henry's." Channing quoted in Van Doren Stern, *The Annotated Walden,* 46.

80. Robbins, "#1 Thoreau Hut Notes," 50.

81. Robbins, "#1 Thoreau Hut Notes," 57.

82. Robbins, "#1 Thoreau Hut Notes," 60.

83. Henry David Thoreau quoted in Robbins, *Discovery at Walden,* 11.

84. Robbins, "#1 Thoreau Hut Notes," 67. Wallace B. Conant was one of Robbins's Concord customers and a founding member of the Thoreau Society, Mr. Allen French was a local historian who lived in Concord, and Mrs. Caleb (Ruth) Wheeler lived in Concord and was a founding member of the Thoreau Society.

85. Robbins, "#1 Thoreau Hut Notes," 76.

86. Robbins, "#1 Thoreau Hut Notes," 77.

87. Robbins, "#1 Thoreau Hut Notes," 79.

88. Robbins, "#1 Thoreau Hut Notes," 84. It is unclear whether Robbins was aware of the archaeological use of the term "posthole" at this point in his career; however, he may have picked it up through his correspondence with members of the Massachusetts Archaeological Society and attendance at their meetings.

89. Roland W. Robbins, "#2 Thoreau Hut Notes," the Roland Wells Robbins Collection, the Thoreau Society, Lincoln, Mass., Feb. 14, 1946. This project marked the first of many contacts between Robbins and the firm of Perry, Shaw, and Hepburn.

90. Robbins, "#2 Thoreau Hut Notes," February 25, 1946.

91. Robbins, "#2 Thoreau Hut Notes," February 25, 1946.

92. Robbins, "#2 Thoreau Hut Notes," March 31, 1946.

93. Robbins, "#2 Thoreau Hut Notes," May 11 to May 30, 1946. Excavation in this area recovered both cut nails and brick about 10 inches deep. Architectural historian W. Barksdale Maynard has speculated that this might be an area leveled by Thoreau to provide a flat assembly area for the timber framing of his house (Maynard, personal communication, 2002).

94. Robbins, "#2 Thoreau Hut Notes," May 11, 1946.

95. Robbins, "#2 Thoreau Hut Notes," May 11, 1946.

96. Robbins, "#2 Thoreau Hut Notes," May 13 to May 14, 1946.

97. W.B.C. (Wallace B. Conant) to Walter Harding, Jan. 14, 1946, the Roland Wells Robbins Collection, the Thoreau Society, Lincoln, Mass.

98. Robbins, "#2 Thoreau Hut Notes," May 31, 1946.

99. Robbins, "#2 Thoreau Hut Notes," June 3, 1946.

100. Robbins, "#2 Thoreau Hut Notes," June 15, 1946.

101. Robbins, "#2 Thoreau Hut Notes," June 17, 1946.

102. Robbins, "#2 Thoreau Hut Notes," June 26, 1946. He calculated this date assuming that the tree had fallen during the hurricane of 1938. This was later confirmed by Miss A. Bruel, who reported that she had visited the house site the day after the hurricane and witnessed two men cutting up the fallen tree. Robbins, "#2 Thoreau Hut Notes," July 13, 1946.

103. Robbins, "#2 Thoreau Hut Notes," June 22, 1946.

104. Robbins, "#2 Thoreau Hut Notes," July 1, 1946. Strickland worked with fellow Harvard Excavator's Club member Henry Hornblower II to excavate the John Howland House in the 1940s. Robbins visited this site during his work at the John Alden House from 1960 to 1964 (see chapter 5).

105. Robbins, "#2 Thoreau Hut Notes," July 1, 1946.

106. Robbins, "#2 Thoreau Hut Notes," July 1, 1946.

107. Robbins, "#2 Thoreau Hut Notes," July 15, 1946. Robbins had commented in his log on the poor condition of the plaster and mortar evidence and was anxious to find a suitable treatment to preserve these artifacts. Orchard recommended that he soak the pieces in a solution of Alvar (polyvinyl acetal) mixed in acetone and then allow them to air dry.

108. Robbins, "#2 Thoreau Hut Notes," July 4, 1946.

109. Robbins, "#2 Thoreau Hut Notes," July 18, 1946.

110. Robbins, "#2 Thoreau Hut Notes," July 15, 1946.

111. Robbins, "#2 Thoreau Hut Notes," July 15, 1946.

112. Robbins, "#2 Thoreau Hut Notes," July 15, 1946. Hosmer's account was published in the *Concord Freeman* (May 6, 1880), thirty-five years after his visit. Architectural historian W. Barksdale Maynard has researched Hosmer's description in some detail and finds it riddled with errors. Maynard, personal communication, 2002.

113. Robbins, "#2 Thoreau Hut Notes," July 15, 1946.

114. Robbins, "#3 Thoreau Hut Notes," Aug. 13, 1946. Robbins moved the stones to the other side of the cairn, shifting it slightly away from the hut site.

115. Roland W. Robbins, "#3 Thoreau Hut Notes," the Roland Wells Robbins Collection, the Thoreau Society, Lincoln, Mass., Aug. 31, 1946. For example, the 1878 "Lake Walden Camp Meeting" was a "Thoreau Pilgrimage" that consisted of readings and songs and the "depositing of a large number of stones, suitably named and dated, upon the cairn which is being formed by visitors to the spot in memory of the illustrious recluse." *Banner of Light* (Aug. 3, 1878), quoted in Robbins, *Discovery at Walden*, 54–56.

116. Robbins, "#3 Thoreau Hut Notes," Sept. 1, 1946.

117. Robbins, "#3 Thoreau Hut Notes," Sept. 1, 1946.

118. Robbins, "#3 Thoreau Hut Notes," Sept. 2, 1946. The note read: "The undersigned have witnessed the excavation of the cellar hole of Henry David Thoreau's Walden cabin on Labor Day, September 2, 1946 by Roland Wells Robbins, who discovered the site of the chimney foundation on November 11, 1945."

119. Robbins, "#3 Thoreau Hut Notes," Sept. 3, 1946. Robbins recorded that he found two coins at the bottom of the cairn, an 1899 nickel and a 1913 penny.

120. Robbins, "#3 Thoreau Hut Notes," Sept. 3, 1946.

121. Robbins, "#3 Thoreau Hut Notes," Sept. 3, 1946.

122. Robbins, "#3 Thoreau Hut Notes," Sept. 3, 1946.

123. Robbins, "#3 Thoreau Hut Notes," Oct. 23, 1946.

124. Robbins, "#3 Thoreau Hut Notes," Oct. 1946 to Apr. 1947.

125. Robbins described the Walden project as his amateur work in several radio interviews. This was also confirmed by his wife Geraldine.

126. Bolton, 1918, quoted in Gruber, "Artifacts Are History," 21–22. This passage could just as easily be describing Robbins's early work. His possession of Calver and Bolton's book, *History Written with Pick and Shovel*, demonstrates that Robbins was aware of the work of these pioneers.

127. Dodson, "The Man Who Found Thoreau," 116.

128. Harrington, "Jamestown Archaeology in Retrospect," 31–32.

129. The large amounts of brick, mortar, and plaster recovered were not generally stored by provenience, but the daily logs record the weight of these artifacts by excavation area.

130. Current work on this is still underway by the author and will be the subject of a forthcoming article. The principal omission by Robbins is the documentation of the entire soil sequence that he excavated, making it difficult to fully understand the stratigraphic relationships between groups of artifacts and features.

131. Roland W. Robbins to Walter Harding, Jan. 26, 1946, the Roland Wells Robbins Collection, the Thoreau Society, Lincoln, Mass.

132. Roland W. Robbins to Walter Harding, Jan. 23, 1946, the Roland Wells Robbins Collection, the Thoreau Society, Lincoln, Mass. In addition to the

National Thoreau Society, Robbins had also unsuccessfully solicited the Guggenheim Foundation, Henry Ford, the Trustees of Public Reservations, the Smithsonian Institution, the Massachusetts Society for the Preservation of Antiquities, and the Fogg Museum at Harvard for funding assistance. He noted in another letter to Harding that an "exhibit of photos [of the excavation] doesn't pay the bills. Robbins to Harding, Jan. 26, 1946.

133. Although he tried to interest several publishing houses in the book idea, he received only rejections, prompting him to publish the book himself. Robbins worked with the firm of George R. Barnstead & Son (Stoneham, Mass.), paying for the cost of typesetting and printing himself. Ten years earlier, the Barnstead company had produced his book of poetry and verse *Thru the Covered Bridge*.

134. Robbins, "#1 Thoreau Hut Notes," 61, 92.

135. Robbins, "#2 Thoreau Hut Notes," July 4, 1946.

136. W. B. C. to Harding, Jan. 14, 1946.

137. Robbins, "#2 Thoreau Hut Notes," 1.

138. Walter Harding, interview with author, Nov. 6, 1992, Geneseo, N.Y.

139. Harding, interview with author, Nov. 6, 1992.

140. Harding, interview with author, Nov. 6, 1992.

141. Harding, interview with author, Nov. 6, 1992.

142. Robbins, *Thru the Covered Bridge*, 61–62.

143. Robbins, *Discovery at Walden*, 3. It was probably not lost on Robbins that Thoreau was thirty-seven years old when he went to live at Walden.

144. Robbins to Harding, Jan. 23, 1946.

145. Robbins, "#1 Thoreau Hut Notes," 61.

146. Robbins to Harding, Jan. 26, 1946.

147. Robbins, *Discovery at Walden*, title page.

148. Robbins, *Discovery at Walden*, 25.

149. The first printing sold out in several years, and Robbins eventually reprinted the book in paperback.

150. Walter Harding to Roland W. Robbins, Feb. 27, 1947, the Roland Wells Robbins Collection, the Thoreau Society, Lincoln, Mass.

151. Walter Harding quoted in Robbins, *Discovery at Walden*, xv–xvi.

152. Clayton Hoagland to Roland W. Robbins, Feb. 19, 1947, the Roland Wells Robbins Collection, the Thoreau Society, Lincoln, Mass.

153. Townsend Scudder, "Review of *Discovery at Walden*," *New England Quarterly* 20 (1947): 274. Interestingly, Scudder's description of *Discovery at Walden*'s "shrewd, homespun, naively humorous quaintness" directly connects with Robbins's earlier book of poems and verse, *Thru the Covered Bridge*, and with his lectures on the Walden discovery and life in rural New England.

154. Roland W. Robbins to Walter Harding, July 23, 1946, the Roland Wells Robbins Collection, the Thoreau Society, Lincoln, Mass.

155. W. B. Conant to Roland W. Robbins, Feb. 5, 1946. The Roland Wells Robbins Collection, the Thoreau Society, Lincoln, Mass.

156. Roland W. Robbins, *Discovery at Walden: A Lecture*, brochure, ca. 1946, the Roland Wells Robbins Collection, the Thoreau Society, Lincoln, Mass.

157. Robbins, *Discovery at Walden: A Lecture*.

158. Robbins, *Discovery at Walden: A Lecture*.

159. Geraldine Robbins, interviews with author, July 31 and Aug. 1 and 3, 1992.

160. Robbins and Jones, *Hidden America*, 11.

Chapter 3. Forging a New Career: Excavating the Ironworks Sites of New England, pp. 58–97

1. Schuyler, "Anthropological Perspectives," 129.

2. Although Robbins focused largely on industrial sites, he also excavated several important domestic sites including the John Alden House site in Duxbury, Massachusetts, the Hancock-Clarke House site in Lexington, Massachusetts, and Shadwell, the Jefferson birthplace in Virginia.

3. Kammen, *Mystic Chords of Memory*, 537.

4. Wallace, "Visiting the Past," 150.

5. Kammen, *Mystic Chords of Memory*, 538; Wallace, "Visiting the Past," 150.

6. Kammen, *Mystic Chords of Memory*, 538; Wallace, "Visiting the Past," 150.

7. Wallace, "Visiting the Past," 150.

8. Wallace, "Visiting the Past," 150.

9. Brown, "A Survey of Historical Archaeology in New England," 6.

10. I discuss Saugus and several other ironworks sites, including the John Winthrop Furnace, Sterling Forest Furnace, and Dover Union Iron Company, in more detail in my article "Forging a Career: Roland W. Robbins and Iron Industry Sites in the Northeastern U.S.," *IA: The Journal of the Society for Industrial Archaeology* 26, no. 1 (2000): 5–36.

11. J. Sanger Attwill to Roland W. Robbins, Aug. 24, 1948, the Roland Wells Robbins Collection, the Thoreau Society, Lincoln, Mass.

12. Marley R. Brown III, ed., "An Evaluation of Roland Wells Robbins Archaeology," 1975, Saugus Iron Works National Historic Site, Saugus, Mass., the Roland Wells Robbins Collection, the Thoreau Society, Lincoln, Mass., 1.

13. During later excavations along Central Street, Robbins located a "First Iron Works" historical marker placed by the Lynn Historical Society in 1898. Roland W. Robbins, "Saugus Ironworks Daily Log, First Iron Works Association, Saugus, Massachusetts—1951," the Roland Wells Robbins Collection, the Thoreau Society, Lincoln, Mass., 65.

14. Stephen P. Carlson, "The Saugus Iron Works Restoration: A Tentative History," 1978, Saugus Iron Works National Historic Site, Saugus Mass., 1978, 1.

15. Carlson, "The Saugus Iron Works Restoration," 1–2. Nutting, unhappy in the ministry, suffered a nervous breakdown; his recovery involved his complete immersion in the civil religion of the past. Edie Clark, "The Man Who Looked Back and Saw the Future," *Yankee* 50, no. 9 (1986): 112.

16. Clark, "The Man Who Looked Back," 174–175.

17. Carlson, "The Saugus Iron Works Restoration," 3.

18. Carlson, "The Saugus Iron Works Restoration," 3.

19. Carlson, "The Saugus Iron Works Restoration," 3.

20. Carlson, "The Saugus Iron Works Restoration," 3–4.

21. Carlson, "The Saugus Iron Works Restoration," 5–6; First Iron Works Association, Inc., fund-raising letter, ca. 1942–1943, the Roland Wells Robbins Collection, the Thoreau Society, Lincoln, Mass.

22. Louise du Pont Crowninshield, the daughter of Henry F. du Pont, was raised at Winterthur. As an adult she lived at the Eleutherian Mills, the original du Pont family home, a site that Robbins investigated briefly in the late 1950s. Mrs. Crowninshield is considered one of the nation's leading historic preservation activists in the first half of the twentieth century.

23. Carlson, "The Saugus Iron Works Restoration," 6. The "Iron Works House" was originally identified as the "Ironmaster's House," but recent dendrochronology on the structure suggests that neither title is likely to be correct as the structure seems to postdate the ironworks period.

24. Quincy Bent was a vice president with Bethlehem Steel; Charles R. Harte was a professional engineer who documented many industrial and iron-making sites, primarily in Connecticut, during the first half of the twentieth century; Edward L. Bartholomew Jr. was an assistant professor of metallurgy at MIT; Walter Renton Ingalls was an engineer; and John Woodman Higgins was the founder of the Higgins Armory Museum in Worcester, Mass. Curtis McKay White, personal communication, 2000.

25. Carlson, "The Saugus Iron Works Restoration," 9.

26. Vincent P. Foley, "On the Meaning of Industrial Archaeology," *Historical Archaeology* 2 (1968): 66–68.

27. David G. Orr, "Philadelphia as Industrial Archaeological Artifact: A Case Study," *Historical Archaeology* 11 (1977): 3–14.

28. Orr, "Philadelphia as Industrial Archaeological Artifact," 3–14.

29. Foley, "On the Meaning of Industrial Archaeology," 66–68; Robert M. Vogel, "On the Real Meaning of Industrial Archaeology," *Historical Archaeology* 3 (1969): 87–93; Vincent P. Foley, "Reply to Vogel," *Historical Archaeology* 3 (1969): 93–94.

30. Foley, "Reply to Vogel," 94.

31. Geraldine Robbins, letter to author, Oct. 26, 1995.

32. Geraldine Robbins, letter to author, Oct. 26, 1995. For instance, Robbins

patented a locking lug nut for automobile wheels in the 1950s and unsuccessfully tried to market it to the major automakers.

33. Thomas Blanding, interview with author, Aug. 10, 1993, Lincoln, Mass.

34. Paul Heberling, interview with author, Nov. 8, 1992, State College, Pa.

35. Evan Jones, interview with author, July 29, 1992, East Hardwick, Vt.

36. Roland W. Robbins, "Report on Research and Excavation, Executed
from September 10, 1848 to October 16, 1948, Old Iron Works Site, Saugus, Massachusetts," the Roland Wells Robbins Collection, the Thoreau Society, Lincoln,
Mass., 1.

37. Roland W. Robbins, "Report of Archaeological Progress at the Old Iron
Works Site, Saugus, Massachusetts, from September 10, 1948 to June 25, 1949,"
the Roland Wells Robbins Collection, the Thoreau Society, Lincoln, Mass.

38. Carlson, "The Saugus Iron Works Restoration," 9. At a cost of $1,500.00.

39. Robbins, "Report of Archaeological Progress," 1; Robbins, "Report on
Research," 4.

40. Robbins, "Report on Research," 5.

41. Carlson, "The Saugus Iron Works Restoration," 9.

42. Robbins, "Saugus Ironworks Daily Log—1949," 24.

43. Robbins worked with several specialists to develop conservation treat-
ments for the wood and metal artifacts. Dr. Elso Barghoorn, an associate professor of botany and curator of paleobotany at Harvard University, developed a
"Paraffin technique" treatment for the waterlogged wood remains. Elso S.
Barghoorn to Roland W. Robbins, May 22, 1951, the Roland Wells Robbins Collection, the Thoreau Society, Lincoln, Mass.). Robbins worked with Professor
Uhlig at MIT to conduct various tests to develop a treatment for the iron artifacts. Robbins, "Saugus Ironworks Daily Log—1951," 21; "Saugus Ironworks
Daily Log—1952," 58; and "Saugus Ironworks Daily Log—1953," 38. One of Robbins workers was assigned to conservation, and they kept a detailed treatment
log of the artifacts. Arthur C. Laura, "Research Notes on Metal Artifacts and
their Restoration," 1952, the Roland Wells Robbins Collection, the Thoreau Society, Lincoln, Mass.

44. Robbins, "Saugus Ironworks Daily Log—1950," 108.

45. Robbins, "Saugus Ironworks Daily Log—1952," 66, 79–80.

46. Robbins, "Saugus Ironworks Daily Log—1952," 93, 95, 105, 108, 114–129;
"Saugus Ironworks Daily Log—1953," 15.

47. In many ways, Robbins's methodology for identifying features differs little
from present practice. Robbins, "Saugus Ironworks Daily Log—1949," 49; "Saugus
Ironworks Daily Log—1950," 40; "Saugus Ironworks Daily Log—1953," 37.

48. Robbins, "Saugus Ironworks Daily Log—1950," 113. Although not within
Robbins's area of interest, prehistoric features were identified on several occasions, and he contacted members of the Massachusetts Archaeological Society

about excavating several features that would be destroyed by the ironworks excavation. Robbins, "Saugus Ironworks Daily Log—1953," 60.

49. The documentation and use of the entire stratigraphic profile is essential for establishing chronological (dating) sequences and the relationships of activities across an archaeological site.

50. Brown, "An Evaluation of Roland Wells Robbins Archaeology," 3.

51. Dodson, "The Man Who Found Thoreau," 116.

52. Robbins, "Saugus Ironworks Daily Log—1950," 102, 215. On several occasions he met with Smithsonian curator C. Malcolm Watkins and his mother Lura Woodside Watkins, who helped with the identification of Saugus artifacts. Robbins, "Saugus Ironworks Daily Log—1952," 30, 127. Both C. Malcolm Watkins and Lura Woodside Watkins were respected ceramics experts. Lura Woodside Watkins, *Early New England Pottery* (Sturbridge, Mass.: Old Sturbridge Village, 1959), and C. Malcolm Watkins, "North Devon Pottery and Its Export to America in the 17th Century," in *Contributions from the Museum of History and Technology,* United States National Museum Bulletin 225 (Washington, D.C.: Smithsonian Institution, 1960).

53. The artifact collection was poorly stored after Robbins's departure, later transferred to the National Park Service facility at Harpers Ferry, and then eventually returned to Saugus; this process resulted in the loss of specific provenience information for parts of the collection. R. J. Barber, *Report on the Saugus Ironworks Collections and their Cataloging,* 1973, on file at New England Museum Services Center, Marine Barracks, Boston National Historical Park, Charlestown Unit, Charlestown, Mass. In addition, during the National Park Service's cataloging project in 1973, portions of the collection were discarded with only samples being retained. Eric S. Johnson, *Archaeological Overview and Assessment of the Saugus Ironworks National Historic Site, Saugus, Massachusetts,* 1997, on file at the New England System Support Office, National Park Service, Boston.

54. Roland W. Robbins to Charles Harte, ca. 1952, the Roland Wells Robbins Collection, the Thoreau Society, Lincoln, Mass.

55. Importantly, these drawings survive and will prove essential in completing a full analysis of the reconstruction's accuracy, as will the records of the Joint Reconstruction Committee and of the architects.

56. Brown, "An Evaluation of Roland Wells Robbins Archaeology," 17.

57. Robbins, "Saugus Ironworks Daily Log—1950," 8.

58. Robbins, "Saugus Ironworks Daily Log—1950," 192. For instance, Robbins's testing around the houses that lined Marion Road, Central Street, and Bridge Street was continuously slowed or stopped by difficulties in getting permission to excavate and by landowner complaints.

59. Robbins, "Saugus Ironworks Daily Log—1950," 152. In fact, the attorney's reputation with the neighbors was such that Robbins was frequently called

upon to act as a negotiator and mediator between the property owners and the attorney, particularly when the association wished to buy the land.

60. Robbins, "Saugus Ironworks Daily Log—1950," 117.

61. Robbins, "Saugus Ironworks Daily Log—1950," 222. They ordered Robbins to backfill his units immediately and abandon the area until they had attended to the problem.

62. Robbins received his introduction to community politics during the Association's campaign to relocate Central Street. Robbins, "Saugus Ironworks Daily Log—1950," 69. Robbins participated in negotiations between the Saugus Iron Works and town officials for several months. Town meetings generated heated debate and opposition from homeowners in the ironworks neighborhood, and town representatives and neighbors visited the site throughout the summer of 1950. Robbins gave them a full tour of the operation and vigorously lobbied for the project. Robbins, "Saugus Ironworks Daily Log—1950," 95–96. With the help of this lobbying effort by Robbins, the road rerouting was approved during a special town meeting on July 27, 1950.

63. Marley R. Brown III, personal communication, 1996.

64. Mary C. Beaudry, "Archaeology and the Documentary Record." In "An Evaluation of Roland Wells Robbins Archaeology," ed. Marley R. Brown III, 1975, manuscript on file, Saugus Iron Works National Historic Site, Saugus, Mass., n.p.

65. Robbins, "Report of Archaeological Progress," 3.

66. Robbins, "Saugus Ironworks Daily Log—1953," 78–81.

67. Brown, "An Evaluation of Roland Wells Robbins Archaeology," 13; Carlson, "The Saugus Iron Works Restoration," 10.

68. Robbins, "Saugus Ironworks Daily Log—1953," 80–81.

69. Robbins, "Saugus Ironworks Daily Log—1950," 119.

70. Robbins, "Saugus Ironworks Daily Log—1951," 80.

71. Robbins, "Saugus Ironworks Daily Log—1951," 109.

72. Robbins, "Saugus Ironworks Daily Log—1951," 109. Robbins was not the only staff member to be irritated by Schock. Chairman Quincy Bent wrote in 1951 that "Mr. Schock's personality leaves much to be desired. He has a rare talent for rubbing people the wrong way, and has clashed on several points with Robbins and Hartley."

73. Robbins, "Saugus Ironworks Daily Log—1952," 18. Conover Fitch was the project architect for Perry, Shaw, Hepburn, Kehoe and Dean, and Harrison Schock worked for Fitch.

74. Robbins, "Saugus Ironworks Daily Log—1952," 23. In mid-1953, committee member and ironworks expert Charles R. Harte resigned because of his own frustrations with the reconstruction designs, particularly the forge layout and furnace. Robbins, "Saugus Ironworks Daily Log—1953," 77.

75. Carlson, "The Saugus Iron Works Restoration," 11.

76. Robbins, "Saugus Ironworks Daily Log—1950," 108–109. In 1950, Bent visited the ironworks over a weekend and found that no one was available to show visitors through the excavations and house. Bent informed Robbins that he wanted him at the ironworks over the weekends for this purpose. Robbins was incensed by the addition of this new responsibility to his many other jobs. Robbins, "Saugus Ironworks Daily Log—1950," 110, 146–148; Roland W. Robbins to Walter S. Tower, Aug. 9, 1950; Walter S. Tower to Roland W. Robbins, Sept. 1, 1950, both in the Roland Wells Robbins Collection, the Thoreau Society, Lincoln, Mass. After talking with his wife, Robbins made the decision to resign "because of the consistent lack of cooperation my department gets from Bent and Attwill." Robbins, "Saugus Ironworks Daily Log—1950," 109. Robbins discussed the situation with Parker and Tower of the American Iron and Steel Institute, and both "wouldn't hear of it [the resignation]. . . . Mr. Tower then told me to sit tight—everything would be taken care of." Robbins, "Saugus Ironworks Daily Log—1950," 109.

77. Roland W. Robbins to Quincy Bent, Aug. 19, 1951, the Roland Wells Robbins Collection, the Thoreau Institute, Lincoln, Mass. Robbins was invited by Dr. William Ritchie of Yale to participate in the ESAF conference to be held at the University of North Carolina.

78. Quincy Bent to Roland W. Robbins, Aug. 20, 1951, the Roland Wells Robbins Collection, the Thoreau Institute, Lincoln, Mass.

79. Walter S. Tower to Roland W. Robbins, July 3, 1951, the Roland Wells Robbins Collection, the Thoreau Society, Lincoln, Mass.

80. Geraldine Robbins to Quincy Bent, Oct. 29, 1953, the Roland Wells Robbins Collection, the Thoreau Society, Lincoln, Mass.

81. Roland W. Robbins to Quincy Bent, Nov. 16, 1953, the Roland Wells Robbins Collection, the Thoreau Society, Lincoln, Mass.

82. After a complete physical, his doctor recommended that he take a vacation and forget about Saugus. Several months later he complained about his "damn nerves . . . kicking up again," and the doctor increased his dose of medication. Robbins finally took a much-needed one-month vacation, but although it helped him regain his strength, he returned to the same set of circumstances that had precipitated his earlier problems. Robbins, "Saugus Ironworks Daily Log—1952," 115; Robbins, "Saugus Ironworks Daily Log—1953," 1, 12, 78–79. He wrote to an associate that "two days after returning from my vacation, I found myself bordering on the rim [sic] of a possible nervous breakdown." Roland W. Robbins to Reverend Charles Jarvis Harriman, Nov. 20, 1952, the Roland Wells Robbins Collection, the Thoreau Society, Lincoln, Mass.

83. Roland W. Robbins to Teresa and Elso Barghoorn, Oct. 27, 1953, the Roland Wells Robbins Collection, the Thoreau Society, Lincoln, Mass.

84. Brown, "An Evaluation of Roland Wells Robbins Archaeology," 15.

85. Dr. Schubert was the historical investigator to the Iron and Steel Insti-

tute (British) and a consultant to the Saugus project. E. Neal Hartley, *Ironworks on the Saugus* (Norman: University of Oklahoma Press, 1957), ix.

86. Robbins, "Saugus Ironworks Daily Log—1952," 68.

87. Roland W. Robbins to Charles Rufus Harte, Aug. 12, 1953, the Roland Wells Robbins Collection, the Thoreau Society, Lincoln, Mass.

88. Robbins, "Saugus Ironworks Daily Log—1952," 31.

89. Hartley, *Ironworks on the Saugus,* 176.

90. As Curtis White points out, the artifactual evidence supports the interpretation of this area as the rolling and slitting mill. White, personal communication, 2000.

91. Robbins, "Saugus Ironworks Daily Log—1950," 122.

92. Brown, "An Evaluation of Roland Wells Robbins Archaeology," 17.

93. Both Brown ("An Evaluation of Roland Wells Robbins Archaeology," 17–19) and Johnson (*Archaeological Overview and Assessment of the Saugus Iron Works,* 32) comment on the problematic aspects of Robbins's landscape renovation and the lack of documentation of this work. For example, it is clear that he not only removed materials and stockpiled this fill but also filled other areas with the stockpiled materials from different portions of the site, a process that had the potential to "alter, obscure, confuse or entirely destroy archaeological context." Johnson, *Archaeological Overview and Assessment of the Saugus Iron Works,* 32.

94. Johnson, *Archaeological Overview and Assessment of the Saugus Iron Works,* 61.

95. Johnson, *Archaeological Overview and Assessment of the Saugus Iron Works,* 61.

96. Robbins worked with Dr. Elso Barghoorn, an associate professor of botany and curator of paleobotany at Harvard University, who was interested in the Saugus site as part of Borghoorn's ongoing research on sea-level changes along the Atlantic coast. Elso S. Barghoorn, "Recent Changes in Sea Level along the New England Coast: New Archaeological Evidence," *Science* 117, no. 3048 (1953): 597–598.

97. Johnson, *Archaeological Overview and Assessment of the Saugus Iron Works,* 32.

98. First Iron Works Association, Inc., and American Iron and Steel Institute, *The Saugus Iron Works Restoration,* 16-mm film (New York: Filmfax Productions, 1955).

99. First Iron Works Association, Inc., and American Iron and Steel Institute, *The Saugus Iron Works Restoration.*

100. Kammen, *Mystic Chords of Memory,* 586–587.

101. Robbins, "Saugus Ironworks Daily Log—1951," 90–91.

102. Barbara Clark Smith, *After the Revolution: The Smithsonian History of Everyday Life in the Eighteenth Century* (New York: Pantheon Books, 1985), xvi.

103. Kammen, *Mystic Chords of Memory,* 586–587.

104. Senator Robert A. Taft, quoted in Paul A. Haley, "Taft Hails Ironworks as Symbol of Freedom," *Lynn (Mass.) Item*, Monday, April 21, 1952, 1.

105. First Iron Works Association, Inc., and American Iron and Steel Institute, *The Saugus Iron Works Restoration*.

106. First Iron Works Association, Inc., and American Iron and Steel Institute, *The Saugus Iron Works Restoration*.

107. First Iron Works Association, Inc., and American Iron and Steel Institute, *The Saugus Iron Works Restoration*.

108. Production of consumer goods increased immediately after World War II with the conversion of factories from wartime production. However, military production continued during this period as well and increased with the growing threats of the Cold War.

109. First Iron Works Association, Inc., and American Iron and Steel Institute, *The Saugus Iron Works Restoration*.

110. Wallace, "Reflections on the History of Historic Preservation," 175.

111. Quoted in Wallace, "Reflections on the History of Historic Preservation," 176.

112. Wallace, "Reflections on the History of Historic Preservation," 176.

113. Jack Frost [pseud.?], *Yankee Homecoming: Official Sketch Book* (Boston: Yankee Homecoming Council, 1958), 4.

114. Frost, *Yankee Homecoming*, 6.

115. Frost, *Yankee Homecoming*, 16.

116. Frost, *Yankee Homecoming*, 31, 76.

117. Frost, *Yankee Homecoming*, 31.

118. Frost, *Yankee Homecoming*, 39.

119. Frost, *Yankee Homecoming*, 33.

120. Frost, *Yankee Homecoming*, 36.

121. Robbins to Harte, Aug. 12, 1953.

122. Roland W. Robbins to Evan Jones, Apr. 30, 1955, the Roland Wells Robbins Collection, the Thoreau Society, Lincoln, Mass.

123. Adolph F. Bandelier quoted in Brian Fagan, *Elusive Treasure: The Story of Early Archaeologists in the Americas* (New York: Charles Scribner's Sons, 1977), 247.

124. Kammen, *Mystic Chords of Memory*, 537.

125. Geraldine Robbins, letter to author, Oct. 26, 1995.

126. Mrs. Robbins noted that "there was no end to his physical and mental energy. . . . his mind was always working. I think it ran all night!" Geraldine Robbins, interviews with author, July 31 and Aug. 1 and 3, 1992. Floyd Johnson, his colleague at Shadwell, remembered that "he was just full of energy, and just vibrated." Floyd Johnson, interview with author, Mar. 9, 1995, Keene, Va.

127. Patterson, "The Last Sixty Years," 116.

128. Schuyler, "Anthropological Perspectives," 74. This meeting was held at Colonial Williamsburg and Jamestown.

129. Harrington, "From Architraves to Artifacts," 11.

130. Schuyler, "Anthropological Perspectives," 74.

131. Schuyler, "Anthropological Perspectives," 76; South, *Pioneers in Histori-cal Archaeology,* vi.

132. J. C. Harrington, "Historic Site Archaeology in the United States," in *Archaeology of the Eastern United States,* ed. James B. Griffin (Chicago: The University of Chicago Press, 1952), 336, 341.

133. Harrington, "Historic Site Archaeology," 341–342.

134. Publication of excavation data was increasingly seen as the ethical responsibility of all archaeologists, as the process of digging destroyed the site forever.

135. Schuyler, "Anthropological Perspectives," 75–76.

136. Schuyler, "Anthropological Perspectives," 76.

137. Schuyler, "Anthropological Perspectives," 77. Everyone was quick to get into the act: Congress established the Jamestown-Williamsburg-Yorktown Celebration Commission, and the Virginia General Assembly created the 350th Virginia Anniversary Commission.

138. Schuyler, "Anthropological Perspectives," 77. The goal of the work at Jamestown was to locate the 1609 fort, reinvestigate the church site, and identify and excavate structures, refuse pits, ditches, and wells across the town site; the results included identification of over 141 structures, many of which were domestic dwellings. In 1958, Cotter produced a site report that went on to become a classic in the field with its detailed descriptive data on the features and structures, thorough illustrations of the fieldwork (drawings and photographs), and careful site interpretation. John L. Cotter, *Archaeological Excavations at Jamestown, Virginia* (1958; reprint, Richmond: Archeological Society of Virginia, Special Publication no. 32, 1994).

139. Schuyler, "Anthropological Perspectives," 77; Cotter, *Archaeological Excavations at Jamestown,* 30.

140. Cotter, *Archaeological Excavations at Jamestown,* 30. Of their excavation work, Cotter noted that "limitations on field methodology were yet another frustration during the 1954–1957 campaign. The field crew, locally hired and carefully trained by the archaeologists, was far smaller than the CCC crews that had assisted in earlier excavations; the workers therefore could not be expected to reduce each grid square stratum by stratum, "onion peeling" the earth in quest of features. Instead, with the archaeologists keeping close watch and often doing most of the trowel work themselves, the crew dug three-foot trenches along grid lines at fifty-foot intervals to undisturbed earth" (31). Like Robbins's trenches at Saugus, these units were designed to identify structural and landscape features, such as ditches, walks, or wells. The overburden removed from these trenches was provenienced only by trench, and the trenches were sometimes several hundred feet long.

141. Schuyler, "Anthropological Perspectives," 79.

142. Robbins appears to have also been familiar with Wheeler's work; he had a copy of Mortimer Wheeler's *Archaeology from the Earth* (London: Penguin Books, 1956) in his library. Wheeler advocated the excavation of natural/ cultural soil layers, arguing that the prehistorian's method of excavating exclusively by arbitrary levels was outmoded and destructive. Prehistorians typically used fixed (arbitrary) levels as a way of providing vertical control for artifacts in deposits that were often not stratified or in which the stratification was difficult to determine. Using this approach with clearly defined historic strata could result in mixing of artifacts between natural/cultural soil layers that were chronologically distinct.

143. Elizabeth A. Schnick, ed., *1997 Current Biography Yearbook* (New York: H. W. Wilson, 1997), 419.

144. Schnick, *1997 Current Biography Yearbook*, 420.

145. Schnick, *1997 Current Biography Yearbook*, 420.

146. Schnick, *1997 Current Biography Yearbook*, 420.

147. Schnick, *1997 Current Biography Yearbook*, 421.

148. Schnick, *1997 Current Biography Yearbook*, 420.

149. Schnick, *1997 Current Biography Yearbook*, 420.

150. Schnick, *1997 Current Biography Yearbook*, 419.

151. Schnick, *1997 Current Biography Yearbook*, 419.

152. Schuyler, "Anthropological Perspectives," 80. Although the use of stratigraphic excavation for chronological control had become standard in American prehistoric archaeology during the first half of the twentieth century, it was not regularly applied in historical archaeology until at least the mid-1950s (see note 142). Willey and Sabloff, *A History of American Archaeology*, 244.

153. Archaeological work in the 1930s had verified the historical interpretation of this site as the Howland family home.

154. James Deetz, "Excavations at the Joseph Howland Site (C5), Rocky Nook, Kingston, Massachusetts, 1959: A Preliminary Report," *Supplement to the Howland Quarterly* 24, nos. 2–3 (1960): 1–11.

155. Schuyler, "Anthropological Perspectives," 91. Deetz's reports on the site are generally presented in summary format, including a brief discussion of the site history (title chain), description of the excavated features and structures, and more detailed presentation of the artifactual information recovered from the site. These reports contain basic sketch maps of the site and plan of the excavations, and one artifact photograph. Deetz, "Excavations at the Joseph Howland Site"; James Deetz, "The Howlands at Rocky Nook: An Archaeological and Historical Study," *Supplement to the Howland Quarterly* 24, no. 4 (1960): 1–8.

156. J. C. Harrington had discovered that the bore diameter of pipes decreased through time and that by measuring the bore diameter of pipe stems it was possible to closely date historic sites.

157. J. C. Harrington, "Archaeology and Local History," *Bulletin of the Amer-*

ican Association for State and Local History, 2, no. 6 (1953): 157. He noted that "experience in this country over the past fifteen or twenty years has demonstrated quite convincingly that the methods and techniques of archaeology can be applied advantageously to the field of local history."

158. Harrington, "Archaeology and Local History," 157–167.

159. Harrington, "Archaeology and Local History," 161–162.

160. Fiske Kimball, "In Search of Jefferson's Birthplace," *Virginia Magazine of History and Biography* 51, no. 4 (1943).

161. It is not clear from either Schumacher's report or field notes whether the trenches were actually excavated by soil strata or layer for vertical artifact control. The trenches may have simply been shoveled to subsoil and profiles drawn of the walls, as described by Cotter at Jamestown.

162. Roland W. Robbins, "Report on 1955 Archaeological Exploration at Shadwell, Birthplace of Thomas Jefferson," the Roland Wells Robbins Collection, the Thoreau Society, Lincoln, Mass., 4–5. By the time that the initial work was completed, Schumacher had exhausted his leave of absence and was not able to extend the work. Floyd E. Johnson to Thomas J. Michie, Mar. 18, 1960, the Roland Wells Robbins Collection, the Thoreau Society, Lincoln, Mass. Johnson's letter provides a summary of the various projects.

163. Robbins W. Robbins to Floyd E. Johnson, June 1, 1954; Floyd E. Johnson to Roland W. Robbins, June 9, 1954; Floyd E. Johnson to Roland W. Robbins, June 30, 1954, the Roland Wells Robbins Collection, the Thoreau Society, Lincoln, Mass.

164. Johnson to Robbins, June 30, 1954.

165. Robbins, "Report on 1955 Archaeological Exploration at Shadwell," 5. The first excavations at the site had been performed for the Thomas Jefferson Memorial Foundation in 1941 under the direction of architect Fiske Kimball. Robbins noted in his report that during these excavations Kimball identified a small stone foundation, a larger brick cellar foundation, and two small brick features. Although Kimball found hints of earlier artifacts, he reported that the majority of the materials dated to the late nineteenth century. As was typical of these early excavation projects, the ceramics were classified by curators at the Philadelphia Museum of Art, where Kimball served as director. Kimball concluded that the large brick foundation was not the mansion house of Peter Jefferson, because it did not face south, "then almost universal in a Virginia dwelling house," and because no evidence of a chimney for the structure had been found. Robbins, "Report on 1955 Archaeological Exploration at Shadwell"; Fiske Kimball, "In Search of Jefferson's Birthplace," 319.

166. Roland W. Robbins to Floyd E. Johnson, Nov. 14, 1954, the Roland Wells Robbins Collection, the Thoreau Society, Lincoln, Mass.

167. Floyd E. Johnson to Roland W. Robbins, Nov. 29, 1954, the Roland Wells Robbins Collection, the Thoreau Society, Lincoln, Mass. Johnson inquired

about Robbins's availability for the work and the fees or charges, and indicated that he would have an engineer plot the two small cellar features and expand the 10-foot grid begun by Schumacher. Following negotiations over expenses, it was decided to begin work in early April 1955.

168. Roland W. Robbins, "Shadwell—1955, Daily Log," the Roland Wells Robbins Collection, the Thoreau Society, Lincoln, Mass., 2. Robbins hired a farmer with a mechanical posthole digger to help complete the tests.

169. Robbins, "Shadwell—1955, Daily Log," 2. Mechanical equipment is now regularly used for the careful removal of plowzone and exposure of the features below, although experiments have shown that there is much to gain from the systematic excavation of the plowzone. "Each square was recorded by its four stake numbers and assigned an additional number designating the chronological order of this work." Robbins, "Report on 1955 Archaeological Exploration at Shadwell," 12. Plowzone sites are typically made up of the upper plowed soils that directly overlie the subsoil. Plowing has mixed the upper layers, and little stratigraphy is evident. Often, features such as cellars or postholes will remain partially intact below the reach of the plow and can be located and excavated by removing the plowzone. Deeply stratified sites are typically made up of multiple intact soil layers that extend to some depth below the plowzone or surface.

170. Robbins, "Report on 1955 Archaeological Exploration at Shadwell," 13. Robbins recorded that "we shall have to be quite careful when taking out the various grid squares to record the related squares that produce the greater bulk of relics indicative of houses or buildings. This way we may be able to pin-point the site of buildings, and come up with pertinent information by studying the basic evidence found 8″, and lower, beneath the existing surface." Robbins, "Shadwell—1955, Daily Log," 9.

171. Robbins, "Report on 1955 Archaeological Exploration at Shadwell," 34. After fire had destroyed the Jefferson home in 1770, he speculated, another house was built at the site; this dwelling was destroyed some years later, and cultivation of the site began. This cultivation and the subsequent erosion, Robbins believed, destroyed the foundation evidence for the Shadwell mansion.

172. Robbins, "Report on 1955 Archaeological Exploration at Shadwell," 5. In 1961, Robbins attended the opening-day activities for the completed reconstruction. Roland W. Robbins, "Shadwell—1961, Daily Log," the Roland Wells Robbins Collection, the Thoreau Society, Lincoln, Mass., 1. Mrs. Robbins recalled that Robbins was never happy with the reconstruction and felt that it did not reflect the archaeology and was just "not quite right." Geraldine Robbins, personal communication, 1993.

173. Robbins, "Shadwell—1955, Daily Log," 2, 6.

174. Robbins, "Shadwell—1955, Daily Log," 13, 14, 16.

175. Kimball, "In Search of Jefferson's Birthplace," 312–325; Paul J. F. Schumacher, "Field Notes, Archaeological Exploration, Shadwell Property, Charlottes-

ville, Va., May 10–June 4, 1954," "1954 Archaeological Exploration at Shadwell," and "Profiles of Trenches, Archaeological Survey for the Jefferson Birthplace Memorial Park Commission, May 1954," Thomas Jefferson Memorial Foundation, Charlottesville, Va.

176. Roland W. Robbins, "Shadwell Grid Data 1955," section in "Shadwell Field Notebook—1955," the Roland Wells Robbins Collection, the Thoreau Society, Lincoln, Mass. Robbins recorded basic sketches in his field notebook and daily log and completed precise mapping of features including elevations. Robbins, "Shadwell—1955, Daily Log," 24, 29.

177. Robbins, "Shadwell—1955, Daily Log," 1. Copies of the photographs and slides were provided to the TJBMPC by Robbins in June 1957. Hope B. Rasor to Roland W. Robbins, June 20, 1957, the Roland Wells Robbins Collection, the Thoreau Society, Lincoln, Mass.; Floyd Johnson, interview with author, Mar. 9, 1995.

178. Robbins, "Report on 1955 Archaeological Exploration at Shadwell," 12.

179. Robbins, "Shadwell—1955, Daily Log," 4, 6.

180. Robbins, "Shadwell Grid Data 1955," 7. For instance, on April 20, 1955, he recorded "Grid Square #12" in his field book, writing "a Fiske Kimball test trench, course outlined by dotted line."

181. Robbins, "Report on 1955 Archaeological Exploration at Shadwell," 12.

182. For example, the "Grid Square #7" artifacts were divided into six bags; the first two (7A and 7B) contained materials from the "grid and above pit," the third and fourth (7C and 7D) contained artifacts from the rubble in clay pit, and the fifth held artifacts that "came from [the] 1–3″ layer of fill at [the] bottom of [the] brick evidence (rubble) and were on [the] floor of [the] clay pit." Robbins, "Shadwell Grid Data 1955," 4.

183. The artifacts were stored in these original bags until the most recent archaeological project at Shadwell.

184. Robbins, "Shadwell—1955, Daily Log," 34. He read extensively on clay tobacco pipes and again enlisted the help of Smithsonian curator C. Malcolm Watkins and his mother Mrs. Lura Watkins with the preliminary identification of ceramics. Robbins also sent six white clay tobacco pipe bowls or bowl fragments to H. Geiger Omwake for analysis. Robbins, "Shadwell—1955, Daily Log," 30. Omwake was an independent researcher whom Robbins probably met through C. Malcolm Watkins. H. Geiger Omwake, "Report on the Examination of White Kaolin Pipes from Shadwell," June 1955, the Roland Wells Robbins Collection, the Thoreau Society, Lincoln, Mass.

185. Robbins, "Report on 1955 Archaeological Exploration at Shadwell," 5.

186. Robbins, "Report on 1955 Archaeological Exploration at Shadwell," n.p. The report is illustrated with black-and-white photographs of the excavations, references are appropriately footnoted, and Omwake's tobacco pipe analysis is included as an appendix.

187. Johnson to Michie, Mar. 18, 1960, 8.

188. Robbins, "Shadwell–1955, Daily Log," 9, 20.

189. Robbins, "Report on 1955 Archaeological Exploration at Shadwell," 35–37.

190. Susan A. Kern, personal communication, 1993.

191. Susan A. Kern, personal communication, 1993.

192. Schuyler, "Anthropological Perspectives," 129.

193. Schuyler, "Anthropological Perspectives," 136.

194. Schuyler, "Anthropological Perspectives," 134.

195. Schuyler, "Anthropological Perspectives," 134.

196. Roland W. Robbins to Evan Jones, May 7, 1955, the Roland Wells Robbins Collection, the Thoreau Society, Lincoln, Mass.

197. Roland W. Robbins, "Site of the Nailery at Monticello," preliminary survey, Apr. 18, 1956, the Roland Wells Robbins Collection, the Thoreau Society, Lincoln, Mass. Working along Mulberry Row, Robbins recorded that "tests show that much of the nailery's southerly foundation survives. It seems likely its entire basic pattern is intact."

198. Floyd E. Johnson to Roland W. Robbins, Jan. 17, 1957, the Roland Wells Robbins Collection, the Thoreau Society, Lincoln, Mass.

199. Jones, "Pick and Shovel Historian," 31.

200. Johnson, interview with author, Mar. 9, 1995.

201. Johnson, interview with author, Mar. 9, 1995.

202. Johnson, interview with author, Mar. 9, 1995.

203. Jones, "Pick and Shovel Historian," 28.

204. Heberling, interview with author, Nov. 8, 1992.

205. Robert L. Schuyler, "The Society for Historical Archaeology, 1967–1992: A Quarter Century of a National Archaeological Society," *Historical Archaeology* 27, no. 1 (1993): 35.

206. Schuyler, "The Society for Historical Archaeology, 1967–1992," 35.

Chapter 4. The Rudiments of a Scientific Approach, pp. 98–130

1. The Dover Union Iron Company was a small, private excavation/restoration project in Dover, Massachusetts, that Robbins completed for Miss Amelia Peabody in 1954.

2. Scott, "The Profession That Vanished," 27–28.

3. This suggestion anticipated Stanley South's "Conference on Historic Site Archaeology" by six years and the formation of the Society for Historical Archaeology by more than thirteen years.

4. Roland W. Robbins to J. C. Harrington, Feb. 8, 1954, the Roland Wells Robbins Collection, the Thoreau Society, Lincoln, Mass.

5. J. C. Harrington to Roland W. Robbins, Feb. 16, 1954, the Roland Wells Robbins Collection, the Thoreau Society, Lincoln, Mass.

6. Burton J. Bledstein, *The Culture of Professionalism: The Middle Class and the Development of Higher Education in America* (New York: W. W. Norton & Company, 1976), 92. "The professional person," writes Bledstein, "absolutely protected his precious autonomy against all assailants. . . . In the service of mankind . . . the professional resisted all corporate encroachments and regulations upon his independence."

7. Everett C. Hughes, "Professions," in *The Professions in America*, ed. Kenneth S. Lynn (Boston: Beacon Press, 1967), 11–12.

8. Roland W. Robbins—"Business Brochures, Replies, 1954–1956," and "Business Brochures—Unanswered Correspondence, 1954–1956," the Roland Wells Robbins Collection, the Thoreau Society, Lincoln, Mass.

9. Robbins, "Business Brochures, Replies—1954–1956"; "Business Brochures—Unanswered Correspondence, 1954–1956"; Roland W. Robbins to the Director of the American Foundation, Feb. 27, 1956, the Roland Wells Robbins Collection, the Thoreau Society, Lincoln, Mass.

10. Roland W. Robbins to Mr. Noel Sargent, National Association of Manufacturers, Sept. 12, 1955, the Roland Wells Robbins Collection, the Thoreau Society, Lincoln, Mass. For example, Robbins obtained a copy of a Virginia Electric and Power Company (1956) advertisement designed to encourage industry to move factories to the Richmond area, highlighting the site of America's first ironworks on Falling Creek with the slogan "the home of America's First Iron Works . . . is a choice industrial home for your plant." He wrote to Virginia Electric, describing his work at other ironworks sites and his previous investigations at Falling Creek, and encouraging them to hire him to excavate the site. Virginia Electric and Power Company, "Advertisement," *Wall Street Journal*, July 18, 1956, 12; Roland W. Robbins to Clark P. Spellman, July 28, 1956; and Clark P. Spellman to Roland W. Robbins, Aug. 1, 1956, the Roland Wells Robbins Collection, the Thoreau Society, Lincoln, Mass.

11. Approximately 50 percent of Robbins's inquiries were not answered, and fewer than 1 percent of those that were answered contained a positive response.

12. Helen D. Bullock to Roland W. Robbins, Feb. 8, 1954, the Roland Wells Robbins Collection, the Thoreau Society, Lincoln, Mass. Bullock went on to inform Robbins that they were working hard on the "difficult educational problem of convincing enthusiastic but untrained preservation organizations that archaeology is not an extravagant luxury, but in many cases an indispensable first step."

13. Bernard Barber, "Some Problems in the Sociology of the Professions," in *The Professions in America*, ed. Kenneth S. Lynn (Boston: Beacon Press, 1967), 18; Gerald L. Geison, ed., *Professions and Professional Ideologies in America* (Chapel Hill: University of North Carolina Press, 1983), 4. Several Deetz students reported that they mocked Robbins's business stationery because it listed his major digs (with small sketches) down one edge of the paper.

14. Paul Heberling, interview with author, Nov. 8, 1992. Heberling said that

this was the academic coming out in him. Yet, from his position as the owner of a private archaeological consulting firm, he was genuinely impressed with Robbins's business acumen.

15. Geison, *Professions and Professional Ideologies*, 5–6.

16. Geison, *Professions and Professional Ideologies*, 5–6; Bledstein, *The Culture of Professionalism*, 298–299. While it is an overstatement to suggest that academic archaeologists were consciously engaged in a conspiratorial and exploitative process, the pursuit of professional self-promotion, book contracts, endowed positions and awards within the university, and grant-funded projects could be seen as no less exploitative than Robbins's tactics.

17. Originally known as Philipse Castle, the property was owned and managed by Sleepy Hollow Restorations (later Historic Hudson Valley).

18. Kammen, *Mystic Chords of Memory*, 550.

19. Hugh Grant Rowell quoted in Kammen, *Mystic Chords of Memory*, 550.

20. Hosmer, *Preservation Comes of Age*, 70.

21. Hosmer, *Preservation Comes of Age*, 70.

22. Hosmer, *Preservation Comes of Age*, 70.

23. Hosmer, *Preservation Comes of Age*, 70.

24. Dana S. Creel quoted in Kammen, *Mystic Chords of Memory*, 340.

25. Roland W. Robbins to Harold Dean Cater, Jan. 7, 1956, the Roland Wells Robbins Collection, the Thoreau Society, Lincoln, Mass.

26. Robert G. Wheeler to Roland W. Robbins, July 23, 1956, the Roland Wells Robbins Collection, the Thoreau Society, Lincoln, Mass. Wheeler had met Robbins during the Saugus project and attended one of his lectures.

27. Roland W. Robbins to Robert G. Wheeler, Aug. 5, 1956, the Roland Wells Robbins Collection, the Thoreau Society, Lincoln, Mass.

28. Robbins and Jones, *Hidden America*, 93–119; Charles Howell and Allan Keller, *The Mill at Philipsburg Manor Upper Mills and A Brief History of Milling.* (Tarrytown, N.Y.: Sleepy Hollow Restorations, 1977), 127–148.

29. See my extended discussions of Robbins's work at Philipsburg. Donald W. Linebaugh, "'The Road to Ruins and Restoration': Roland Wells Robbins and the Professionalization of Historical Archaeology" (Ph.D diss., College of William and Mary, 1996), 231–344; Donald W. Linebaugh, "Walden Pond and Beyond: The Restoration Archaeology of Roland W. Robbins" in *The Reconstructed Past: Reconstructions in the Public Interpretation of Archaeology and History*, ed. John H. Jameson Jr. (Walnut Creek, Calif.: AltaMira Press, 2004); and Meta Janowitz, Allan S. Gilbert, and Donald W. Linebaugh, "Compositional Analysis of Redwares for the Philipsburg Manor Upper Mills Sites, Sleepy Hollow, New York," in *Scientific Tools in Historical Archaeology*, ed. Timothy James Scarlett (Pensacola: University Press of Florida, forthcoming).

30. Roland W. Robbins, "Voice of America," Sidney Diamond, moder., audio tape of June 27, 1962, the Roland Wells Robbins Collection, the Thoreau Society, Lincoln, Mass.

31. Robbins completed sample excavations of the entire sequence before using the heavy equipment; however, he did not consistently save artifacts from all levels in these tests nor completely document the stratigraphy in each excavation area.

32. As part of a project to chemically sample redware ceramics from PMUM, the author studied the proveniencing information for specific artifacts in selected contexts. A discussion of this can be found in Janowitz, Gilbert, and Linebaugh, "Compositional Analysis of Redwares."

33. Roland W. Robbins, "Sleepy Hollow Restorations Daily Log—1956," the Roland Wells Robbins Collection, the Thoreau Society, Lincoln, Mass., 1. "The Philipse Castle Land and Structures," 1956, manuscript prepared by the Research Department, Sleepy Hollow Restorations, Tarrytown, N.Y., the Roland Wells Robbins Collection, the Thoreau Society, Lincoln, Mass.

34. Robbins, "Sleepy Hollow Restorations Daily Log—1956," 1–9; Roland W. Robbins, "Bay Trench M3, 10/3/56 to 10/31/56," field notes; "2nd Dock Site at Mill (Section thru M3 Trench), 10/5/56," field notes; and "Bay and River Course Tests (Section—Looking N.W.), 9/13/56," field notes, Historic Hudson Valley Archives, Sleepy Hollow, N.Y.

35. Robbins, "Sleepy Hollow Restorations Daily Log—1956," 18.

36. Robbins, "Sleepy Hollow Restorations Daily Log—1956," 18.

37. Robbins, "Sleepy Hollow Restorations Daily Log—1956," 27–28. Robbins and Wheeler prepared an annual budget of $37,500.00, including engineering, machinery, equipment, photography, labor, and the archaeologist's fee ($12,000/year @ $50/day) and expenses ($3,000/year).

38. R. G. W. (Bob Wheeler) to H. D. C. (Harold Cater), memo titled "Proposed Philipse Castle Archaeological Budget," dated Dec. 18, 1956, the Roland Wells Robbins Collection, the Thoreau Society, Lincoln, Mass.

39. Robbins, "Sleepy Hollow Restorations Daily Log—1956," 33.

40. Robert G. Wheeler to Dr. Harold Dean Cater, Feb. 8, 1957, the Roland Wells Robbins Collection, the Thoreau Society, Lincoln, Mass.

41. Robbins had been in contact with Old Salem in North Carolina and with Historic Bethlehem in Pennsylvania about excavation projects; he eventually worked on a small project at Historic Bethlehem in the late 1950s and early 1960s.

42. Robbins, "Sleepy Hollow Restorations Daily Log—1957," 12.

43. Robbins, "Sleepy Hollow Restorations Daily Log—1957," 7, 92; "Sleepy Hollow Restorations Daily Log—1958," 13, 25, 76; "Sleepy Hollow Restorations Daily Log—1960," 67.

44. Robbins, "Sleepy Hollow Restorations Daily Log—1957," 77. Each section was then divided into ninety-six 10-foot-square units that could be subsequently divided into sixteen 2.5-foot-square units. Thus, the designation 45–50–1 represents the 2.5-foot box (1) within the 10-foot unit (50) with the 80-by-120-foot section (45). Robbins, "Sleepy Hollow Restorations Daily Log—

1957," 92; "Sleepy Hollow Restorations Daily Log—1958," 13, 25, 76; "Sleepy Hollow Restorations Daily Log—1960," 67.

45. Robbins, "Sleepy Hollow Restorations Daily Log—1958," 38.

46. Robbins, "Sleepy Hollow Restorations Daily Log—1959," 14, 17.

47. Robbins, "Sleepy Hollow Restorations Daily Log—1960," 30.

48. Roland W. Robbins and Harvey Zorbaugh, "The Empire State," audio tape of educational television program presented by the Board of Education, Garden City, N.Y., Feb. 24, 1960, the Roland Wells Robbins Collection, the Thoreau Society, Lincoln, Mass.

49. Robbins, "Sleepy Hollow Restorations Daily Log—1957," 13, 26, 73. Soils were raked and hand sorted as well as passed through one-quarter-inch-mesh screen to recover artifacts. Robbins, "Sleepy Hollow Restorations Daily Log—1958," 78, 82, 85.

50. Robbins, "Sleepy Hollow Restorations Daily Log—1960," 10, 13. For instance, "Trench 3, Section 43, North Side of Pond, Contact Surface, Thursday, 6/26/58." About two years into the project, Robbins developed an artifact bag stamp that included the section, location (box or site), original grade and depth, photos (color slide or print or black-and-white), excavator, date, bag number, and comments.

51. Unfortunately, many of the original field bags were disposed of during this period along with important provenience information, particularly vertical or stratigraphic data.

52. Robbins, "Sleepy Hollow Restorations Daily Log—1959," 63.

53. Robbins, "Sleepy Hollow Restorations Daily Log—1961," 9.

54. Roland W. Robbins, "Artifact Inventory Cards—Philipsburg Manor Upper Mills," n.d.. Historic Hudson Valley Archives, Sleepy Hollow, N.Y. The artifact bag labels and catalog inventory cards confirm both horizontal and vertical control of the artifacts. For instance, the artifact inventory card for section 45, foundation 1, box 2, lists two levels; the second level, designated 45-F1 2–2, "began at el. −1.47 which was surface of mucks with peat and which were from 8–11″ deep."

55. While many proveniences do not have specific vertical information, these data can often be deduced from the field notes, daily logs, and plans from the excavation. For instance, feature fill was often recorded with reference only to the section, box number, and feature name on the artifact bag, yet the top and bottom elevations of the features were usually recorded in the daily field records or on the plan drawing and can often be used to link the artifacts to specific strata.

56. Helen McKearin, "Miscellaneous Research Notes—1960. Supplement I. Helen McKearin Identification of Glass Artifacts Recovered at Philipsburg Manor," Folder—Misc. Lists, Historic Hudson Valley Archives, Sleepy Hollow, N.Y.

57. Robbins, "Sleepy Hollow Restorations Daily Log—1958," 33. Richard R.

Fenska to Roland W. Robbins, June 3, 1958, Historic Hudson Valley Archives, Sleepy Hollow, N.Y. Fenska, a former professor of forest engineering at Syracuse University, took borings and provided Robbins with detailed reports of the findings. The pencil-thin bore samples are still retained in Robbins's original files at Historic Hudson Valley.

58. Robbins, "Sleepy Hollow Restorations Daily Log— 1958," 66, 80, 78–85. Leon A. Hausman to Roland W. Robbins, Jan. 23, 1959, Historic Hudson Valley Archives, Sleepy Hollow, N.Y. Dr. Hausman was a retired zoology professor from Rutgers University. Robbins reported that "a microscopic examination of these soils . . . showed that they contained fragments of pumpkin seeds. Also what may be seed-coats of rye and common wheat." Roland W. Robbins, "Report of Archaeological Work Conducted for the Sleepy Hollow Restorations During 1959," the Roland Wells Robbins Collection, the Thoreau Society, Lincoln, Mass., xii.

59. Robbins, "Report of Archaeological Work Conducted for the Sleepy Hollow Restorations During 1959"; Robbins, "Sleepy Hollow Restorations Daily Log—1960," 18, 23–24. A series of three "measured drawings of 17th & 18th century sill, log, and driven saplings found on the peat bed of the Hudson River," including a plan of the excavated features, conjectural drawing of the features, and plan showing the location of waterwheel parts, mill building timbers, and wooden artifacts, provides specific data on this portion of the work. A plan of section 45 contains evidence for the mills on the property, ca. 1940, ca. 1875, ca. 1840, and ca. 1700–1750. Robbins, "Report of Archaeological Work Conducted for the Sleepy Hollow Restorations During 1959," vi–ix, xv–xvii.

60. Roland W. Robbins and Robert Wheeler, "First Draft of Outline for Final Archaeological Report for Philipsburg Manor, Upper Mills," n.d., Historic Hudson Valley Archives, Sleepy Hollow, N.Y. Wheeler went on to write an "Archaeological Report" on the site after Robbins's departure with the help of artifact cataloger Paula Sampson. In 1974, Jacob Judd and Paula Sampson completed another report on the archaeology. These last two reports, as well as a later review of the archaeology by Mary Ostrander, contain many errors related to Robbins's provenience system and methods. Robert Wheeler and Paula Sampson, "Archaeological Report—Philipsburg Manor Upper Mills"; Jacob Judd and Paula Sampson, "Archaeological Study of Philipsburg Manor Upper Mills, 1974"; Mary Ostrander "The PMUM Case," 1974, Historic Hudson Valley Archives, Sleepy Hollow, N.Y.

61. Although most archaeologists never visited the site to inspect the work closely, the publication of photographs of the work, showing large mechanical equipment used for excavation, certainly gave the impression that there was little archaeological about the excavations at PMUM.

62. Perry, Shaw, Hepburn, Kehoe and Dean partner T. Mott Shaw had assisted Robbins with the Thoreau memorial at Walden.

63. Robbins, "Sleepy Hollow Restorations Daily Log—1961," 58.

64. Robbins, "Sleepy Hollow Restorations Daily Log—1960," 98. Robbins worked with Perry, Shaw, and Hepburn on several occasions, particularly Saugus (see chapter 3).

65. Robbins, "Sleepy Hollow Restorations Daily Log—1960," 99.

66. Robbins, "Sleepy Hollow Restorations Daily Log—1961," 32.

67. Robbins, "Sleepy Hollow Restorations Daily Log—1961," 46.

68. Robbins, "Sleepy Hollow Restorations Daily Log—1961," 52.

69. Robbins, "Sleepy Hollow Restorations Daily Log—1961," 55.

70. Robbins, "Sleepy Hollow Restorations Daily Log—1961," 57.

71. Robbins, "Sleepy Hollow Restorations Daily Log—1961," 59–63. He notes that "Collins thought that the final report could probably be written in 6 weeks; Wheeler said two months; I said it probably would be nearer 3 months."

72. Robbins, "Sleepy Hollow Restorations Daily Log—1961," 67.

73. Robbins, "Sleepy Hollow Restorations Daily Log—1961," 68.

74. Robbins, "Sleepy Hollow Restorations Daily Log—1961," 68.

75. Robbins, "Sleepy Hollow Restorations Daily Log—1961," 68.

76. Bledstein, The Culture of Professionalism, 102.

77. Robbins, "Sleepy Hollow Restorations Daily Log—1961," 69.

78. Roland W. Robbins, "Sleepy Hollow Restorations: Robbins's Vacation [1962]," the Roland Wells Robbins Collection, the Thoreau Society, Lincoln, Mass., 1–9.

79. Jack B. Collins to Roland W. Robbins, Mar. 13, 1962, the Roland Wells Robbins Collection, the Thoreau Society, Lincoln, Mass.

80. Robbins, "Sleepy Hollow Restorations: Robbins's Vacation," 8.

81. Robbins, "Sleepy Hollow Restorations: Robbins's Vacation," 10.

82. Roland W. Robbins to Dana S. Creel, Feb. 5, 1965, the Roland Wells Robbins Collection, the Thoreau Society, Lincoln, Mass.

83. Dana S. Creel to Roland W. Robbins, Mar. 3, 1965, the Roland Wells Robbins Collection, the Thoreau Society, Lincoln, Mass.

84. Robbins, "Sleepy Hollow Restorations Daily Log—1956," 31. Robbins and Wheeler speculated that the archaeological program was "not bringing the kind of publicity he [Chamberlain] would like to have." Roland W. Robbins to Evan Jones, Apr. 7, 1957, the Roland Wells Robbins Collection, the Thoreau Society, Lincoln, Mass.

85. Robbins, "Sleepy Hollow Restorations Daily Log—1956," 33.

86. Robbins, "Sleepy Hollow Restorations Daily Log—1958," 67.

87. Robbins, "Sleepy Hollow Restorations Daily Log—1958," 69; "Sleepy Hollow Restorations Daily Log—1959," 45, 48; "Sleepy Hollow Restorations Daily Log—1960," 81. For instance, Robbins was frequently constrained by lack of access to portions of the property, resulting from lack of coordination among SHR staff.

88. Robbins, "Sleepy Hollow Restorations Daily Log—1959," 16. Try as he

might to accurately predict the time and effort involved with various sections of the work, Robbins was frequently surprised by new features, complex stratigraphy, and major weather problems that delayed the excavations. Robbins, "Sleepy Hollow Restorations Daily Log—1959," 64; "Sleepy Hollow Restorations Daily Log—1960," 60, 66, 72, 74–75.

89. Robbins, "Sleepy Hollow Restorations Daily Log—1960," 2, 3, 44, and 45. In June 1960, Wheeler reported to Robbins that board member Setzer and director Cater had asked him if he thought that through "additional technical assistance . . . the major points of concern . . . [could] be completed by . . . [September 31, 1960]." Aggravated by what he perceived as additional pressure from management to finish the work in an unrealistic amount of time, Robbins told Wheeler that "I couldn't help but get the feeling that somebody has got the idea that I haven't been pushing the work hard enough and that things that I have been suggesting for the last couple of years suddenly come out as the brilliant brainchild of some other person."

90. Robbins, "Sleepy Hollow Restorations Daily Log—1958," 11, 52–53; "Sleepy Hollow Restorations Daily Log—1960," 13, 65, 70, 76, 105. In 1958, Robbins reported that he had not been eating or sleeping well and had been "very keyed up." Robbins, "Sleepy Hollow Restorations Daily Log—1958," 53. In 1960, he noted that he was tired, worn out, and had frayed nerves.

91. Robbins, "Sleepy Hollow Restorations Daily Log—1960," 86.

92. Robbins, "Sleepy Hollow Restorations Daily Log—1961," 1.

93. Robbins, "Sleepy Hollow Restorations Daily Log—1961," 15.

94. Jones, interview with author, July 29, 1992.

95. Jones, interview with author, July 29, 1992.

96. Robbins, interviews with author, July 31 and Aug. 1 and 3, 1992.

97. Joseph Butler, personal communication, 1991.

98. Butler, personal communication, 1991.

99. Robbins, "Sleepy Hollow Restorations Daily Log—1960," 42.

100. Kammen, *Mystic Chords of Memory*, 550.

101. Kammen, *Mystic Chords of Memory*, 550.

102. Susan Colby to Carl Ginsburg, Oct. 1957, the Roland Wells Robbins Collection, the Thoreau Society, Lincoln, Mass.

103. Kammen, *Mystic Chords of Memory*, 550–551.

104. Kammen, *Mystic Chords of Memory*, 550.

105. Kammen, *Mystic Chords of Memory*, 550–551.

106. Mrs. Robbins recalled a visit to the site in the 1980s during a tour of Robbins's past projects that they undertook following his major heart ailment. He was, she remembered, particularly upset to discover during his visit to Philipsburg Manor that there was no mention of his work in any of the museum displays or literature. He had been effectively written out of the project. Geraldine Robbins, interview with author, Aug. 3, 1992.

107. Robbins, "Sleepy Hollow Restorations Daily Log—1957," 22, 33; "Sleepy Hollow Restorations Daily Log—1958," 5.

108. Robbins, "Sleepy Hollow Restorations Daily Log—1957," 19.

109. Merrill Folsom, "Dig It Yourself: Philipsburg Manor's Visitors Welcome to Lend Archaeologists a Hand," New York Times, Sept. 8, 1957, section 2, p. 26.

110. Roland W. Robbins to Mrs. Beth Gonet, n.d., the Roland Wells Robbins Collection, the Thoreau Society, Lincoln, Mass. Robbins also reported that he had his laborers resift all the "soils that the visitors had gone through." Kammen perpetuates the myth that Robbins allowed the public to dig on the site, writing that "amateur archaeologists were even permitted to 'dig' under controlled circumstances, a practice not allowed elsewhere and one that administrators at Colonial Williamsburg regarded as a highly problematic precedent." Kammen, Mystic Chords of Memory, 550–551.

111. Robbins, "Sleepy Hollow Restorations Daily Log—1958," 74. In late 1958, Robbins recorded that he counted "as many as 100 diggers at our dig-it-yourself soils at one time!"

112. Cynthia Lowry, "Variation of Do-It-Yourself Turns Up in Archaeology, Project Works," Danville (Va.) Register, Oct. 2, 1958.

113. Donald S. Smith to Roland W. Robbins, Apr. 4, 1956, the Roland Wells Robbins Collection, the Thoreau Society, Lincoln, Mass.

114. Robbins and Jones, Hidden America.

115. Robbins, "Sleepy Hollow Restorations Daily Log—1956," 29. Knopf had contacted Robbins to write a book after seeing a New York Times article about his work (Henry Robbins to Roland W. Robbins, Nov. 21, 1956, the Roland Wells Robbins Collection, the Thoreau Society, Lincoln, Mass.).

116. Robbins, "Sleepy Hollow Restorations Daily Log—1957," 27.

117. Robbins, "Sleepy Hollow Restorations Daily Log—1959," 42, 64, 69.

118. Robbins, "Sleepy Hollow Restorations Daily Log—1959," 81, 84.

119. Sales records indicate that approximately ten thousand copies were sold.

120. Raymond Holden, "Amateurs at Work," New York Times Book Review, Oct. 25, 1959, 20.

121. Holden, "Amateurs at Work," 20.

122. Jimmy Magette to Roland W. Robbins, Jan. 13, 1961, and Michael Cohn to Roland W. Robbins, Oct. 22, 1959, the Roland Wells Robbins Collection, the Thoreau Society, Lincoln, Mass.

123. Cotter, "Review of Hidden America," 221–222.

124. Cotter, "Review of Hidden America," 221–222. Robbins does distinguish between archaeological research and pothunting, pointing out the need for extreme care and precision in excavation, detail and thoroughness in recording, and skill in analysis and interpretation.

125. Lawrence H. Leder, "Review of Hidden America," New York History, Apr. 1960, 243–244. Leder worked as a historian at Philipsburg Manor for two years during Robbins's excavation project.

126. Leder, "Review of *Hidden America*," 243–244. Interestingly, both Robbins and Jones had advocated for a book devoted solely to Robbins's archaeological projects.

127. Leder, "Review of *Hidden America*," 243–244.

128. Lowry, "Variation of Do-It-Yourself."

129. Barber, "Some Problems in the Sociology of the Professions," 21.

130. Cotter, "Review of *Hidden America*," 221–222.

131. Bledstein, *The Culture of Professionalism*, 328.

132. Scott, "The Professional That Vanished," 27–28.

133. Evan Jones, "Dig-It-Yourself Archaeologists," *New York Times Magazine*, Feb. 16, 1958, 48.

134. Robbins, "Roland Wells Robbins and the Saugus Iron Works Restoration," xiv.

135. Dodson, "The Man Who Found Thoreau," 116.

136. Robbins and Jones, *Hidden America*, 11.

Chapter 5. Historical Archaeology Comes of Age, pp. 131–168

1. James Deetz, *Flowerdew Hundred: The Archaeology of a Virginia Plantation, 1619–1864* (Charlottesville: University of Virginia Press, 1993).

2. Brown, "A Survey of Historical Archaeology in New England," 15.

3. Willey and Sabloff, *A History of American Archaeology*, 181; Patterson, "The Last Sixty Years," 19.

4. Charles F. Hayes III, "Review of *Pilgrim John Alden's Progress: Archaeological Excavations in Duxbury*," *Historical Archaeology* 5 (1971): 115.

5. Roland W. Robbins to Evan Jones, audiotape, ca. 1958, the Roland Wells Robbins Collection, the Thoreau Society, Lincoln, Mass.

6. Bullock to Robbins, Feb. 8, 1954.

7. Robbins was actually still working at PMUM while he completed the Alden House dig.

8. Kammen, *Mystic Chords of Memory*, 494–496.

9. Cedric Larson, 1938, quoted in Kammen, *Mystic Chords of Memory*, 421.

10. Roland W. Robbins to Mrs. Ernest Bailey, May 26, 1960, the Roland Wells Robbins Collection, the Thoreau Society, Lincoln, Mass.

11. Roland W. Robbins and Evan Jones, *Pilgrim John Alden's Progress: Archaeological Excavations in Duxbury* (Plymouth: Pilgrim Society, 1969), 8–9; Alden Kindred of America, "The John Alden House, Duxbury, Massachusetts: A Narrative History," www.alden.org/heritage/househistory.htm. (Duxbury: Alden Kindred of America, Inc., n.d.).

12. Roland W. Robbins, "John Alden—1st House in Duxbury, Daily Log, 1960," the Roland Wells Robbins Collection, the Thoreau Society, Lincoln, Mass., 1.

13. Robbins, "John Alden—1960," 1–2.

14. Russell Edwards to Roland W. Robbins, Mar. 21, 1960, the Roland Wells Robbins Collection, the Thoreau Society, Lincoln, Mass. Robbins often used his "preliminary surveys" as an opportunity to introduce his work to potential clients and demonstrate his abilities.

15. Robbins, "John Alden—1960," 3.

16. Robbins, "John Alden—1960," 3.

17. Roland W. Robbins to Russell Edwards, Apr. 19, 1960, the Roland Wells Robbins Collection, the Thoreau Society, Lincoln, Mass.

18. Robbins, "John Alden—1960," 3.

19. Robbins to Bailey, May 26, 1960.

20. Robbins, "John Alden—1960," 4. Robbins and Jones, *Pilgrim John Alden's Progress,* 46.

21. Robbins, "John Alden—1960," 4.

22. Robbins, "John Alden—1960," 5; Roland W. Robbins to Russell Edwards, Aug. 2, 1960, the Roland Wells Robbins Collection, the Thoreau Society, Lincoln, Mass.

23. Roland W. Robbins to Mrs. Ernest Bailey, Aug. 1, 1960, the Roland Wells Robbins Collection, the Thoreau Society, Lincoln, Mass. Robbins likely used several sources that were in his library, including John L. Cotter and J. Paul Hudson's *New Discoveries at Jamestown* (Washington, D.C.: National Park Service, 1957) and J. C. Harrington's *Glassmaking at Jamestown* (Richmond, Va.: Dietz Press, 1952).

24. Robbins to Bailey, Aug. 1, 1960.

25. Russell Edwards to Roland W. Robbins, Aug. 8, 1960; Roland W. Robbins to Mrs. Ernest Bailey, Aug. 19, 1960; Mrs. Ernest Bailey to Roland W. Robbins, Aug. 30, 1960, the Roland Wells Robbins Collection, the Thoreau Society, Lincoln, Mass.

26. Robbins, "John Alden—1960," 6.

27. Robbins, "John Alden—1960," 6–7.

28. Robbins, "John Alden—1960," 7.

29. Robbins, "John Alden—1960," 8.

30. Roland W. Robbins to Mrs. Ernest Bailey, Oct. 19, 1960, the Roland Wells Robbins Collection, the Thoreau Society, Lincoln, Mass.

31. Robbins, "John Alden—1961," 1, 3.

32. J. Paul Hudson to Roland W. Robbins, Apr. 5, 1961, the Roland Wells Robbins Collection, the Thoreau Society, Lincoln, Mass.

33. Robbins, "John Alden—1961," 1; "John Alden—1963," 1.

34. Hall's excavation of the Standish site in ca. 1853 is considered one of the first historical archaeology projects in New England. Robbins, "John Alden—1963," 5; "John Alden—1962," 1, 2; "John Alden—1960," 8.

35. Robbins, "John Alden—1963," 4.

36. Robbins, "John Alden—1963," 5–6.

37. Roland W. Robbins and Evan Jones, "Pilgrim John Alden's First Home in Duxbury and Its Archaeological Excavation," Mar. 1964, the Roland Wells Robbins Collection, the Thoreau Society, Lincoln, Mass.

38. Robbins, "John Alden—1966," 6; Roland W. Robbins, "Larry Geller—Pilgrim Society Daily Log, 1969," the Roland Wells Robbins Collection, the Thoreau Society, Lincoln, Mass., 1–3.

39. Robbins, "Larry Geller—Pilgrim Society Daily Log, 1969," 4–5.

40. Robbins, "John Alden—1964," 1.

41. Robbins to Jones, audiotape, ca. 1958.

42. Robbins, "John Alden—1960," 3.

43. Robbins and Jones, *Pilgrim John Alden's Progress*, 17.

44. Robbins and Jones, *Pilgrim John Alden's Progress*, 17–19, 61.

45. Robbins and Jones, *Pilgrim John Alden's Progress*, 24; Robbins, "John Alden—1960," 6.

46. Robbins, "John Alden—1960," 4–5, 8; Robbins and Jones, *Pilgrim John Alden's Progress*, 60–63; Roland W. Robbins, "John Alden Duxbury House Excavations, Sat., April 16, 1960," the Roland Wells Robbins Collection, the Thoreau Society, Lincoln, Mass. Robbins recorded basic sketches in his field notebook, photo logs, and daily log, and he completed a precise mapping of features, including elevations using a transit.

47. Robbins, "John Alden—1963," 2–3.

48. Robbins and Jones, *Pilgrim John Alden's Progress*, 41–42, 50–55; Robbins, "John Alden—1963," 1.

49. Robbins, "John Alden—1961," 1; "John Alden—1963," 1; Robbins and Jones, *Pilgrim John Alden's Progress*, 31, 33, 35. The list includes J. Paul Hudson at Jamestown, Ivor and Audrey Noël Hume at the Colonial Williamsburg Foundation, Harold Peterson at the National Park Service in Washington, C. Malcolm Watkins at the Smithsonian, and Lura Watkins, a noted New England ceramics researcher. J. Paul Hudson wrote a brief summary of the artifacts by type, providing both overall impressions, specific identifications, and suggestions for additional study. Hudson to Robbins, Apr. 5, 1961.

50. Robbins and Jones, *Pilgrim John Alden's Progress*, 36–39. Robbins used the original plan and artifacts from the Standish House (James Hall), reports on the John Howland site by Sidney T. Strickland ("Excavations at Site of Home of Pilgrim John Howland, Rocky Nook," in *The Howlands in America*, comp. William Howland [Detroit: Pilgrim John Howland Society, 1939]) and James Deetz ("The Howlands at Rocky Nook"), and a report on the Joseph Howland site by James Deetz ("Excavations at the Joseph Howland Site"). He also referenced Cotter and Hudson's *New Discoveries at Jamestown*.

51. Robbins and Jones, *Pilgrim John Alden's Progress*, 36–39.

52. Robbins, "John Alden—1961," 2; Robbins, "John Alden—1963," 4; Robbins and Jones, *Pilgrim John Alden's Progress*, 43, 48, 62.

53. Robbins, "John Alden—1960," 8; "John Alden—1963," 5; Robbins and Jones, *Pilgrim John Alden's Progress*, 36–39. Hudson to Robbins, Apr. 5, 1961.

54. Hayes, "Review of *Pilgrim John Alden's Progress*," 115.

55. Hayes, "Review of *Pilgrim John Alden's Progress*," 115.

56. Robbins's site reports were structured to tell a story, while the standard academic report was intended to present the excavation and all its data in a manner that could be used by other researchers. Although Robbins did often include detailed lists of artifacts and maps of the excavations, he also relied heavily on the use of photographs and dramatic devices to convey his story.

57. Hayes, "Review of *Pilgrim John Alden's Progress*," 115.

58. Hayes, "Review of *Pilgrim John Alden's Progress*," 115.

59. Robbins to Bailey, Aug. 1, 1960.

60. Hayes, "Review of *Pilgrim John Alden's Progress*," 115.

61. Brown, "A Survey of Historical Archaeology in New England," 15.

62. Bledstein, *The Culture of Professionalism*, 96, 303.

63. J. C. Harrington, *Archaeology and the Historical Society* (Nashville, Tenn.: American Association for State and Local History, 1965).

64. Harrington, *Archaeology and the Historical Society*, 4.

65. Harrington, *Archaeology and the Historical Society*, 5.

66. Harrington, *Archaeology and the Historical Society*, 35.

67. By the late 1960s, several schools, including the University of Pennsylvania, were offering limited training in historical archaeology within their departments of anthropology, and these schools were increasingly called on to investigate historic sites as a result of federal and state preservation and antiquities legislation.

68. Schuyler, "Anthropological Perspectives," 139. The excavation, or more aptly rescue project, identified two buildings, a main house and a kitchen structure, dating to the first half of the eighteenth century.

69. Schuyler, "Anthropological Perspectives," 140.

70. C. Malcolm Watkins and Ivor Noël Hume, "The 'Poor Potter' of Yorktown," *Contributions from the Museum of History and Technology* 54 (1967): 73–112.

71. Schuyler, "Anthropological Perspectives," 141. In what is an excellent example of the increasing research orientation and advances in field techniques of the discipline, archaeologist Norman Barka of the College of William and Mary began a decade-long study of the site in 1970. Norman F. Barka, Edward Ayres, and Christine Sheridan, *The "Poor Potter" of Yorktown: A Study of a Colonial Pottery Factory*, Yorktown Research Series, no. 5 (Williamsburg, Va.: College of William and Mary, Department of Anthropology, 1984); and Norman F. Barka, "The Kiln and Ceramics of the 'Poor Potter' of Yorktown: A Preliminary Report," in *Ceramics in America*, ed. Ian M. G. Quimby (Charlottesville: University of Virginia Press, 1973).

72. Ivor Noël Hume, *Here Lies Virginia: An Archaeologist's View of Colonial Life and History* (New York: Alfred A. Knopf, 1963).

73. Schuyler, "Anthropological Perspectives," 141; Noël Hume, *Historical Archaeology.*

74. Schuyler, "Anthropological Perspectives," 141; Noël Hume, *Historical Archaeology.*

75. Ivor Noël Hume, *A Guide to Artifacts of Colonial America* (New York: Alfred A. Knopf, 1969).

76. Schuyler, "Anthropological Perspectives," 141.

77. Schuyler, "Anthropological Perspectives," 142.

78. Schuyler, "Anthropological Perspectives," 142–143.

79. Schuyler, "Anthropological Perspectives," 143; James Deetz, "Ceramics from Plymouth, 1635–1835," in *Ceramics in America,* ed. Ian M. C. Quimby (Charlottesville: University of Virginia Press, 1973). In his study of ceramics recovered at these sites, which dated from 1635 to 1835, Deetz argued that they reflected the development of three successive and different cultural systems that he called Stuart Yeoman, Anglo-American, and Georgian.

80. Robbins, "John Alden—1961," 2.

81. Schuyler, "Anthropological Perspectives," 143.

82. Robbins completed several small test excavations at the Brothers House from 1958 to 1959 for Historic Bethlehem, Inc.

83. Schuyler, "Anthropological Perspectives," 144.

84. Schuyler briefly mentions Robbins's work at Strawbery Banke and describes him as a "famous amateur archaeologist." Schuyler, "Anthropological Perspectives," 145.

85. Schuyler, "Anthropological Perspectives," 145.

86. Daniel W. Ingersoll Jr., "Settlement Archaeology at Puddle Dock" (Ph.D. diss., Harvard University, 1971), 15–16.

87. Schuyler, "Anthropological Perspectives," 145–146.

88. Roland W. Robbins to Dorothy M. Vaughan, Feb. 12, 1963, the Roland Wells Robbins Collection, the Thoreau Society, Lincoln, Mass.

89. Carl A. Johnson to Roland W. Robbins, Oct. 21, 1965, the Roland Wells Robbins Collection, the Thoreau Society, Lincoln, Mass.

90. Johnson to Robbins, Oct. 21, 1965.

91. Roland W. Robbins to Carl A. Johnson, Oct. 23, 1965, the Roland Wells Robbins Collection, the Thoreau Society, Lincoln, Mass.

92. Richard M. Candee, "Urban Landscapes and Vernacular Building in Portsmouth, N.H., 1660–1990: A Field Guide for Tours of Portsmouth." Prepared for the Vernacular Architecture Forum 13th Annual Meeting and Conference, Portsmouth, N.H., May 13–16, 1992, 49–51.

93. Carl A. Johnson, "Agreement Between Strawbery Banke, Inc., and The Department of History, University of New Hampshire, April 1966," the Roland Wells Robbins Collection, the Thoreau Society, Lincoln, Mass.

94. Ann Marie Nielsen, "Puddle Dock Dig—an Adventure in Colonial Site Archaeology," *New Hampshire Alumnus* 42, no. 8 (1966): 12–13.

95. Johnson, "Agreement Between Strawbery Banke, Inc., and The Department of History." Half of the funding was allocated for mechanical equipment and the other half for Robbins's services.

96. Johnson, "Agreement Between Strawbery Banke, Inc., and The Department of History." It appears that Robbins had made some commitments about the work before he realized that the funds were limited. However, he often performed this type of preliminary survey work as a way of building business relationships with the hope of future work if the project expanded. Robbins also seemed to be very interested in working with the college students; he had dreamed of founding a "College of Archaeology" since the late 1950s. Roland W. Robbins and Evan Jones, "Big Joe Program," taped interview, Nov. 22, 1959, WABC, New York; Johnson, "Agreement Between Strawbery Banke, Inc., and The Department of History."

97. Roland W. Robbins, "Strawbery Banke, Inc. Daily Log, 1966," the Roland Wells Robbins Collection, the Thoreau Society, Lincoln, Mass., 1.

98. Robbins, "Strawbery Banke, Inc. Daily Log, 1966," 1.

99. Robbins, "Strawbery Banke, Inc. Daily Log, 1966," 2.

100. Robbins, "Strawbery Banke, Inc. Daily Log, 1966," 2.

101. Robbins numbered all features, such as foundations, roadways, bulkheads, and wharfs, in the order in which they were found. For instance, W1 = the first wharf found.

102. Robbins, "Strawbery Banke, Inc. Daily Log, 1966," 3.

103. Nielsen, "Puddle Dock Dig," 13.

104. Robbins, "Strawbery Banke, Inc. Daily Log, 1966," 4–5.

105. Robbins, "Strawbery Banke, Inc. Daily Log, 1968," 1.

106. Robbins, "Strawbery Banke, Inc. Daily Log, 1968," 1.

107. James L. Garvin to Roland W. Robbins, Jan. 31, 1972, the Roland Wells Robbins Collection, the Thoreau Society, Lincoln, Mass.

108. Garvin to Robbins, Jan. 31, 1972.

109. Garvin to Robbins, Jan. 31, 1972.

110. Robbins, "Strawbery Banke, Inc. Daily Log, 1965," 1; "Strawbery Banke, Inc. Daily Log, 1966," 1, 3.

111. Colonel George L. Prindle quoted in Ingersoll, "Settlement Archaeology at Puddle Dock," 5. The "thousands of artifacts" recovered from these excavations have unfortunately been lost over the years, making it impossible to directly assess their provenience information. Ingersoll, "Settlement Archaeology at Puddle Dock," 15.

112. Ingersoll, "Settlement Archaeology at Puddle Dock," 15.

113. This was the case in deep excavations at Philipsburg Manor Upper Mills (see chapter 4).

114. Roland W. Robbins, "Profile of 39-W2, Friday, May 6, 1966," the Roland Wells Robbins Collection, the Thoreau Society, Lincoln, Mass. However, this is impossible to determine without the original artifact assemblage.

115. On several occasions, however, Robbins also explained that artifacts should not be sought in and of themselves, and provided a bonus only if they were recovered in the context of features.

116. Schuyler, "Anthropological Perspectives," 152.

117. Carl A. Johnson to Roland W. Robbins, Apr. 22, 1966, the Roland Wells Robbins Collection, the Thoreau Society, Lincoln, Mass.

118. Ingersoll, "Settlement Archaeology at Puddle Dock," 5, 15; Garvin to Robbins, Jan. 31, 1972.

119. Schuyler, "Anthropological Perspectives," 181.

120. Schuyler, "Anthropological Perspectives," 181. The integration of historical archaeology into anthropology was still contended at this point (and for some still is today), and many scholars felt that history was a more appropriate disciplinary home. As seen at Strawbery Banke, the University of New Hampshire's History Department was training historical archaeologists, as was the History Department at the College of William and Mary.

121. Schuyler, "Anthropological Perspectives," 182.

122. Schuyler, "Anthropological Perspectives," 182.

123. Johnson, interview with author, Mar. 9, 1995.

124. Robert Dickens, *Thoreau: The Complete Individualist* (New York: Exposition Press, 1974).

125. Kammen, *Mystic Chords of Memory*, 537.

126. Nathan O. Hatch, "Introduction: The Professions in a Democratic Culture," in *The Professions in American History*, ed. Nathan O. Hatch (Notre Dame, Ind.: University of Notre Dame Press, 1988), 4–5.

127. Bledstein, *The Culture of Professionalism*, 106.

128. Bledstein, *The Culture of Professionalism*, 27.

129. Jones, interview with author, July 29, 1992.

130. Heberling, interview with author, Nov. 8, 1992.

131. John H. Meade to Roland W. Robbins, Jan. 13, 1967, the Roland Wells Robbins Collection, the Thoreau Society, Lincoln, Mass.

132. John H. Meade to Roland W. Robbins, Apr. 11, 1967, the Roland Wells Robbins Collection, the Thoreau Society, Lincoln, Mass.

133. Ed McCaffrey, "The Monsignor Said It Rather Well," *Concord (Mass.) Journal*, July 1, 1965, 2a.

134. The Right Reverend George W. Casey quoted in McCaffrey, "The Monsignor Said It Rather Well."

135. Roland W. Robbins to E. Gilbert Barker, Aug. 29, 1971, the Roland Wells Robbins Collection, the Thoreau Society, Lincoln, Mass.

136. Bradford Torrey and Francis Allen, eds., *The Journal of Henry D. Thoreau*, Dec. 14, 1841 (Boston: Houghton Mifflin, 1949), 1: 294. In his eulogy of Robbins, friend Thomas Blanding noted Robbins's intense interest in Thoreau and their kindred spirit: "I think that Roland not only enjoyed Thoreau, and admired him, but believed him—and believed in him. They both had the courage

of their convictions, besides many other traits in common. . . . They were Yankees through and through—their characters grew out of that tradition."
Thomas Blanding, "Eulogy for Roland Wells Robbins, Read at Memorial Service, Trinitarian Congregational Church, Concord Massachusetts, March 21,
1987," manuscript in the collection of Thomas Blanding, Concord, Mass.

137. Van Doren Stern, *The Annotated Walden*, 289.

138. Van Doren Stern, *The Annotated Walden*, 386–387.

139. John Albee, 1852, quoted in Robert D. Richardson Jr., *Emerson: The
Mind on Fire* (Berkeley: University of California Press, 1995), 281–282.

140. Henry Petroski, "H. D. Thoreau, Engineer," *Invention and Technology*
(Fall 1989): 8–16; Harry B. Chase, "Henry Thoreau Surveyor," *Surveying and
Mapping* 25 (June 1965): 219–222.

141. Geraldine Robbins, personal communication, 1995.

142. Roland W. Robbins to Joseph A. Masi, Nov. 13, 1968, the Roland Wells
Robbins Collection, the Thoreau Society, Lincoln, Mass., 16.

143. Kammen, *Mystic Chords of Memory*, 538–544.

144. Lowenthal, *The Past Is a Foreign Country*, 197.

145. Lowenthal, *The Past Is a Foreign Country*, 197, 210.

146. Lowenthal, *The Past Is a Foreign Country*, 197, 210.

147. Dean MacCannell, *The Tourist: A New Theory of the Leisure Class* (New
York: Schocken Books, 1989), 83.

148. Kammen, *Mystic Chords of Memory*, 538–544.

149. Kammen, *Mystic Chords of Memory*, 538–544.

150. Roland W. Robbins, "The Oliver Mill Park Restoration: A Report," December 1969, the Roland Wells Robbins Collection, the Thoreau Society, Lincoln, Mass., 2.

151. Robbins to Barker, Aug. 29, 1971.

152. Henry D. Thoreau, quoted in Robbins, "The Oliver Mill Park Restoration: A Report," 8.

153. Robbins, "The Oliver Mill Park Restoration: A Report," 8.

154. Robbins, "The Oliver Mill Park Restoration: A Report," 8.

155. Robbins, "The Oliver Mill Park Restoration: A Report," 8.

156. Robbins to Barker, Aug. 29, 1971.

157. Robbins, "The Oliver Mill Park Restoration: A Report," 1.

158. Robbins, "The Oliver Mill Park Restoration: A Report," 2.

159. Ben Ford and Matthew A. Kierstead, *Oliver Mill Park Restoration Project
Archaeological Monitoring of Machine Excavations*, technical report produced
by PAL, Pawtucket, R.I., 2001, on file at the Massachusetts Historical Commission, Boston, 1–2.

160. Ford and Kierstead, *Oliver Mill Park Restoration Project Archaeological
Monitoring*, 1–3.

161. Robbins to Masi, Nov. 13, 1968, 1–2.

162. Robbins to Masi, Nov. 13, 1968, 2.

163. Robbins to Masi, Nov. 13, 1968, 2.

164. Robbins to Masi, Nov. 13, 1968, 2. He sent a brief summary of the work to Mr. Masi, emphasizing the importance of completing the excavations before the winter to avoid damage to the site, to allow for proper completion of the preliminary study, and to begin interpretation of the site to the public. Roland W. Robbins to Joseph A. Masi, Sept. 23, 1967, the Roland Wells Robbins Collection, the Thoreau Society, Lincoln, Mass.

165. Robbins to Masi, Nov. 13, 1968, 2. He developed a proposal and cost estimate of $30,000 for a two-year program that would complete the first phase of the restoration in time for the town's three-hundredth anniversary in 1969.

166. Robbins to Masi, Nov. 13, 1968, 8.

167. Joe Masi to Roland W. Robbins, Oct. 1, 1968, the Roland Wells Robbins Collection, the Thoreau Society, Lincoln, Mass.

168. Robbins to Masi, Nov. 13, 1968.

169. Robbins to Masi, Nov. 13, 1968, 16.

170. Cotter, "Review of *Hidden America*," 221–222.

171. Robbins to Masi, Nov. 13, 1968, 16.

172. Roland W. Robbins to Richard Humphrey, Nov. 12, 1968, the Roland Wells Robbins Collection, the Thoreau Society, Lincoln, Mass.

173. Roland W. Robbins, "The Oliver Mill Park Restoration—Daily Log, 1969," the Roland Wells Robbins Collection, the Thoreau Society, Lincoln, Mass., x.

174. Brown, personal communication, 2004.

175. Brown, personal communication, 2004. Brown points out, however, that Deetz was clearly able to supervise much reconstruction of another kind at Plymouth.

176. Robbins, "The Oliver Mill Park Restoration: A Report," 10–26.

177. Brown, personal communication, 2004.

178. This loss of vertical and stratigraphic provenience makes it very difficult or impossible to understand the chronology and the relationships between and among features. These relationships can in some cases be reconstructed using Robbins's field records and photos; however, the complete loss of provenience information due to improper storage of the artifacts makes this difficult.

179. Ford and Kierstead, *Oliver Mill Park Restoration Project Archaeological Monitoring.*

180. Roland W. Robbins to Lucy Moran, Redpath Lyceum Bureau, Dec. 17, 1964, the Roland Wells Robbins Collection, the Thoreau Society, Lincoln, Mass.

181. Walter Harding, *The Days of Henry Thoreau: A Biography* (Princeton, N.J.: Princeton University Press, 1992), 142–143, 412–420.

182. Roland W. Robbins, "Lecture Folders—1945–1980," the Roland Wells Robbins Collection, the Thoreau Society, Lincoln, Mass. These figures are drawn

from Robbins's meticulous lecture notes that record the attendance at all his lectures.

183. Smith to Robbins, Apr. 4, 1956.

184. Roland W. Robbins to Mrs. Addison Simmons, Jan. 28, 1954, the Roland Wells Robbins Collection, the Thoreau Society, Lincoln, Mass.; "Advertisement," *Yankee*, Nov. 1962, 139. Following publication of Evan Jones's 1955 *Collier's* article "Pick and Shovel Historian," Robbins began to designate himself as the "Pick and Shovel" historian. Searching for ways to expand his lecture business, Robbins also began to advertise his lectures in the publications and programs of civic organizations, and expanded direct advertisements in print media. In 1955, he contacted local lecture bureaus, which soon began distributing Robbins's publicity circulars to clubs, businesses, and schools throughout New England. Robbins, "Lecture Folder—1955." The Redpath Lyceum was founded in 1868 by James Redpath. Redpath had published some of Thoreau's early essays, and Emerson used the Redpath Lyceum Bureau to manage his bookings. Bledstein, *The Culture of Professionalism*, 81; Harding, *The Days of Henry Thoreau*, 422; Richardson, *Emerson*, 418–419. A. H. Handley to Roland W. Robbins, Mar. 8, 1955, the Roland Wells Robbins Collection, the Thoreau Society, Lincoln, Mass.

185. Harrington, *Archeology and the Historical Society*, 35.

186. Robbins, "Lecture Folders—1945–1980." Approximately 35.5 percent of Robbins's lectures were sponsored by historical and patriotic societies, 50.3 percent by clubs and organizations, and 14.2 percent by schools and colleges.

187. Jones, interview with author, July 29, 1992. For instance, Robbins spoke on his Saugus work to the State Museum of New Jersey as part of its exhibit New Jersey Iron, 1674–1850; on his work at the Philipsburg Manor site to a conference, "The Tradition of the American Home: The Influence of the Dutch," at the New Jersey Historical Society; to the First Annual Meeting of the American Association of State and Local History at Sturbridge Village; and to the Second and Third Annual Symposium on Historic Sites Archaeology held at Bear Mountain Park, N.Y.

188. Robbins, *Discovery at Walden*, 60.

189. Roland W. Robbins, "On the Photographs of Herbert Wendell Gleason," in *The Illustrated Maine Woods*, ed. Joseph J. Moldenhauer (Princeton, N.J.: Princeton University Press, 1974), ix. The Walden Cabin enterprise was only one of Robbins's ventures during this period of slower archaeological consulting work. He also focused his attention on marketing his collection of Herbert Gleason's photographs. Beginning in 1899, Gleason had visited and photographed national parks in the United States and Canada as well as gardens and estates in the Northeast. Robbins was very successful at marketing the publication rights for the photographs to companies preparing new illustrated editions of many of Thoreau's works. Geraldine Robbins, personal communi-

cation, 1995; Moldenhauer, *The Illustrated Maine Woods;* Thea Wheelwright, ed., *Thoreau's Cape Cod: With the Early Photographs of Herbert W. Gleason* (Barre, Mass.: Barre Publishers, 1971).

190. Roland W. Robbins, *The Thoreau–Walden Cabin,* brochure (Concord, Mass.: House of Thoreau, ca. 1964), the Roland Wells Robbins Collection, the Thoreau Society, Lincoln, Mass.

191. Robbins, *The Thoreau–Walden Cabin.*

192. Robbins, *The Thoreau–Walden Cabin.* Robbins sold the complete frame unit and left the selection and completion of exterior siding, roofing, and interior finish to the individual.

193. Robbins got the idea for the first replica from a visitor, who looked out the back window at the small stable in their yard and remarked, "Oh, you have built your own Walden Cabin out back." Harding, interview with author, Nov. 6, 1992. The first Thoreau Cabin replica was actually built in Carlisle, Mass., in 1964.

194. Roland W. Robbins to Walter Harding, Apr. 20, 1964, the Walter Harding Collection, the Thoreau Institute, Lincoln, Mass. Robbins prepared an informational brochure with pictures of his replica cabin and a plan of the Walden Pond excavation site. Although he had many requests for information, Robbins sold few kits. He reported that he had received seventy-two inquires from an ad placed in *Yankee* magazine. In 1980, Robbins renewed his cabin project, hoping that sales would boost his declining income and help provide for his retirement years. Although he received hundreds of inquiries from articles in *Country Living,* the *New York Times,* and *Yankee* magazine, Robbins found that they did not turn into orders.

195. Timothy Clemmer and Jack Troy to Walter Harding, June 19, 1964, the Walter Harding Collection, the Thoreau Institute, Lincoln, Mass. Ironically, it was Walter Harding who put a notice in the *Thoreau Society Bulletin* about the cabins, not Robbins. Walter Harding to Roland W. Robbins, June 8, 1964, the Roland W. Robbins Collection, the Thoreau Society, Lincoln, Mass. Mrs. Robbins reported that Roland offered Troy and Clemmer an opportunity to discuss their feelings about the cabin replica at the Thoreau Society meeting, and asked that they reserve judgment until they saw the replica at his house. Troy came to the house and apologized for the letter, and both he and Clemmer became close friends of Robbins. Troy invited Robbins to Juniata College to lecture in 1976. Geraldine Robbins, personal communication, 1994.

196. Anonymous to Roland W. Robbins, July 21, 1981, the Roland Wells Robbins Collection, the Thoreau Society, Lincoln, Mass. This letter may be from Thoreauvian Mary Sherwood.

197. Harding, interview with author, Nov. 6, 1992.

198. Blanding, interview with author, Aug. 10, 1993.

199. Blanding, interview with author, Aug. 10, 1993.

200. Blanding, interview with author, Aug. 10, 1993.

201. Clement W. Meighan, ed. "Notes and News." *American Antiquity* 24, no. 1 (1958): 103.

202. Jones, interview with author, July 29, 1992.

203. Heberling, interview with author, Nov. 8, 1992. Professionals mocked Robbins's reports for their quaint storylike character and their lack of specific scientific data. The level of Robbins's excavation documentation is not apparent in most of his reports, and this has contributed to his poor reputation among archaeologists.

Chapter 6. A "Thoreau Yankee" Meets the Academy, pp. 169–202

1. Bradley Dean, personal communication, 2001.

2. Jones, interview with author, July 29, 1992.

3. Edward Jelks, 1976, quoted in Stanley South, "Strange Fruit: Historic Archaeology, 1972–1977," *Historical Archaeology* 27, no. 1 (1993): 16.

4. Barber, "Some Problems in the Sociology of the Professions," 22.

5. Barber, "Some Problems in the Sociology of the Professions," 23.

6. Barber, "Some Problems in the Sociology of the Professions," 23–24.

7. Bledstein, *The Culture of Professionalism*, 325; Barber, "Some Problems in the Sociology of the Professions," 20.

8. Bledstein, *The Culture of Professionalism*, 325.

9. Members need to demonstrate a command of the language of the profession, to know and use the proper terminology or jargon. This scholarly shorthand is important for clear communication between members of a discipline or profession and serves to differentiate them from nonmembers, whether the general public or amateur practitioners.

10. Robbins's excavations at Strawbery Banke were completed as part of an undergraduate teaching program that was organized by the History Department at the University of New Hampshire.

11. Several schools, including the College of William and Mary and the University of Massachusetts at Boston, still maintain historical archaeology programs within the history department. Proponents of this approach point out that it is possible to receive an anthropology degree in historical archaeology without taking a single graduate-level course in American or world history.

12. Kathleen Deagan, "Retrospective on the Society for Historical Archaeology, 1977–1982," *Historical Archaeology* 27, no. 1 (1993): 19.

13. South, "Strange Fruit" 15–16.

14. Brown, "A Survey of Historical Archaeology in New England," 4.

15. Brown, "A Survey of Historical Archaeology in New England," 7.

16. Brooke S. Blades, "Doctor Williams' Privy: Cultural Behavior as Re-

flected in Artifact Deposition at the Dr. Thomas Williams House, Deerfield, Massachusetts," in *New England Historical Archaeology,* ed. Peter Benes, The Dublin Seminar for New England Folklife Annual Proceedings, vol. 2 (Boston: Boston University, 1977), 56; Brown, "A Survey of Historical Archaeology in New England," 8.

17. Brown, "A Survey of Historical Archaeology in New England," 9.

18. Bert Salwen, "Has Historical Archaeology Survived the Bicentennial? An Inquiry into the Development of Historical Archaeology in the United States," *Northeast Historical Archaeology* 12 (1983): 6.

19. Brown, "A Survey of Historical Archaeology in New England," 9.

20. Brown, "A Survey of Historical Archaeology in New England," 9–10.

21. Brown, "A Survey of Historical Archaeology in New England," 10–12.

22. Brown, "An Evaluation of Roland Wells Robbins Archaeology."

23. Brown, "An Evaluation of Roland Wells Robbins Archaeology." Marley R. Brown III prepared the evaluation of the archaeology, while his classmate Mary C. Beaudry discussed the relationship between the archaeology and documentary record.

24. Brown, "An Evaluation of Roland Wells Robbins Archaeology," 1.

25. The authors interviewed Robbins and used his records for some of their work. They were also aware that Robbins would receive a copy of the finished report.

26. William Hampton Adams, "Historical Archaeology Strove for Maturity in the Mid-1980s," *Historical Archaeology* 27, no. 1 (1993): 29.

27. Adams, "Historical Archaeology Strove for Maturity in the Mid-1980s," 23.

28. Adams, "Historical Archaeology Strove for Maturity in the Mid-1980s," 23.

29. Adams, "Historical Archaeology Strove for Maturity in the Mid-1980s," 30–31.

30. Adams, "Historical Archaeology Strove for Maturity in the Mid-1980s," 29; James Deetz, "Scientific Humanism and Humanistic Science: A Plea for Paradigmatic Pluralism in Historical Archaeology," *Geoscience and Man* 23 (1983): 27–34.

31. Adams, "Historical Archaeology Strove for Maturity in the Mid-1980s," 29.

32. Barber, "Some Problems in the Sociology of the Professions," 24.

33. Barber, "Some Problems in the Sociology of the Professions," 24.

34. Barber, "Some Problems in the Sociology of the Professions," 24.

35. Charles W. Eliot, 1869, quoted in Bledstein, *The Culture of Professionalism,* 323.

36. Daniel Mouer, "Re:Educational Requirements," comments to Histarch listserve (histarch@asuvm.inre.asu.edu), Apr. 27, 1998.

37. Daniel Mouer, "Re:Educational Requirements."

38. Steve Boxley, "Re:Educational Requirements," comments to Histarch listserve (histarch@asuvm.inre.asu.edu), Apr. 28, 1998.

39. Heberling, interview with author, Nov. 8, 1992.

40. Robbins, "Larry Geller–Pilgrim Society Daily Log, 1969," 3–4. Pilgrim Society director Larry Geller recommended Robbins to the committee; Geller had collaborated with Robbins on the John Alden House report, which the Pilgrim Society then published.

41. Robbins, "Larry Geller—Pilgrim Society Daily Log, 1969," 9.

42. Robbins, "Larry Geller—Pilgrim Society Daily Log, 1969," 11.

43. Robbins, "Larry Geller—Pilgrim Society Daily Log, 1969," 13–14.

44. Roland W. Robbins to Larry Geller, Feb. 25, 1970, the Roland W. Robbins Collection, the Thoreau Society, Lincoln, Mass., 1.

45. Robbins to Geller, Feb. 25, 1970, 1–2. Robbins included an estimate for the reconstruction of the mill but explained that the cost would depend "upon the results of the preliminary survey and the archaeological explorations."

46. Robbins, "Larry Geller—Pilgrim Society Daily Log, 1970," 5.

47. Robbins, "Larry Geller—Pilgrim Society Daily Log, 1970," 5. Ironically, James Deetz used and cited Robbins's Alden site data in his classic book, *In Small Things Forgotten: The Archaeology of Early American Life* (Garden City, N.Y.: Anchor Books, 1977).

48. Robbins, "Larry Geller—Pilgrim Society Daily Log, 1970," 6.

49. Robbins, "Larry Geller—Pilgrim Society Daily Log, 1970," 6.

50. Robbins, "Larry Geller—Pilgrim Society Daily Log, 1970," 6.

51. Robbins, "Larry Geller—Pilgrim Society Daily Log, 1970," 6.

52. Roland W. Robbins, "Hancock-Clarke House Site Daily Log—1964," the Roland Wells Robbins Collection, the Thoreau Society, Lincoln, Mass., 1.

53. Robbins, "Hancock-Clarke House Site Daily Log—1964," 1.

54. Robbins, "Hancock-Clarke House Site Daily Log—1964," 1.

55. Robbins, "Hancock-Clarke House Site Daily Log—1965," 2–3.

56. Robbins, "Hancock-Clarke House Site Daily Log—1965," 4. This cellar was designated 6-F1 for grid section 6, foundation 1.

57. Robbins, "Hancock-Clarke House Site Daily Log—1965," 4.

58. Robbins, "Hancock-Clarke House Site Daily Log—1965," 5.

59. Robbins, "Hancock-Clarke House Site Daily Log—1965," 5.

60. Robbins, "Hancock-Clarke House Site Daily Log—1965," 6. He noted that this cellar (designated 6-F3) was apparently "older than the 1698 cellar, being dry laid and the artifacts being older than those yet found."

61. Robbins, "Hancock-Clarke House Site Daily Log—1965," 7. This cellar was designated 3-F1.

62. Robbins, "Hancock-Clarke House Site Daily Log—1965," 7.

63. Roland W. Robbins, "Surveys at Hancock-Clarke Homestead—1966," the Roland Wells Robbins Collection, the Thoreau Society, Lincoln, Mass., 2.

64. Robbins, "Surveys at Hancock-Clarke Homestead—1966," 2.

65. Robbins, "Surveys at Hancock-Clarke Homestead—1966," 3–5; "Surveys at Hancock-Clarke Homestead—1967," 1.

66. Robbins, "Hancock-Clarke House Site Daily Log—1969," 1.

67. Robbins, "Hancock-Clarke House Site Daily Log—1969," 2. Following the completion of the excavation, Robbins prepared a plan of the well excavation.

68. Roland W. Robbins, "The Archaeological Excavations of the Hancock-Clarke Homestead [1966]," the Roland Wells Robbins Collection, the Thoreau Society, Lincoln, Mass.

69. Robbins, "The Archaeological Excavations of the Hancock-Clarke Homestead."

70. Ruth Morey and Roland Wells Robbins, "Agreement by and Between the Lexington Historical Society and Roland Wells Robbins," Nov. 10, 1965, the Roland Wells Robbins Collection, the Thoreau Society, Lincoln, Mass.

71. The society voted to return the house to the original site in 1974.

72. Charles W. Tremer, "A Brief Analysis of the Foundations of the Hancock-Clarke House: Recommendations for Future Plans of Same [1971]," the Roland Wells Robbins Collection, the Thoreau Society, Lincoln, Mass. Tremer, an archaeologist at Muhlenberg College, had evidently been working on a site in Minuteman National Historical Park at the time that he was asked to prepare this report. Robbins did not receive a copy of the report until 1973.

73. Tremer, "A Brief Analysis of the Foundations of the Hancock-Clarke House," n.p.

74. Tremer, "A Brief Analysis of the Foundations of the Hancock-Clarke House," n.p.

75. Tremer, "A Brief Analysis of the Foundations of the Hancock-Clarke House," n.p.

76. Tremer, "A Brief Analysis of the Foundations of the Hancock-Clarke House," n.p.

77. Tremer, "A Brief Analysis of the Foundations of the Hancock-Clarke House," n.p.

78. Tremer, "A Brief Analysis of the Foundations of the Hancock-Clarke House," n.p.

79. Tremer, "A Brief Analysis of the Foundations of the Hancock-Clarke House," n.p.

80. Tremer, "A Brief Analysis of the Foundations of the Hancock-Clarke House," n.p.

81. Tremer, "A Brief Analysis of the Foundations of the Hancock-Clarke House," n.p.

82. James Deetz, "Summary Report: Conference of October 15, 1973, Hancock-Clarke House, Lexington, Mass. [1973]," the Roland Wells Robbins Collection, the Thoreau Society, Lincoln, Mass., 1.

83. Deetz, "Summary Report," 2.

84. Deetz, "Summary Report," 2.

85. Deetz, "Summary Report," 2–3.

86. Deetz, "Summary Report," 3.

87. It is unclear whether Deetz or Tremer were aware of the society's goals to identify foundations or the limited budget that Robbins had available to him. Unlike the "worst tradition" of Williamsburg, where artifacts were haphazardly saved and provenienced only to the house lot, Robbins's procedure at the Hancock-Clarke site was systematic in screening for artifacts, and these materials were provenienced by cellar or feature (although not by level in the feature).

88. Robbins, "Hancock-Clarke House Site Daily Log—1964," 1–2; "Hancock-Clarke House Site Daily Log—1965," 4.

89. Robbins, "Hancock-Clarke House Site Daily Log—1964," 1–2; "Hancock-Clarke House Site Daily Log—1965," 4. Although late-nineteenth-century sites are now considered to have potential research value, historical archaeologists of the 1960s and 1970s generally disregarded them altogether.

90. Deetz, "Summary Report," 3; Robbins, "The Archaeological Excavations of the Hancock-Clarke Homestead," 25–31.

91. Deetz, "Summary Report," 4. Excavation of the chimneys might provide a reliable terminus post quem for the construction of the cellar and structure, and reexcavation of the cellars would be worthwhile if Robbins had not reached the bottom.

92. Deetz, "Summary Report," 6. Deetz's student Vernon G. Baker analyzed the ceramics from Hancock-Clarke in 1975. Vernon G. Baker, "South's Ceramic Dating Formula: An Application and Addition," Society for Historical Archaeology Newsletter 8, no. 2 (1975): 12–17. He found that even though they lacked specific vertical position within the cellar features, the artifacts were clearly provenienced by feature or cellar, allowing him to address some temporal and functional questions. The ceramic artifacts, along with those from the Alden House, were later used by Sarah Peabody Turnbaugh in her study of ideo-cultural variation and change in the seventeenth- and eighteenth-century Massachusetts Bay Colony. Sarah Peabody Turnbaugh, "Ideo-Cultural Variation and Change in the Massachusetts Bay Colony," in The Conference on Historic Site Archaeology Papers, vol. 11, ed. Stanley South (Columbia: Institute of Archaeology and Anthropology, University of South Carolina, 1976).

93. Charles H. Cole II to Roland B. Greeley, Dec. 4, 1973, the Roland Wells Robbins Collection, the Thoreau Society, Lincoln, Mass.

94. Cole to Greeley, Dec. 4, 1973.

95. Cole to Greeley, Dec. 4, 1973. Cole's attitude demonstrates the ethical standards of the older and more organized profession of architecture. The immediate notification of an ethics charge is now accepted procedure in disputes adjudicated by the Register of Professional Archaeologists.

96. Cole to Greeley, Dec. 4, 1973.

97. Cole to Greeley, Dec. 4, 1973.

98. Cole to Greeley, Dec. 4, 1973.

99. David Starbuck, personal communication, 2001.

100. Robert A. Gross, personal communication, 1996.

101. Gross, personal communication, 1995; Deetz, *In Small Things Forgotten*.

102. Deetz, *In Small Things Forgotten*, 96–97.

103. Deetz, *In Small Things Forgotten*, 30–31. Mystery Hill has, according to Deetz, "been the center of controversy for years."

104. Deetz, *In Small Things Forgotten*, 4–6.

105. Michael B. Schiffer and George J. Gumerman, eds., *Conservation Archaeology: A Guide for Cultural Resource Management Studies* (New York: Academic Press, 1977), 3–8. The National Historic Preservation Act established the National Register of Historic Places, and Section 106 required federal agencies to consider the effect of their projects on properties listed on the National Register. NEPA was the first comprehensive federal policy dealing with land use and resource planning, and required that environmental, historical, and cultural values be weighed against the economic and technological benefits of any proposed federally funded projects, or those requiring federal licenses. The passage of Executive Order 11593 in 1973 tied these two pieces of legislation together and extended their interpretation to include properties that were eligible for nomination to the National Register.

106. Salwen, "Has Historical Archaeology Survived the Bicentennial?" 5.

107. Salwen, "Has Historical Archaeology Survived the Bicentennial?" 5.

108. Salwen, "Has Historical Archaeology Survived the Bicentennial?" 6.

109. Brown, personal communication, 1995. Brown University established its contract archaeology program in 1975.

110. Schiffer and Gumerman, *Conservation Archaeology*, 9–11. Willey and Sabloff reported in 1974 that "the profession already is trying to cope with the mundane problems of setting standards for the fulfilling of contracts and the elimination of shoddy fieldwork and reporting." Willey and Sabloff, *A History of American Archaeology*, 262.

111. William J. Morris to Roland W. Robbins, June 15, 1970, and Roland W. Robbins to Senator Edward W. Brooke, Aug. 6, 1970, 3, the Roland Wells Robbins Collection, the Thoreau Society, Lincoln, Mass.

112. Robbins to Brooke, Aug. 6, 1970, 3; Morris to Robbins, June 15, 1970.

113. Morris to Robbins, June 15, 1970.

114. Roland W. Robbins to William J. Morris, July 7, 1970, the Roland Wells Robbins Collection, the Thoreau Society, Lincoln, Mass.

115. Robbins noted in several pieces of correspondence that he had magazine articles with photographs showing Park Service archaeologists using heavy equipment.

116. Robbins to Brooke, Aug. 6, 1970, 4.

117. Robbins to Brooke, Aug. 6, 1970, 4.

118. Senator Edward W. Brooke to Roland W. Robbins, Aug. 25, 1970, the Roland Wells Robbins Collection, the Thoreau Society, Lincoln, Mass.

119. Roland W. Robbins to Senator Edward W. Brooke, Sept. 29, 1970, and Feb. 6, 1971, the Roland Wells Robbins Collection, the Thoreau Society, Lincoln, Mass.

120. Raymond L. Freeman to Senator Edward W. Brooke, Apr. 15, 1971; Senator Edward W. Brooke to Roland W. Robbins, Apr. 18, 1971, the Roland Wells Robbins Collection, the Thoreau Society, Lincoln, Mass.

121. Freeman to Brooke, Apr. 15, 1971.

122. William J. Morris to Roland W. Robbins, Apr. 30, 1971, the Roland Wells Robbins Collection, the Thoreau Society, Lincoln, Mass.

123. Roland W. Robbins to Senator Edward W. Brooke, May 26, 1971, the Roland Wells Robbins Collection, the Thoreau Society, Lincoln, Mass.

124. Robbins to Brooke, May 26, 1971, 2.

125. Raymond L. Freeman to Senator Edward W. Brooke, July 8, 1971, the Roland Wells Robbins Collection, the Thoreau Society, Lincoln, Mass.

126. Freeman to Brooke, July 8, 1971.

127. These agencies were responsible for review of Section 106 projects. In general review and oversight of CRM work was fairly lax in the first ten to fifteen years of CRM practice, allowing Robbins to work on several small projects.

128. Interestingly, Troy was one of the Thoreau Society members to complain about Robbins's Walden Cabin Kit.

129. Heberling, interview with author, Nov. 8, 1992.

130. Heberling, interview with author, Nov. 8, 1992.

131. Heberling, interview with author, Nov. 8, 1992. Heberling later excavated the Greenwood Furnace and found Robbins's predictions to be extremely accurate.

132. Heberling, interview with author, Nov. 8, 1992.

133. Heberling, interview with author, Nov. 8, 1992.

134. James Robert, "People's Archaeology," in *Old Glory: A Pictorial Report on the Grass Roots History Movement and the First Hometown History Primer,* ed. James Robert (New York: Warner Paperback, 1973), 103.

135. Robert, "People's Archaeology," 104.

136. Robert, "People's Archaeology," 104.

137. Leder, "Review of *Hidden America,*" 243–244.

138. Hatch, "Introduction," 5. Hatch argues that this quest has "become a central organizing principal in our society."

139. Jones, interview with author, July 29, 1992.

140. Robbins to Barker, Aug. 29, 1971.

141. "New England Historical Archaeology," the Dublin Seminar for New England Folklife, organized by Peter Benes and Marley R. Brown III, Dublin School, Dublin, N.H., June 25–26, 1977.

142. Marley R. Brown III to Roland W. Robbins, May 18, 1977, the Roland Wells Robbins Collection, the Thoreau Society, Lincoln, Mass. Brown remem-

bered that he was against inviting Robbins to speak. At the time, he recalled, "I thought that anyone who was not a trained or schooled archaeologist, like Robbins, was a pot hunter." Brown, personal communication, 1995.

143. Roland W. Robbins to Marley R. Brown III, June 7, 1977, the Roland Wells Robbins Collection, the Thoreau Society, Lincoln, Mass.

144. Roland W. Robbins, "Daily Journal for Dublin Seminar, 1977," the Roland Wells Robbins Collection, the Thoreau Society, Lincoln, Mass., 1.

145. Robbins, "Daily Journal for Dublin Seminar," 1.

146. Robbins, "Daily Journal for Dublin Seminar," 1.

147. Brown, personal communication, 1995.

148. Brown, personal communication, 1995. Archaeologist David Starbuck has a much different recollection of the conference, suggesting that the students and professionals involved were quite derisive and disrespectful of Robbins. Starbuck, personal communication, 2001.

149. Stephen R. Pendry, personal communication, 1996. Pendry reported that Deetz frequently disparaged Robbins in class.

150. Brown, personal communication, 1995.

151. In recent years, faced with a lack of university and government positions for its students, the academy has had to adopt cultural resource management as a legitimate approach to archaeological research. However, the Society for American Archaeology (SAA) did not establish a standing committee on cultural resource management until 1994, and with a few exceptions universities have just begun to offer courses on CRM.

152. Gross, personal communication, 1996.

153. Estimates of archaeologists employed in CRM range from 30 percent to 70 percent. Polls by the SAA and SHA suggest the lower to middle end of the range; however, they principally reflect membership rolls in these societies. Julie Zimmer, Richard Wilk, and Ann Pyburn, "A Survey of Attitudes and Values in Archaeological Practice," *SAA Bulletin* 13, no. 5 (1995): 10. The high costs of membership exclude many practicing archaeologists (B.A. and M.A.), particularly those in entry-level positions.

154. Dodson, "The Man Who Found Thoreau," 116.

155. Joseph Wood Krutch, ed. *Thoreau: Walden and Other Writings* (New York: Bantam Books, 1962), 132.

156. Krutch, *Thoreau*, 144.

157. The Munroe Tavern excavation, performed for the Lexington Historical Society in the mid-1980s, is a very interesting example of the relationships that Robbins maintained with local historical societies and museums in the last years of his career. It had been less than ten years since members of the society had hired professional, university-based archaeologists Charles W. Tremer and James Deetz to review Robbins's work at their Hancock-Clarke House property. His reemployment by the society as a consultant for the Munroe Tavern project

is particularly interesting in light of the extremely negative assessment by these reviewers. It points out both the confidence that the society members had in Robbins and in his ability to adequately complete their project, and their disregard for the opinion of professional archaeologists. Of equal importance is the generally small budget of local historical societies and their inability to pay the high costs of professional archaeologists. Roland W. Robbins, "Munroe Tavern Notes—1982," and "Munroe Tavern, A Preliminary Search for the Site of its Masonic Hall [1984]," the Roland Wells Robbins Collection, the Thoreau Society, Lincoln, Mass.

158. Dean, personal communication, 2001.

159. Geraldine Robbins, interviews with author, July 31 and Aug. 1 and 3, 1992.

160. This was a bitter pill for Robbins to swallow; he wrote more than eighteen letters before he appeared to give up on the idea.

161. Joyce, interview with author, Aug. 8, 1993.

162. Heberling, interview with author, Nov. 8, 1992.

163. Geraldine Robbins, interviews with author, July 31 and Aug. 1 and 3, 1992.

164. Roland W. Robbins, "Lecture Folders—1967," Feb. 24, 1967.

165. Geraldine Robbins, interviews with author, July 31 and Aug. 1 and 3, 1992.

166. Foley, "On the Meaning of Industrial Archaeology," 66–68.

167. Orr, "Philadelphia as Industrial Archaeological Artifact," 3–14.

168. Blanding, interview with author, Aug. 10, 1993.

169. Heberling, interview with author, Nov. 8, 1992.

170. Linebaugh, "Forging a Career."

171. Dodson, "The Man Who Found Thoreau," 116.

172. Blanding, interview with author, Aug. 10, 1993.

173. An entire literature has developed on public archaeology. These works range from Mark P. Leone's "Method as Message: Interpreting the Past with the Public," *Museum News* 62, no. 1 (1983): 34–41, to Parker B. Potter Jr.'s *Public Archaeology in Annapolis: A Critical Approach to History in Maryland's Ancient City* (Washington, D.C.: Smithsonian Institution Press, 1994), and to John H. Jameson Jr.'s edited volume, *Presenting Archaeology to the Public: Digging for Truths* (Walnut Creek, Calif.: AltaMira Press, 1997). The literature also includes a growing number of texts for younger readers and teaching manuals.

174. J. C. Harrington had seen the need for public participation in Jamestown in the 1930s and opened portions of the excavations for public tours. Harrington, "Jamestown Archaeology in Retrospect." The post-processual "critical theorists" have argued for the importance of taking "into account its [American archaeology's] contemporary social context." Potter, *Public Archaeology,* 27.

175. Robert C. Olsen, "Digging Up the Past—Archaeology in Outdoor Education," *Science Teacher* 37, no. 8 (1970).

176. Malcolm Katz to Roland W. Robbins, June 7, 1967, the Roland Wells Robbins Collection, the Thoreau Society, Lincoln, Mass.

177. Harry M. Johnson to Roland W. Robbins, Nov. 29, 1967, the Roland Wells Robbins Collection, the Thoreau Society, Lincoln, Mass.

178. Heberling, interview with author, Nov. 8, 1992.

179. Heberling, interview with author, Nov. 8, 1992.

180. Deetz, *Flowerdew Hundred,* 171–172.

181. Roland W. Robbins, "Interview on Martha Dean Show," audiotape, Aug. 8, 1960 (New York: WOR Radio), the Roland Wells Robbins Collection, the Thoreau Society, Lincoln, Mass.

182. Deetz, *Flowerdew Hundred,* 172–173.

183. It seems fairly clear that Robbins did excavate by level and layer at many sites and clearly used this data to guide his work. He also provenienced materials by level and layer at various sites. However, he did not consistently record the stratigraphic profile in its entirety and consistently provenience and mark all artifacts within these soil layers. Some of this data can be recovered from the use of Robbins's field notes, maps, and photographs.

184. Cotter, "Review of *Hidden America,*" 221.

185. Robbins's reports and publications unfortunately do not convey the overall quality of his records and record keeping. Robbins also had an undeserved reputation for hoarding his records and not sharing them with researchers or the organizations that sponsored the work. In almost every case, Robbins provided the records of his work, at the very least his maps and photographs, to the sponsoring organizations, historical societies, or museums. For instance, in 1975 Robbins received a letter from Bruce Gill, the archaeologist at Historic Bethlehem, Inc., inquiring after records and photographs from his 1957 excavations. He replied that he was shocked that Historic Bethlehem had not retained its copies of these materials, particularly the black-and-white photographs taken by one of its own employees. It is indeed fortunate that Robbins provided copies of documentation to his clients and retained the originals in his personal archives. Although Robbins was willing to share the requested information with Historic Bethlehem and provided a detailed summary in his letter to Gill, his time was valuable, he said, and he could not spend it re-creating Historic Bethlehem's files. Roland W. Robbins to Bruce Cooper Gill, Apr. 28, 1975, the Roland Wells Robbins Collection, the Thoreau Society, Lincoln, Mass. Likewise, Strawbery Banke, Inc., had no record of the site and plan maps that Robbins had sent, nor did it retain most of the artifacts from the dig.

186. Harrington, "Jamestown Archaeology in Retrospect," 29.

187. Brown, "A Survey of Historical Archaeology in New England," 14.

188. Robbins quoted in Turner, *Spirit of Place,* 48.

189. Heberling, interview with author, Nov. 8, 1992.

190. Heberling, interview with author, Nov. 8, 1992.

191. Robbins quoted in Turner, *Spirit of Place,* 48.

192. Heberling, interview with author, Nov. 8, 1992.

193. Heberling, interview with author, Nov. 8, 1992.

194. Blanding, "Eulogy for Roland Wells Robbins."

195. Henry David Thoreau, *Walden,* ed. J. Lyndon Shanley (Princeton, N.J.: Princeton University Press, 1971), 323.

Bibliography

Adams, William Hampton. "Historical Archaeology Strove for Maturity in the Mid-1980s." *Historical Archaeology* 27, no. 1 (1993): 29.

Alden Kindred of America. "The John Alden House, Duxbury, Massachusetts: A Narrative History," www.alden.org/heritage/househistory.htm. Duxbury: Alden Kindred of America, Inc., n.d.

Bacon, Edwin. *Historic Pilgrimages in New England; Among Landmarks of Pilgrim and Puritan Days and of the Provincial and Revolutionary Periods.* New York and Boston: Silver, Burdett & Co., 1898.

Baker, Vernon G. "South's Ceramic Dating Formula: An Application and Addition." *Society for Historical Archaeology Newsletter* 8, no. 2 (1975): 12–17.

Barber, Bernard. "Some Problems in the Sociology of the Professions." In *The Professions in America,* ed. Kenneth S. Lynn, 15–34. Boston: Beacon Press, 1967.

Barber, R. J. *Report on the Saugus Ironworks Collections and their Cataloging,* 1973. On file at New England Museum Services Center, Marine Barracks, Boston National Historical Park, Charlestown Unit, Charlestown, Mass.

Barghoorn, Elso S. "Recent Changes in Sea Level along the New England Coast: New Archaeological Evidence." *Science* 117, no. 3048 (1953): 597–598.

Barka, Norman F., Edward Ayres, and Christine Sheridan. *The "Poor Potter" of Yorktown: A Study of a Colonial Pottery Factory.* Yorktown Research Series, no. 5. Williamsburg, Va.: College of William and Mary, Department of Anthropology, 1984.

Beaudry, Mary C. "Archaeology and the Documentary Record." In "An Evaluation of Roland Wells Robbins Archaeology," ed. Marley R. Brown III, n.p., 1975. Manuscript on file, Saugus Iron Works National Historic Site, Saugus, Mass.

Becker, Carl. "Everyman His Own Historian." *American Historical Review* 37, no. 2 (1932): 221–236.

Blades, Brooke S. "Doctor Williams' Privy: Cultural Behavior as Reflected in Artifact Deposition at the Dr. Thomas Williams House, Deerfield, Massachusetts." In *New England Historical Archaeology,* ed. Peter Benes, 56–65. The

Dublin Seminar for New England Folklife Annual Proceedings, vol. 2. Boston: Boston University, 1978.

Blanding, Thomas. "Eulogy for Roland Wells Robbins. Read at Memorial Service, Trinitarian Congregational Church, Concord, Massachusetts, Saturday, March 21, 1987." Manuscript in the collection of Thomas Blanding, Concord, Mass.

———. Interview with author. Aug. 10, 1993, Lincoln, Mass.

Bledstein, Burton J. *The Culture of Professionalism: The Middle Class and the Development of Higher Education in America.* New York: W. W. Norton & Company, 1976.

Bonfield, Lynn A., and Mary C. Morrison. *Roxanna's Children: The Biography of a Nineteenth-Century Vermont Family.* Amherst: University of Massachusetts Press, 1995.

Boxley, Steve. "Re:Educational Requirements." Comments to Histarch listserve (histarch@asuvm.inre.asu.edu), Apr. 28, 1998.

Brown, Marley R., III, ed. "An Evaluation of Roland Wells Robbins Archaeology," 1975. Manuscript on file, Saugus Iron Works National Historic Site, Saugus, Mass.

———. Personal communication, 1995, 1996, 2004.

———. "A Survey of Historical Archaeology in New England." In *New England Historical Archaeology,* ed. Peter Benes, The Dublin Seminar for New England Folklife: Annual Proceedings, vol. 2: 4–15. Boston: Boston University, 1978.

Buell, Lawrence. "The Thoreauvian Pilgrimage: The Structure of an American Cult." *American Literature* 61, no. 2 (1989): 175–199.

Burlington Free Press. "More Vermont Verse," n.d., editorial page.

Butler, Joseph. Personal communication, 1991.

Calver, William L., and Reginald P. Bolton. *History Written with Pick and Shovel; military buttons, belt plates, badges and other relics excavated from Colonial, Revolutionary, and War of 1812 camp sites by the Field Exploration Committee of the New-York Historical Society.* New York: New-York Historical Society, 1950.

Candee, Richard M. "Urban Landscapes and Vernacular Building in Portsmouth, N.H., 1660–1990: A Field Guide for Tours of Portsmouth." Prepared for the Vernacular Architecture Forum 13th Annual Meeting and Conference, Portsmouth, N.H., May 13–16, 1992.

Carlson, Stephen P. "The Saugus Iron Works Restoration: A Tentative History," 1978. Saugus Iron Works National Historic Site, Saugus, Mass.

Chase, Harry B. "Henry Thoreau Surveyor." *Surveying and Mapping* 25 (June 1965): 219–222.

Cheyfitz, Eric. "Matthiessen's *American Renaissance:* Circumscribing the Revolution." *American Quarterly* 41 (1989): 341–361.

Clark, Edie. "The Man Who Looked Back and Saw the Future." *Yankee* 50, no. 9 (1986): 108–181.

Conforti, Joseph A. *Imagining New England: Explorations of Regional Identity from the Pilgrims to the Mid-Twentieth Century.* Chapel Hill: University of North Carolina Press, 2001.

Cotter, John L. *Archaeological Excavations at Jamestown, Virginia.* Washington, D.C.: National Park Service, 1958; reprint, Richmond: Archaeological Society of Virginia, Special Publication no. 32, 1994.

————. Personal communication, 1996.

————. "Review of *Hidden America.*" *Archaeology* 14 (1961): 221–222.

Cotter, John L., and J. Paul Hudson. *New Discoveries at Jamestown.* Washington, D.C.: National Park Service, 1957.

Dawson, James. "A History of the Cairn." *Thoreau Society Bulletin,* no. 232 (Summer 2000): 1–3.

Deagan, Kathleen. "Retrospective on the Society for Historical Archaeology, 1977–1982." *Historical Archaeology* 27, no. 1 (1993): 19–22.

Dean, Bradley. Personal communication, 2001.

Deetz, James. "Ceramics from Plymouth, 1635–1835." In *Ceramics in America,* ed. Ian M. C. Quimby, 15–40. Charlottesville: University of Virginia Press, 1973.

————. "Excavations at the Joseph Howland Site (C5), Rocky Nook, Kingston, Massachusetts, 1959: A Preliminary Report." *Supplement to the Howland Quarterly* 24, nos. 2–3 (1960): 1–11.

————. *Flowerdew Hundred: The Archaeology of a Virginia Plantation, 1619–1864.* Charlottesville: University of Virginia Press, 1994.

————. "The Howlands at Rocky Nook: An Archaeological and Historical Study." *Supplement to the Howland Quarterly* 24, no. 4 (1960): 1–8.

————. *In Small Things Forgotten: The Archaeology of Early American Life.* Garden City, N.Y.: Anchor Books, 1977.

————. "Scientific Humanism and Humanistic Science: A Plea for Paradigmatic Pluralism in Historical Archaeology." *Geoscience and Man* 23 (1983): 27–34.

————. "Summary Report: Conference of October 15, 1973, Hancock-Clarke House, Lexington, Mass [1973]." The Roland Wells Robbins Collection, the Thoreau Society, Lincoln, Mass.

Derry, Linda, and Marley R. Brown III. "Excavation at Colonial Williamsburg Thirty Years Ago: An Archaeological Analysis of Cross-Trenching Behind the Peyton Randolph Site," 1987. Office of Archaeological Research, Colonial Williamsburg Foundation, Williamsburg, Va.

Dickens, Robert. *Thoreau: The Complete Individualist.* New York: Exposition Press, 1974.

Dodson, James. "The Man Who Found Thoreau." *Yankee* 49 (1985): 62–65, 116–123.

Fagan, Brian. *Elusive Treasure: The Story of Early Archaeologists in the Americas.* New York: Charles Scribner's Sons, 1977.

First Iron Works Association, Inc. Fund-raising letter, ca. 1942–1943. The Roland Wells Robbins Collection, the Thoreau Society, Lincoln, Mass.

First Iron Works Association, Inc., and American Iron and Steel Institute. *The Saugus Iron Works Restoration.* 16-mm film. New York: Filmfax Productions, 1955.

Foley, Vincent P. "On the Meaning of Industrial Archaeology." *Historical Archaeology* 2 (1968): 66–68.

———. "Reply to Vogel." *Historical Archaeology* 3 (1969): 93–94.

Folsom, Merrill. "Dig It Yourself: Philipsburg Manor's Visitors Welcome to Lend Archaeologists a Hand." *New York Times,* Sept. 8, 1957, section 2, p. 26.

Ford, Ben, and Matthew A. Kierstead. *Oliver Mill Park Restoration Project Archaeological Monitoring of Machine Excavations.* Technical report produced by PAL, Pawtucket, R.I., 2001. On file at the Massachusetts Historical Commission, Boston.

Frost, Jack [pseud.?]. *Yankee Homecoming: Official Sketch Book.* Boston: Yankee Homecoming Council, 1958.

Geison, Gerald L. "Introduction." In *Professions and Professional Ideologies in America,* ed. Gerald L. Geison, 1–11. Chapel Hill: University of North Carolina Press, 1983.

Gross, Robert A. Personal communications, 1995 and 1996.

Gruber, Jacob W. "Artifacts Are History: Calver and Bolton in New York." In *The Scope of Historical Archaeology: Essays in Honor of John L. Cotter,* ed. David G. Orr and Daniel G. Crozier, 13–27. Philadelphia: Laboratory of Anthropology, Temple University, 1984.

Hard, Walter, Jr., and J. Kevin Graffagnino. *Walter Hard's Vermont People.* Middlebury: Vermont Books, 1981.

Harding, Walter. *The Days of Henry Thoreau: A Biography.* Princeton, N.J.: Princeton University Press, 1992.

———. Interview with author. Nov. 6, 1992, Geneseo, N.Y.

Harding, Walter, and Michael Meyer. *The New Thoreau Handbook.* New York: New York University Press, 1980.

Harrington, J. C. "Archaeology and Local History." *Bulletin of the American Association for State and Local History* 2, no. 6 (1953): 157–167.

———. *Archaeology and the Historical Society.* Nashville, Tenn.: American Association for State and Local History, 1965.

———. "From Architraves to Artifacts: A Metamorphosis." In *Pioneers in Historical Archaeology: Breaking New Ground,* ed. Stanley South, 1–14. New York: Plenum Press, 1994.

———. *Glassmaking at Jamestown.* Richmond, Va.: Dietz Press, 1952.

———. "Historic Site Archaeology in the United States." In *Archaeology of the Eastern United States,* ed. James B. Griffin, 335–344. Chicago: University of Chicago Press, 1952.

———. "Jamestown Archaeology in Retrospect." In *The Scope of Historical Archaeology: Essays in Honor of John L. Cotter,* ed. David G. Orr and Daniel G.

Crozier, 29–51. Philadelphia: Laboratory of Anthropology, Temple University, 1984.

Hartley, E. Neal. *Ironworks on the Saugus*. Norman: University of Oklahoma Press, 1957.

Hatch, Nathan O. "Introduction: The Professions in a Democratic Culture." In *The Professions in American History*, ed. Nathan O. Hatch, 1–13. Notre Dame, Ind.: University of Notre Dame Press, 1988.

Hayes, Charles F., III. "Review of *Pilgrim John Alden's Progress: Archaeological Excavations in Duxbury*." *Historical Archaeology* 5 (1971): 115.

Heberling, Paul. Interview with author. Nov. 8, 1992, State College, Pa.

Holden, Raymond. "Amateurs at Work." *New York Times Book Review*, Oct. 25, 1959, 20.

Hosmer, Charles B., Jr. *Presence of the Past: A History of the Preservation Movement in the United States before Williamsburg*. New York: G. P. Putnam's Sons, 1965.

———. *Preservation Comes of Age: From Williamsburg to the National Trust, 1926–1949*. Charlottesville: University of Virginia Press, 1981.

Howell, Charles, and Allan Keller. *The Mill at Philipsburg Manor Upper Mills and A Brief History of Milling*. Tarrytown, N.Y.: Sleepy Hollow Restorations, 1977.

Hughes, Everett C. "Professions." In *The Professions in America*, ed. Kenneth S. Lynn, 1–14. Boston: Beacon Press, 1967.

Ingersoll, Daniel W., Jr. "Settlement Archaeology at Puddle Dock." Ph.D. diss., Harvard University, 1971.

Jackson, J. A. *Professions and Professionalization*. Cambridge: Cambridge University Press, 1970.

James, Robert, ed. *Old Glory: A Pictorial Report of the Grass Roots History Movement and the First Hometown History Primer*. New York: Warner Paperback, 1973.

Janowitz, Meta, Allan S. Gilbert, and Donald W. Linebaugh. "Compositional Analysis of Redwares for the Philipsburg Manor Upper Mills Sites, Sleepy Hollow, New York." In *Scientific Tools in Historical Archaeology*, ed. Timothy James Scarlett. Pensacola: University Press of Florida, forthcoming.

Jelks, Edward B. "The Founding Meeting of the Society for Historical Archaeology." *Historical Archaeology* 27, no. 1 (1993): 10–11.

Johnson, Carl A. "Agreement Between Strawbery Banke, Inc., and The Department of History, University of New Hampshire, April 1966." The Roland Wells Robbins Collection, the Thoreau Society, Lincoln, Mass.

Johnson, Eric S. *Archaeological Overview and Assessment of the Saugus Ironworks National Historic Site, Saugus, Massachusetts, 1997*. On file at the New England System Support Office, National Park Service, Boston.

Johnson, Floyd. Interview with author. Mar. 9, 1995, Keene, Va.

Jones, Evan. "Dig-It-Yourself Archaeologists." *New York Times Magazine*, Feb. 16, 1958, 48.

————. Interview with author. July 29, 1992, East Hardwick, Vt.

————. "Pick and Shovel Historian." *Collier's,* Aug. 5, 1955, 28–31.

Joyce, Kristina. Interview with author. Aug. 8, 1993, Lincoln, Mass.

Judd, Jacob, and Paula Sampson. "Archaeological Study of Philipsburg Manor Upper Mills, 1974." Historic Hudson Valley Archives, Sleepy Hollow, N.Y.

Kammen, Michael. *Mystic Chords of Memory: The Transformation of Tradition in American Culture.* New York: Alfred A. Knopf, 1991.

Kern, Susan A. Personal communication, 1993.

Kimball, Fiske. "In Search of Jefferson's Birthplace." *Virginia Magazine of History and Biography* 51, no. 4 (1943): 312–325.

King, Thomas F. *Cultural Resource Laws and Practice: An Introductory Guide.* Walnut Creek, Calif.: AltaMira Press, 1998.

Krutch, Joseph Wood, ed. *Thoreau: Walden and Other Writings.* New York: Bantam Books, 1962.

Laura, Arthur C. "Research Notes on Metal Artifacts and Their Restoration," 1952. The Roland Wells Robbins Collection, the Thoreau Society, Lincoln, Mass.

Lears, T. J. Jackson. *No Place of Grace: Antimodernism and the Transformation of American Culture, 1880–1920.* New York: Pantheon Books, 1981.

Leder, Lawrence H. "Review of *Hidden America.*" *New York History,* Apr. 1960, 243–244.

Leone, Mark P. "Method as Message: Interpreting the Past with the Public." *Museum News* 62, no. 1 (1983): 34–41.

Lindgren, James M. "'A Constant Incentive to Patriotic Citizenship': Historic Preservation in Progressive-Era Massachusetts." *New England Quarterly* 64, no. 4 (1991): 594–608.

————. "The Gospel of Preservation in Virginia and New England: Historic Preservation and the Regeneration of Traditionalism." Ph.D. diss., College of William and Mary, 1984.

————. *Preserving Historic New England: Preservation, Progressivism, and the Remaking of Memory.* New York: Oxford University Press, 1995.

————. *Preserving the Old Dominion: Historic Preservation and Virginia Traditionalism.* Charlottesville: University of Virginia Press, 1993.

Linebaugh, Donald W. "Forging a Career: Roland Wells Robbins and Iron Industry Sites in the Northeastern U.S." *IA: The Journal of the Society for Industrial Archaeology* 26, no. 1 (2000): 5–36.

————. "'The Road to Ruins and Restoration': Roland Wells Robbins and the Professionalization of Historical Archaeology." Ph.D. diss., College of William and Mary, 1996.

————. "Walden and Beyond: The Restoration Archaeology of Roland Wells Robbins." In *The Reconstructed Past: Reconstructions in the Public Interpretation of Archaeology and History,* ed. John H. Jameson Jr., 21–46. Walnut Creek, Calif.: AltaMira Press, 2004.

Littlefield, Louise Hall. *The Triad Anthology of New England Verse.* Portland, Maine: Falmouth Book House, 1938.

Lowenthal, David. *The Past Is a Foreign Country.* Cambridge: Cambridge University Press, 1985.

Lowry, Cynthia. "Variation of Do-It-Yourself Turns Up in Archaeology, Project Works." *Danville (Va.) Register,* Oct. 2, 1958.

Lynn, Kenneth S., ed. *The Professions in America.* Boston: Beacon Press, 1967.

MacCannell, Dean. *The Tourist: A New Theory of the Leisure Class.* New York: Schocken Books, 1989.

Maynard, W. Barksdale. Personal communication, 2002.

McCaffrey, Ed. "The Monsignor Said It Rather Well." *Concord (Mass.) Journal,* July 1, 1965, 2a.

McKearin, Helen. "Miscellaneous Research Notes—1960. Supplement I. Helen McKearin Identification of Glass Artifacts Recovered at Philipsburg Manor." Folder—Misc. Lists, Historic Hudson Valley Archives, Sleepy Hollow, N.Y.

Mero, Everett B. *Celebrating a 300th Anniversary: A Report on the Massachusetts Bay Tercentenary of 1930.* Boston: Tercentenary Conference of City and Town Committees, 1931.

Moldenhauer, Joseph J., ed. *The Illustrated Maine Woods.* Princeton, N.J.: Princeton University Press, 1974.

Morey, Ruth, and Roland W. Robbins. "Agreement by and Between the Lexington Historical Society and Roland Wells Robbins," Nov. 10, 1965. The Roland Wells Robbins Collection, the Thoreau Society, Lincoln, Mass.

Mouer, Daniel. "Re:Educational Requirements." Comments to Histarch listserve (histarch@asuvm.inre.asu.edu), Apr. 27, 1998.

Murtagh, William J. *Keeping Time: The History and Theory of Preservation in America.* Pittstown, N.J.: Main Street Press, 1988.

National Education Association. "Salaries Paid and Salary Practices in Universities, Colleges, and Junior Colleges, 1955–1956." *National Education Association Research Bulletin* 34, no. 3 (1956): 118.

Nielsen, Ann Marie. "Puddle Dock Dig—an Adventure in Colonial Site Archaeology." *New Hampshire Alumnus* 42, no. 8 (1966): 12–13.

Noël Hume, Ivor. "Excavations at Clay Bank, Gloucester County, Virginia." *Contributions from the Museum of History and Technology* 52 (1966): 1–28.

———. *A Guide to Artifacts of Colonial America.* New York: Alfred A. Knopf, 1969.

———. *Here Lies Virginia: An Archaeologist's View of Colonial Life and History.* New York: Alfred A. Knopf, 1963.

———. *Historical Archaeology.* New York: Alfred A. Knopf, 1968.

———. *The Virginia Adventure, Roanoke to James Towne: An Archaeological and Historical Odyssey.* New York: Alfred A. Knopf, 1994.

Olsen, Robert C. "Digging Up the Past—Archaeology in Outdoor Education." *Science Teacher* 37, no. 8 (1970): n.p.

Omwake, H. Geiger. "Report on the Examination of White Kaolin Pipes from Shadwell," June 1955. The Roland Wells Robbins Collection, the Thoreau Society, Lincoln, Mass.

Orr, David G. "Philadelphia as Industrial Archaeological Artifact: A Case Study." *Historical Archaeology* 11 (1977): 3–14.

Ostrander, Mary. "The PMUM Case," 1974. Historic Hudson Valley Archives, Sleepy Hollow, N.Y.

Patterson, Thomas C. "The Last Sixty Years: Toward a Social History of Americanist Archaeology in the United States." *American Anthropologist* 88 (1986): 7–26.

Pendry, Stephen R. Personal communication, 1996.

Petroski, Henry. "H. D. Thoreau, Engineer." *Invention and Technology* (Fall 1989): 8–16.

"The Philipse Castle Land and Structures [1956]." Manuscript prepared by the Research Department, Sleepy Hollow Restorations, Tarrytown, N.Y. The Roland Wells Robbins Collection, the Thoreau Society, Lincoln, Mass.

Potter, Parker B., Jr. *Public Archaeology in Annapolis: A Critical Approach to History in Maryland's Ancient City.* Washington, D.C.: Smithsonian Institution Press, 1994.

Richardson, Robert D., Jr. *Emerson: The Mind on Fire.* Berkeley: University of California Press, 1995.

Robbins, Irwin. Interview with author. July 26, 1994, Portland, Maine.

Robbins, Geraldine. Interviews with author. July 2, 1990, July 31 and Aug. 1 and 3, 1992, and Feb. 2, 1996, Lincoln, Mass.

———. Letter to author. Oct. 26, 1995.

———. Personal communications. 1993–1996.

Robbins, Roland W. "The Archaeological Excavations of the Hancock-Clarke Homestead [1966]." The Roland Wells Robbins Collection, the Thoreau Society, Lincoln, Mass.

———. "Artifact Inventory Cards—Philipsburg Manor Upper Mills," n.d. Historic Hudson Valley Archives, Sleepy Hollow, N.Y.

———. "Bay and River Course Tests (Section—Looking N.W.), 9/13/56." Field notes. Historic Hudson Valley Archives, Sleepy Hollow, N.Y.

———. "Bay Trench M3, 10/3/56 to 10/31/56." Field notes. Historic Hudson Valley Archives, Sleepy Hollow, N.Y.

———. "Business Brochures—Replies, 1954–1956." The Roland Wells Robbins Collection, the Thoreau Society, Lincoln, Mass.

———. "Business Brochures—Unanswered Correspondence, 1954–1956." The Roland Wells Robbins Collection, the Thoreau Society, Lincoln, Mass.

———. "Daily Journal for Dublin Seminar, 1977." The Roland Wells Robbins Collection, the Thoreau Society, Lincoln, Mass.

———. *Discovery at Walden.* Stoneham, Mass.: George R. Barnstead & Son, 1947.

———. *Discovery at Walden: A Lecture* [1946]. Brochure. The Roland Wells Robbins Collection, the Thoreau Society, Lincoln, Mass.

————. General Correspondence, 1935–1980. The Roland Wells Robbins Collection, the Thoreau Society, Lincoln, Mass.

————. "Hancock-Clarke House Site Daily Log—1964–69." The Roland Wells Robbins Collection, the Thoreau Society, Lincoln, Mass.

————. "Interview on Martha Dean Show," audiotape, Aug. 8, 1960. New York: WOR Radio. The Roland Wells Robbins Collection, the Thoreau Society, Lincoln, Mass.

————. "John Alden—1st House in Duxbury, Daily Log [1960–1970]." The Roland Wells Robbins Collection, the Thoreau Society, Lincoln, Mass.

————. "John Alden Duxbury House Excavations, Sat., April 16, 1960." The Roland Wells Robbins Collection, the Thoreau Society, Lincoln, Mass.

————. "John Alden House, Supplemental Test Pits—June 17, 1962." The Roland Wells Robbins Collection, the Thoreau Society, Lincoln, Mass.

————. "Larry Geller—Pilgrim Society Daily Log, 1969–1970." The Roland Wells Robbins Collection, the Thoreau Society, Lincoln, Mass.

————. "Lecture Folders—1945–1980." The Roland Wells Robbins Collection, the Thoreau Society, Lincoln, Mass.

————. "Munroe Tavern, A Preliminary Search for the Site of its Masonic Hall [1984]." The Roland Wells Robbins Collection, the Thoreau Society, Lincoln, Mass.

————. "Munroe Tavern Notes—1982." The Roland Wells Robbins Collection, the Thoreau Society, Lincoln, Mass.

————. "#1 Thoreau Hut Notes [1945]." Notebook kept by Roland Robbins from Aug. to Nov. 1945. The Roland Wells Robbins Collection, the Thoreau Society, Lincoln, Mass.

————. "#2 Thoreau Hut Notes [1946]." Notebook kept by Roland Robbins from Dec. 1945 to July 1946. The Roland Wells Robbins Collection, the Thoreau Society, Lincoln, Mass.

————. "#3 Thoreau Hut Notes [1947]." Notebook kept by Roland Robbins from Aug. 1946 to Oct. 1947. The Roland Wells Robbins Collection, the Thoreau Society, Lincoln, Mass.

————. "The Oliver Mill Park Restoration: A Report," December 1969. The Roland Wells Robbins Collection, the Thoreau Society, Lincoln, Mass.

————. "The Oliver Mill Park Restoration—Daily Log, 1969." The Roland Wells Robbins Collection, the Thoreau Society, Lincoln, Mass.

————. "On the Photographs of Herbert Wendell Gleason." In *The Illustrated Maine Woods,* ed. Joseph J. Moldenhauer, ix–x. Princeton, N.J.: Princeton University Press, 1974.

————. "Profile of 39-W2, Friday, May 6, 1966 [Strawbery Banke]." The Roland Wells Robbins Collection, the Thoreau Society, Lincoln, Mass.

————. "Report of Archaeological Progress at the Old Iron Works Site, Saugus, Massachusetts, from September 10, 1948 to June 25, 1949." The Roland Wells Robbins Collection, the Thoreau Society, Lincoln, Mass.

278 • Bibliography

———. "Report of Archaeological Work Conducted for the Sleepy Hollow Restorations During 1959 [1960]." The Roland Wells Robbins Collection, the Thoreau Society, Lincoln, Mass.

———. "Report on 1955 Archaeological Exploration at Shadwell, Birthplace of Thomas Jefferson." The Roland Wells Robbins Collection, the Thoreau Society, Lincoln, Mass.

———. "Report on Research and Excavation, Executed from September 10, 1948 to October 16, 1948, Old Iron Works Site, Saugus, Massachusetts." The Roland Wells Robbins Collection, the Thoreau Society, Lincoln, Mass.

———. "Roland Wells Robbins and the Saugus Iron Works Restoration," n.d. The Roland Wells Robbins Collection, the Thoreau Society, Lincoln, Mass.

———. "Saugus Ironworks Daily Log, First Iron Works Association, Saugus, Massachusetts [1948–1953]." The Roland Wells Robbins Collection, the Thoreau Society, Lincoln, Mass.

———. "2nd Dock Site at Mill (Section thru M3 Trench), 10/5/56." Field notes. Historic Hudson Valley Archives, Sleepy Hollow, N.Y.

———. "Shadwell, Daily Log," 1955 and 1961. The Roland Wells Robbins Collection, the Thoreau Society, Lincoln, Mass.

———. "Shadwell Grid Data 1955," section in "Shadwell Field Notebook—1955." The Roland Wells Robbins Collection, the Thoreau Society, Lincoln, Mass.

———. "Site of the Nailery at Monticello," preliminary survey, Apr. 18, 1956. The Roland Wells Robbins Collection, the Thoreau Society, Lincoln, Mass.

———. "Sleepy Hollow Restorations Daily Log [1956–1961]." The Roland Wells Robbins Collection, the Thoreau Society, Lincoln, Mass.

———. "Sleepy Hollow Restorations: Robbins's Vacation [1962]." The Roland Wells Robbins Collection, the Thoreau Society, Lincoln, Mass.

———. The Story of the Minute Man. New London, N.H.: Country Press, 1945.

———. "Strawbery Banke, Inc. Daily Log, 1965, 1966, 1968." The Roland Wells Robbins Collection, the Thoreau Society, Lincoln, Mass.

———. "Surveys at Hancock-Clarke Homestead—1966–67." The Roland Wells Robbins Collection, the Thoreau Society, Lincoln, Mass.

———. "Tennis Notebook [1961–1968, 1970]." The Roland Wells Robbins Collection, the Thoreau Society, Lincoln, Mass.

———. The Thoreau–Walden Cabin. Brochure. Concord, Mass.: House of Thoreau, ca. 1964. The Roland Wells Robbins Collection, the Thoreau Society, Lincoln, Mass.

———. Thru the Covered Bridge. Stoneham, Mass.: George R. Barnstead & Son, 1938; reprint, Rutland, Vt.: Academy Books, 1986.

———. "Voice of America," Sidney Diamond, moder., audiotape of June 27, 1962. The Roland Wells Robbins Collection, the Thoreau Society, Lincoln, Mass.

Robbins, Roland W., and Evan Jones. "Big Joe Program." Taped interview, Nov. 22, 1959. WABC, New York.

————. *Hidden America.* New York: Alfred Knopf, 1959.

————. "Pilgrim John Alden's First Home in Duxbury and Its Archaeological Excavation," Mar. 1964. The Roland Wells Robbins Collection, the Thoreau Society, Lincoln, Mass.

————. *Pilgrim John Alden's Progress: Archaeological Excavations in Duxbury.* Plymouth, Mass.: Pilgrim Society, 1969.

Robbins, Roland W., and Lexington Historical Society. "Agreement Between Roland Wells Robbins and Lexington Historical Society, November 10, 1965." The Roland Wells Robbins Collection, the Thoreau Society, Lincoln, Mass.

Robbins, Roland W., and Robert Wheeler. "First Draft of Outline for Final Archaeological Report for Philipsburg Manor, Upper Mills [n.d.]." Historic Hudson Valley Archives, Sleepy Hollow, N.Y.

Robbins, Roland W., and Harvey Zorbaugh. "The Empire State." Audiotape of educational television program presented by the Board of Education, Garden City, N.Y., Feb. 24, 1960. The Roland Wells Robbins Collection, the Thoreau Society, Lincoln, Mass.

Robert, James, ed. *Old Glory: A Pictorial Report on the Grass Roots History Movement and the First Hometown History Primer.* New York: Warner Paperback, 1973.

Salwen, Bert. "Has Historical Archaeology Survived the Bicentennial? An Inquiry into the Development of Historical Archaeology in the United States." *Northeast Historical Archaeology* 12 (1983): 3–6.

Schiffer, Michael B., and George J. Gumerman, eds. *Conservation Archaeology: A Guide for Cultural Resource Management Studies.* New York: Academic Press, 1977.

Schnick, Elizabeth A., ed. *1997 Current Biography Yearbook.* New York: H. W. Wilson, 1997.

Schumacher, Paul J. F. "Field Notes, Archaeological Exploration, Shadwell Property, Charlottesville, Va., May 10–June 4, 1954." Thomas Jefferson Memorial Foundation, Charlottesville, Va.

————. "1954 Archaeological Exploration at Shadwell." Thomas Jefferson Memorial Foundation, Charlottesville, Va.

————. "Profiles of Trenches, Archaeological Survey for the Jefferson Birthplace Memorial Park Commission, May 1954." Thomas Jefferson Memorial Foundation, Charlottesville, Va.

Schuyler, Robert L. "Anthropological Perspectives in Historical Archaeology." Ph.D. diss., University of California at Santa Barbara, 1975.

————. "The Society for Historical Archaeology, 1967–1992: A Quarter Century of a National Archaeological Society." *Historical Archaeology* 27, no. 1 (1993): 35–40.

Scott, Donald M. "The Profession That Vanished: Public Lecturing in Mid-Nineteenth-Century America." In *Professions and Professional Ideologies in*

America, ed. Gerald L. Geison, 12–28. Chapel Hill: University of North Carolina Press, 1983.

Scudder, Townsend. "Review of *Discovery at Walden.*" *New England Quarterly* 20 (1947): 274–276.

Smith, Barbara Clark. *After the Revolution: The Smithsonian History of Everyday Life in the Eighteenth Century.* New York: Pantheon Books, 1985.

South, Stanley, ed. *Pioneers in Historical Archaeology: Breaking New Ground.* New York: Plenum Press, 1994.

———. "Strange Fruit: Historic Archaeology, 1972–1977." *Historical Archaeology* 27, no. 1 (1993): 15–18.

Starbuck, David. Personal communication, 2001.

Strawbery Banke, Inc. "Agreement Between Strawbery Banke, Inc, and The Department of History, University of New Hampshire, April 1966." The Roland Wells Robbins Collection, the Thoreau Society, Lincoln, Mass.

Strickland, Sidney T. "Excavations at Site of Home of Pilgrim John Howland, Rocky Nook." In *The Howlands in America,* comp. William Howland, 26–30. Detroit: Pilgrim John Howland Society, 1939.

Thoreau, Henry David. *Walden,* ed. J. Lyndon Shanley. Princeton, N.J.: Princeton University Press, 1971.

Torrey, Bradford, and Francis Allen, eds. *The Journal of Henry D. Thoreau.* Boston: Houghton Mifflin, 1949.

Town of Acton. "Annual Report, 1929." Town of Acton, Mass.

Tremer, Charles W. "A Brief Analysis of the Foundations of the Hancock-Clarke House: Recommendations for Future Plans of Same [1971]." The Roland Wells Robbins Collection, the Thoreau Society, Lincoln, Mass.

Turnbaugh, Sarah Peabody. "Ideo-Cultural Variation and Change in the Massachusetts Bay Colony." In *The Conference on Historic Site Archaeology Papers,* vol. 11, ed. Stanley South, 169–235. Columbia: Institute of Archaeology and Anthropology, University of South Carolina, 1976.

Turner, Frederick. *Spirit of Place: The Making of an American Literary Landscape.* Washington, D.C.: Island Press, 1992.

Van Doren Stern, Philip, ed. *The Annotated Walden: Walden; or, Life in the Woods.* 1970. Reprint, New York: Marboro Books Corp., 1992.

Virginia Electric and Power Company. "Advertisement." *Wall Street Journal,* July 18, 1956, 12.

Vogel, Robert M. "On the Real Meaning of Industrial Archaeology." *Historical Archaeology* 3 (1969): 87–93.

Wallace, Michael. "Reflections on the History of Historic Preservation." In *Presenting the Past: Essays on History and the Public,* ed. Susan Porter Benson, Stephen Brier, and Roy Rosenzweig, 165–202. Philadelphia: Temple University Press, 1986.

———. "Visiting the Past: History Museums in the United States." In *Present-*

ing the Past: Essays on History and the Public, ed. Susan Porter Benson, Stephen Brier, and Roy Rosenzweig, 137–164. Philadelphia: Temple University Press, 1986.

Watkins, C. Malcolm. "North Devon Pottery and Its Export to America in the 17th Century." In *Contributions from the Museum of History and Technology*, United States National Museum Bulletin 225. Washington, D.C.: Smithsonian Institution, 1960.

Watkins, C. Malcolm, and Ivor Noël Hume. "The 'Poor Potter' of Yorktown." *Contributions from the Museum of History and Technology* 54 (1967): 73–112.

Watkins, Lura Woodside. *Early New England Pottery*. Sturbridge, Mass.: Old Sturbridge Village, 1959.

Wheeler, Sir Mortimer. *Archaeology from the Earth*. London: Penguin Books, 1956.

Wheeler, Robert. Letter to Roland W. Robbins, July 23, 1956. The Roland Wells Robbins Collection, the Thoreau Society, Lincoln, Mass.

————. Memo to Harold Cater, "Proposed Philipse Castle Archaeological Budget," Dec. 18, 1956. The Roland Wells Robbins Collection, the Thoreau Society, Lincoln, Mass.

Wheeler, Robert, and Paula Sampson. "Archaeological Report—Philipsburg Manor Upper Mills [n.d.]." Historic Hudson Valley Archives, Sleepy Hollow, N.Y.

Wheelwright, Thea, ed. *Thoreau's Cape Cod: With the Early Photographs of Herbert W. Gleason*. Barre, Mass.: Barre Publishers, 1971.

White, Curtis McKay. Personal communication, 2000.

Whiteside, Clara Walker. *Touring New England on the Trail of the Yankee*. Philadelphia: Penn Publishing Co., 1926.

Wilderson, Paul W. "Archaeology and the American Historian: An Interdisciplinary Challenge." *American Quarterly* 27 (1975): 115–132.

Willey, Gordon R., and Jeremy A. Sabloff. *A History of American Archaeology*. San Francisco: W. H. Freeman and Co., 1974.

Wolfe, Theodore F. *Literary Shrines: The Haunts of Some Famous American Authors*. Philadelphia: Lippincott, 1895.

Yonge, Samuel H. *The Site of Old "James Towne."* Richmond, Va.: Association for the Preservation of Virginia Antiquities, 1930.

Zimmer, Jeanne M. "A History of Thoreau's Hut and Hut Site." *ESQ* 18 (1972): 134–140.

Zimmer, Julie, Richard Wilk, and Ann Pyburn. "A Study of Attitudes and Values in Archaeological Practice." *SAA Bulletin* 13, no. 5 (1995): 10.

Index

Page numbers in italics refer to illustrations.